REMEMBRANCE
OF
GAMES
PAST

REMEMBRANCE

OF

GAMES

PAST

On Tour with the Tennis Grand Masters

JOHN SHARNIK

MACMILLAN PUBLISHING COMPANY   New York

Macmillan Publishing Company
866 Third Avenue, New York, N.Y. 10022
Collier Macmillan Canada, Inc.

Library of Congress Cataloging-in-Publication Data
Sharnik, John.
Remembrance of games past.
Includes index.
1. Tennis—History.   2. Tennis players.   I. Title.
GV992.S45   1986   796.342   86-12809
ISBN 0-02-610040-1

Macmillan books are available at special discounts for bulk purchases
for sales promotions, premiums, fund-raising, or educational use.
For details, contact:

Special Sales Director
Macmillan Publishing Company
866 Third Avenue
New York, N.Y. 10022

10 9 8 7 6 5 4 3 2 1

Designed by Jack Meserole

Printed in the United States of America

For my tennis companion
on the courts and in the stands,
my wife, Barbara

CONTENTS

AUTHOR'S NOTES

If this story were being told on the television screen—my usual medium—rather than in print, the credits would include the name of Ned Chase, the editor, who steered me past historical and technical pitfalls. There would also be a lengthy list of my fellow players at the Heights Casino in Brooklyn, N.Y., who stimulated me with good tennis and good tennis talk.

Sharp-eyed readers may notice that my spelling of the last name of Richard (Pancho) Gonzalez differs from the way they have usually seen it on the sports pages, where it most often appeared with a final "s" rather than a "z." I have chosen to use the spelling Pancho himself prefers as true to the name's Spanish origins. It's *his* name, so I figure it's his choice.

This book contains references to the published memoirs of various tennis players. Rather than clutter up the pages with footnotes, I list those books here:

Kramer, Jack, and Frank DeFord, *The Game: My 40 Years in Tennis*, New York: Putnam, 1979; Mulloy, Gardnar, *The Will to Win*, New York: A. S. Barnes, 1960; Riggs, Robert L., with George McGann, *Court Hustler*, Philadelphia: Lippincott, 1973; Seixas, Vic, with Joel H. Cohen, *Prime Time Tennis*, New York: Scribner's, 1983; Talbert, William F., with John Sharnik, *Playing for Life: Billy Talbert's Story*, Boston: Little, Brown, 1959.

PART I

Masters of the Game

Delayed Replay

YOU WOULDN'T HAVE PICKED either one of them out of a line of customers buying peat moss and touch-up paint at your local hardware on a Saturday morning. Or out of a crowd of parents at Homecoming Day on your kid's college campus. There was nothing to distinguish these two slight, unprepossessing men edging into their middle years along with the rest of us.

Well, maybe they *were* making the transition a little more gracefully than most guys. That much might have occurred to you if you took notice of the flat stomachs, the jowlless jaw lines. Not a bulge in their immaculate warm-up suits. Figure the dark-haired guy at about five feet seven and 145 pounds—the one with the kind of lean, weathered face that looks as if it belongs behind the wheel of a pickup truck. Give the red-haired gent, the slightly younger one, another inch, another ten to twelve pounds. Yes, come to think of it, they do look in pretty good shape for a couple of old dads, old grads, whatever they are.

It was only when the two men stripped down to their tennis whites and began hitting balls to each other with long fluid strokes—it was only then that they would really command your attention.

After a while you could not help but notice how they tested themselves and challenged each other, sometimes with shots of surprising force, sometimes with spins and angles that stenciled the court with patterns of skillful geometry. You would watch them move with remarkably quick short steps, starting toward the ball at that critical moment just as it was hit—before anyone else could tell where it was going—and reaching it just when you were sure it was past them. Reaching it with a burst of measured speed or a lunge of boyish abandon.

Even if your own experience on a tennis court was limited to a few sets at some holiday resort—a little exercise to clear away the buzz of last night's pina coladas—you would still realize that you were witnessing something special.

If you were one of those ardent club players who consider any week unfulfilled unless it includes three or four hours of hard singles, to whom tennis is part of the fundamental routine of life, like a day at the office or dinner with your family, if you counted yourself among those devotees of the game—as I do— then you would realize you were in the presence of art.

And if you also happened to have any sense of history, as far as tennis is concerned, then you would recognize these two ordinary-looking, aging citizens as a pair of living monuments of the game. Two compact-size Australians from similar blue-collar backgrounds, with the similar habits of loners and comparable records of achievement. Two remarkable ex-champions named Rod Laver and Ken Rosewall.

They were playing as if a couple of decades had been erased from the books, and we were all back in the Sixties together.

Thwack! The serve explodes off Laver's racquet like anti-tank fire aimed straight into Rosewall's body. You might almost expect it to burn a hole right through his bony ribs. Behind the service Laver strains toward the net but is forced to hold his ground.

With a mere shift of his weight, a movement as graceful and effortless as a bullfighter's, Rosewall has taken the ball on the rise and stroked a perfect backhand return deep into the corner, nailing Laver to the baseline.

They are into the second set, and Rosewall is still probing for ways to neutralize his opponent's deadly power.

Laver and Rosewall. The names are forever linked in the story of the game.

If you want to place their rivalry in its historic context, then think back to the era when the front-page names were Kennedy, Johnson and Nixon—the span from Dallas to Watergate.

Vietnam and civil rights were riding the American conscience.

The Middle East crisis meant Israel versus Egypt. Oil was still just the raw material of a thirty-cent item you filled your gas tank with, not yet a weapon of political warfare.

There was Go-Go action in the stock market as well as in the bedazzling new pleasure palaces called discotheques.

It was the time of flower power in the streets, "Sergeant Pepper" on the record players, "Bonanza" on the picture tube.

In baseball it was the era of Mickey Mantle and Roger Maris, Willy Mays and Hank Aaron, Sandy Koufax and Bob Gibson. The Green Bay Packers clobbered the Kansas City Chiefs in Superbowl I. In basketball the heroes were Wilt Chamberlain and Bill Russell. And it was Cassius Clay versus Sonny Liston in the ring.

Tennis was in the throes of a revolution. The sport was soon to cast off its own debilitating form of segregation. On one side of the wall were the big prestigious amateur tournaments like Wimbledon and Forest Hills. On the other, the "tainted" professionals with their barnstorming tours and their lesser, infrequent tournaments—first-class players shut off in their own second-class world. The sport was reaching toward an integrated state called "open tennis," which, when it finally did happen, would prove unimaginably rich in competition, in profits—and in intramural conflicts.

The Laver-Rosewall rivalry was part of the drama of the transition period.

For more than a decade, from 1963 to 1974, these two friendly antagonists conducted a cordial vendetta before tennis fans around the world. They clashed week-in, week-out on the professional barnstorming tours. After 1968, in the less hectic, more structured atmosphere of open tennis, they often collided in the finals of big tournaments. Many of their meetings were major events in the early history of the open era.

Between matches they were mates—in their fashion. They

would practice together, discuss their games. But basically both were solitary types. Laver, withdrawn and fidgety, would fuss to himself over details like the crease in his tennis shorts, or the texture on the grip of his racquet handle. Rosewall, withdrawn and brooding, would lie on a bench with a towel over his eyes while the locker room noise swirled around him.

Then they would go punch each other out for a couple of hours on the tennis court.

For most of its twelve-year span the Laver-Rosewall competition was also a contest for the position of Number 1 in the game; the leader in the rivalry was widely regarded as the world's best tennis player, pro or amateur. At first it was clearly Rosewall, the darker, slightly smaller and by four years the older of the pair. A kind of infant prodigy, he had achieved world-class ranking in his teens, had turned pro early and, by the time Laver arrived to challenge him, had already survived six years of pitfighting on the pro tour. Not only survived it but emerged as top dog.

Laver, a redheaded lefty with a flamboyant style, arrived fresh and feisty from a spectacular sweep of the four major national championships: British, American, French, Australian —a rare Grand Slam, an achievement recorded by only one other man in tennis history, the great Don Budge. But Rosewall beat back Laver's challenge, winning the majority of their head-to-head matches on their first two pro tours.

Then Rod adjusted to the rigors of the pro game and knocked Rosewall off his perch. For the next five years, from 1965 until the turn of the Seventies, Laver ruled tennis absolutely, first as king of the pros and then, after 1968, as sovereign of the new, consolidated domain of open tennis. In 1969 he established that unarguable claim by winning his *second* Grand Slam, something *no* other player ever accomplished, not even Don Budge. Meanwhile, the aging Rosewall was slipping into his inevitable decline.

Or was it inevitable? Was he really slipping? The outlines of a legend were about to emerge—an image of Ken Rosewall as a hero impervious to time.

As Laver, forcing his way into the net, slashes a crosscourt volley, Rosewall moves toward the ball with the instinct of a cat outguessing a mouse. He reaches it with his racquet already drawn back in perfect position to hit a passing shot down the line. Instead, at the moment of contact, he adjusts the pitch of his racquet and slices a little offensive lob in a perfect arc over Laver's head.

Rod, caught off balance, flings his forty-five-year-old body into sudden reverse. He scoots back and manages to get behind the shot as it nicks the baseline. Turning his shoulders into the stroke, he sees that Rosewall has come in to the net. Laver, apparently set to hit one of his patented whiplash passing shots, chooses instead to spin a little lob of his own.

Now it's Kenny's turn to scramble. Every seam in his forty-nine-year-old face shows with the effort. When the ball drops in the farthest corner of the court, he is there and in position to make the return.

What he chooses to hit is not a high defensive lob or a go-for-it passing shot, but still another attacking lob—perfectly disguised, perfectly controlled.

After so many years, so many hundreds of matches, they know each other's every stroke, every move and countermove. But they still haven't given up trying to trick each other.

Laver versus Rosewall. It was one of the great matchups in sports history. Like all great rivalries it had its unexpected climaxes, its unforeseen swings and turns.

Rosewall's apparent decline, after the start of open tennis, turned out to be only a midcareer slump. In his late thirties, an age when most tennis players have long since put serious competition behind them, Kenny experienced an astonishing revival. So did the Laver-Rosewall competition. It was still going strong when, on May 14, 1972, the two old gladiators—Kenny now thirty-seven, Rod thirty-three—crossed swords in Dallas to determine the winner of the World Championship Tennis Finals, the season-ending playoff of the WCT tour involving most of the world's top ten pros.

At Dallas the stage was set for history. They were playing for the sport's biggest purse ever—the $50,000 first prize was twice as much as the U.S. Open would offer that same year. Laver, who had dominated the tour, was favored to take the fifty grand to the bank.

Another epochal fact: The television audience of 20 million (in addition to the substantial crowd of 7,800 eyewitnesses at Moody Coliseum) was by far the greatest number to have viewed any tennis match to that date. For many of those millions it was their first taste of high-level tennis.

What they saw was one of the most fiercely contested matches in the whole Laver-Rosewall record, and one of the landmark events in the history of the game. It helped to establish tennis as a sport with mass appeal, instead of the cultish ritual it had once been considered. The Dallas match supplied impetus to the tennis boom, already in motion, which was to be one of the social phenomena of the 1970s.

So compelling was the drama of that match, the result was almost incidental. But it was Rosewall, the aging underdog, who walked away with the prize. *Stumbled away*, more accurately, after five roller-coaster sets, almost four hours of exhausting effort.

Laver or Rosewall—in the end, who came out on top?

The issue was never really resolved, only suspended, a couple of years after the Dallas spectacular. Time simply ran out.

Rosewall's incredible renascence had carried him back to the summit of the game—at least to the uppermost slopes—as a finalist at Wimbledon and the U.S. Open in 1974, as he was about to turn forty, an almost unheard-of age at that level of tennis. But within a year or so, Laver, suffering from chronic injuries and a form of burnout, eased himself off the circuit. After that the two old competitors met only once or twice a year in special tournaments involving world-class players over thirty-five (Rosewall giving away five or ten years to the rest of the field).

Meanwhile, the great game had marched on. The circuits of open tournaments flourished in spite of running conflicts of power between the professionals and the old amateur tennis establishment. The competition for Numero Uno passed on to a succession of other contenders: Smith and Nastase, Newcombe and Ashe, Connors and Borg, McEnroe and Lendl.

Laver and Rosewall were not merely history, they were ancient history.

So what were they doing here in the spring of 1984 in an elegant little tennis arena in Nashville, Tennessee—two middle-aged citizens starting a season on the tennis circuit, playing the finals of yet another tournament before a paying crowd of enthusiasts, with big bucks again on the line?

The time machine had slipped its gears, the wheels were spinning crazily.

Laver once again seems to be penned into his forehand corner—no chance to seize the net, no option but to keep the ball in play. He and his old rival are locked in a crosscourt rally, baseline to baseline. Laver's lefty forehand to Rosewall's dangerous backhand.

Finally, one shot off Laver's racquet lands a bit short. Rosewall, seizing the opening, slices an approach shot down the line to Laver's backhand, and charges the net.

Laver takes the ball on the run, his thinning red hair streaming straight out behind him. There is a flick of the racquet, like the paw of an animal. The ball hurtles past Rosewall in a blur. A unanimous shout of astonishment escapes from the crowd.

"Game, Laver," the umpire announces in his judicial monotone. "He leads, four games to one, second set."

Laver versus Rosewall, 1984. This is an era in which training and fitness, like all aspects of sport, have become professionalized, technologized, industrialized. When all fields are being mastered by waves of superbly conditioned men and women in their twenties. When tennis in particular is populated by teenage prodigies pounding the hell out of the ball with exercise-machine-made muscles.

Then what are these two grownups doing here—Rosewall now verging on fifty, Laver some months past forty-five—both of them stretched-out and sweating like a couple of circuit rookies trying to qualify for their first Grand Prix tournament?

It's as if you were watching Koufax pitching against Gibson again, or Mantle taking his cuts against Dean Chance, or Bart Starr suiting up for the Pack once more. As if Sonny Liston and the fighter now called Muhammad Ali were climbing back into the ring, both of them in fighting trim. It is world-class sport being played at an age when most men are taken over in mind and spirit by grownup cares.

At the changeover, Laver mops his face briefly with a towel, tosses it aside. Abruptly he becomes aware of a flickering thought that is threatening to intrude into his concentration: something about the schedule for tomorrow's business trip to North Carolina. He erases the thought from his mind as deliberately and completely as if he were erasing it from a blackboard, and busies himself for a few moments by roughening the grip of his racquet against the net post. Then, with brisk, bandy-legged little strides, he moves to the receiver's position on the court.

In a courtside box Wilma Rosewall deliberately removes her mind from the match. She clicks off a few stitches on her knitting.

Without actually watching, in her mind's eye she can follow the precise patterns of her husband's movements as he folds his towel, places it on his chair, and moves to the server's position, where he proceeds to go to work like a mechanic at a workbench.

Twenty-five tough minutes later, Kenny has fought his way back into the match: 4–all, 5–all, 6–all.

Brace yourself! It's Laver and Rosewall in a tiebreaker.

This is the finals of the opening tournament on the 1984 schedule of the Tennis Grand Masters—former champions now past the age of forty-five. We are on the first stop of a tour that I am going to follow on its irregular circuit across the country throughout the year. And the tour is beginning just the way any tennis fan would have hoped: like a replay—not an instant replay but a long delayed one, a reprise of games fondly remembered from the receding past. Ken Rosewall, the established leader of the Grand Masters, is facing a rookie challenger, Rod Laver.

More than a moment of nostalgia, it is an event that radiates hope for all of us grownups who dream about being boys again. For anybody who has ever entertained the fantasy of stopping time and age in their tracks.

Born Again

No MATTER HOW you sugarcoat it, there is something sad about growing old, and there is something heroic about people who refuse to give in to the process. They are putting up a fight against the most implacable of enemies: time. They are trying to maintain skills and powers that we'd all like to hang on to.

That explains the poignancy of aging pitchers or linebackers struggling to make the cut in the training camps. It also accounts for the prevalent fantasy about middle-aged athletic prodigies with a magical pitch or a sudden talent for laying fastballs up against an outfield fence—as in the reemergence of Roy Hobbs, "The Natural," in his late thirties, or the phenomenon of Joe Hardy, even older, who changed the course of the pennant race in *Damn Yankees*.

James Thurber once wrote that most American husbands put themselves to sleep at night striking out the Yankees batting order. Not exactly. In my case it happens to be by breaking the service of the U.S. Open tennis champion at love. Piece of cake. Two deft chip returns, one sweeping crosscourt passing shot, and a surprise charge to the net that pays off in a crushing volley. Just imagining it produces a remarkable feeling of rejuvenation that medical science cannot hope to approximate by any mere hormone injection or organ transplant.

The closest thing I know of to that experience in real life is a vicarious one. It comes from watching tournaments involving the troupe of overage athletes called the Tennis Grand Masters —Laver, Rosewall and a roster of other players from their era.

At a time of life when most people have come to settle for

nothing more strenuous than an occasional set of social doubles, these players are still performing, or *again* performing, as professional athletes, competing for substantial purses before paying crowds of enthusiasts; playing serious, sometimes punishing matches that go into the official records of the sport; hitting shots that provoke cheers of approval and sometimes tears of memory and wonder.

To compete in a Grand Masters tournament, you have to be at least forty-five years old, but you cannot simply show up with a couple of racquets and a birth certificate. To qualify for an invitation you must also be a former winner of some recognized national or international championship. Some of the old champions are in their middle or late fifties, and a few have competed in their sixties.

Their example has been followed by senior athletes in such fields as golf, skiing, swimming and track. But the Tennis Grand Masters are the originals, and they remain unique in the annals of sport and gerontology: They are the oldest group of professional athletes engaged in regular, organized, strenuous competition.

The Golden Age of any sport is the period that ended when you became older than the players. The Grand Masters defined that chronological boundary for me in tennis.

The circuit was organized in 1973, and the early tournament draws included some names I could remember reading on the sport pages as a teenager in the late 1930s, when the front-page news was about Hitler's armies on the march toward World War II. The names were Don Budge and Bobby Riggs, Frank Parker and Bitsy Grant, Billy Talbert and Gardnar Mulloy. (As with Laver and Rosewall, tennis names tend to leap to mind in pairs, linked as rivals or doubles partners, sometimes both.) I had even glimpsed some of these players in action, in minor tournaments or exhibitions at tennis clubs in New England, where I grew up.

Those august names—American heroes of the old amateur circuit and the international Davis Cup competition—were sprinkled among players of a slightly later vintage, the 1940s

and 1950s. They included Vic Seixas, Tony Trabert and Budge
Patty, Pancho Gonzalez and Pancho Segura, all of them also
Americans—in Patty's case an expatriate, in Segura's an
adopted son.

There were some lesser-known Americans, too: Tom
Brown, Hugh Stewart, Whitney Reed.

And there was a bloc of fine foreign players—Australians
like Frank Sedgman, Mervyn Rose and Rex Hartwig; South
Africa's Abe Segal, Mexico's Gustavo Palafox, and the Chilean
Luis Ayala; Sven Davidson, Torsten Johannson and Lennart
Bergelin of Sweden; Kurt Nielsen and Torben Ulrich of Denmark; Italy's Beppe Merlo and Nicola Pietrangeli; the Czech
exile Jaroslav Drobny, who, during the Cold War years, played
out of Egypt and, later on, England.

I thought of that whole group of Grand Masters as My Generation of tennis players. Some were a few years older than I
and some a few years younger. Their playing careers encompassed a period, familiar to me, when the game was still tied to
the old traditions, for better or for worse. When tennis was a
game played in white flannel shorts, and the standard warm-up
outfit was a white cable-knit cricket sweater. When players de-
ferred to officials and sometimes gave points away to opponents
whom they felt had been deprived by an errant call. When the
valued prizes at Wimbledon and what was then called the U.S.
Nationals at Forest Hills consisted of rather homely pieces of
silverplate.

Officially, tennis was then an amateur sport, though it was
sometimes administered like an exclusive club or a religion of
the elect, and there were rumors of payoffs to the leading contestants. The Davis Cup was a Holy Grail, pursued by national
teams of earnest seekers in a competition almost as rich in international color as the Olympics.

In the Grand Masters' revival of that era only a few obvious
names were missing—players inhibited from getting back into
competition by some physical disability, or, in a few cases, an
emotional one. Call it pride, which rejects any thought of playing below your old championship standard, or call it "image,"
a fear of losing prestige among your old peers.

The preeminent no-shows were Jack Kramer, his old partner Ted Schroeder, ex-Wimbledon champ Dick Savitt, and the spectacular Australian Lew Hoad.

The absence of Kramer, sidelined from the courts by severe arthritis long before the Grand Masters got started, was a gaping one as far as history was concerned. For he was *the* towering figure of the whole postwar era: an amateur champion of the late 1940s who took immediate command of the professional ranks and was still king of the pros when he retired in the mid-1950s—in effect, undefeated heavyweight champ. As a tennis promoter, furthermore, Kramer was instrumental in the arduous, long-delayed conversion of the game to open status.

Too badly incapacitated to play in the Grand Masters, Kramer nevertheless had a role in its origins as the promoter of several Grand Masters tournaments involving some of his old chums and antagonists.

Where had they been during their decades off the circuit, these old white-flannel campaigners?

Most of them had run the standard course for tennis stars of the preopen era. They competed as amateurs until their middle twenties, then barnstormed with the pros for a few years, and finally retired from the game, usually in their early thirties. Then they faded into the margins of the sports pages. Bobby Riggs turned up there occasionally in the role of promoter or in anecdotes about hustling bets on club courts. The two Panchos, Gonzalez and Segura, became high-priced teaching pros at expensive resorts. Gardnar Mulloy, after hanging in on the amateur circuit longer than any high-ranked player in modern times, eventually did the same.

Some players gradually, quietly disappeared beneath the surface of business life, as Talbert and Seixas did without ever having turned pro, as Sven Davidson did in Sweden, as Frank Sedgman did in Australia after his barnstorming days ended.

These men were all *creatures* of tennis. In or out of the game, their careers had been launched by tennis—tennis contacts, tennis fame. They stayed in touch with the game. And eventually, in one way or another, they drifted back into it. As club pros or racquet club proprietors, as representatives of sporting goods companies, as officials in their various national tennis organizations. And finally as players, once again, in the Grand Masters competition, whether for a moment or for a whole new phase of their careers.

Some of the older generation—Budge, Bitsy Grant, Talbert and Parker—made only a ceremonial appearance or two in Grand Masters tournaments. A couple of their contemporaries, Riggs and Mulloy, played every so often right into the 1982 season before finally dropping out. Gardnar by then had reached the ripe old age of sixty-seven. Riggs was a mere sixty-four.

Some of the 1940s–1950s generation lasted only a few tournaments—just long enough to discover that the level of play and the pace of competition required much more than a casual commitment. Some of them just couldn't hack it any longer; some couldn't spare the time and effort they saw it would take to get in condition and retool their strokes.

But a hard core of forty-five-to-fifty-year-olds—Sedgman, Seixas, Gonzalez, Ulrich, Davidson, plus a changing cast of supernumeraries—settled into an annual competition. They were back on the circuit again. It was a kind of renascence, a locker room version of the religious experience that converts describe as "born again."

When you look at the names on the draw sheet of a Grand Masters tournament, you have a sense of revisiting the past. As soon as play starts, you are sure of it. The atmosphere is that different from the brawling hassles of contemporary tennis, the sheer nastiness that sometimes pervades the court and the stands.

If you are one of those sports fans who are turned on by churlish behavior; if you come in hopes of seeing bad blood oozing like sweat; if you buy your ticket as a permit to boo and harass the heroes as a way of publically venting your resentment of your boss, your wife, the injustices of life; if this is your idea of sports, then save yourself for hockey, for that legitimized form of bar-fighting called tough-man contests, or for tennis matches involving John McEnroe, Ilie Nastase or other

Visigoths of the game. The Grand Masters will not be your cup of tea.

The atmosphere at these tournaments is characterized not by hostility but by a mood of celebration. There are no angry sounds from the stands. Tension, yes. Excitement. Awe. Astonishment. Occasionally disappointment, when a sure putaway is missed or a rally suddenly dies. But not hostility, because there is nothing to provoke it.

Line calls are challenged—*if* they are challenged—by a look of doubt or surprise, or by a simple question to the official: "Are you sure?" When a linesman hesitates, a player will sometimes help out with a call in favor of his opponent: "That ball was in."

The only time I can remember seeing an official strong-armed at a Grand Masters match, it was done with kindness. It happened during a doubles match in which a linesman called "Fault!" on a first serve down the middle which all four players saw as a clean ace. So did everybody else in the house. With a mere exchange of glances at each other, the players very quickly changed positions on the court and moved on to the next point, pausing only to salute the mistaken official. The gesture said, in effect, "Hey, everybody misses one now and then."

Some reporters of the tennis scene find the Grand Masters' style of play as sedate as their court manners—a little *too* genteel for the modern taste. "Like Grand Prix tennis played under water," in the phrase of one jaded observer, "or viewed in slow motion."

That wasn't the way I saw it.

Watching Sven Davidson—crew cut and still muscular, at fifty still looking like a varsity oarsman—leap for an overhead and pound it deep into the opponent's court, I had the feeling that time, the universal enemy, had somehow been held at bay. It was hard to believe that Davidson had ever leaped any higher for that shot or hit it any harder, even when he was winning the French championship or the doubles at Wimbledon, in the late Fifties.

From the distance of the stands, Seixas seemed hardly any older, hardly a pound heavier or a step slower, than my own recollection of him at Forest Hills two decades before, scooting around the court hitting his slightly unorthodox but economical strokes.

Gonzalez, though visibly not in shape, could still crank up the service that had once been the most formidable in the game. What's more, he didn't hesitate to come in behind it to volley away the return.

And Frank Sedgman! With the pigeon-toed grace that characterizes many great athletes, he glided in to hit devastating volleys from midcourt. The first time I saw Sedgman hit those incredible volleys, back in the Fifties, I found myself thinking that the making of an Australian tennis player must begin by implanting steel pins in his wrists. Twenty-five years later it looked as if the pins hadn't even loosened.

Grand Masters, I thought, after seeing them play a couple of tournaments, not only appeared to lose neither speed nor strength, they didn't get bald like some of us. Hell, they hardly even seemed to turn gray!

I once discussed this impression of agelessness with Torben Ulrich, a Danish original who is distinguished for physical fitness even among his well-preserved colleagues. In his midfifties, Ulrich wears a biblical brown beard and a long 1960s-style pigtail, which seem out of character with his exercise-chart body. They give him the look of a muscular troll, or a hippy on a health kick. That afternoon he had played an imaginative, energetic singles match that would have taxed a well-conditioned twenty-five-year-old, and followed it by teaming with Sven Davidson for three tough sets of doubles, in which he performed acrobatically. With that performance in mind, I asked Ulrich how much longer he thought he could continue to cheat the aging process.

"Oh, I don't feel I'm cheating age," he said with a cheery, ingenuous air. "Just like everybody else, I'm on a curve of declining potential. I am only struggling, you see, to stay as close to the curve as I can. The satisfaction is in the struggle.

It's like tennis itself. I never get some special feeling out of winning—only out of playing well."

Ulrich is a professing Buddhist. His Zen approach to life and to tennis (which includes meditating while staring at a ball) sometimes seems merely whimsical. His denials notwithstanding, I found it difficult to resist the notion that the Tennis Grand Masters must have discovered some sort of jocks' Shangri-la. Presumably they were subject to the usual forms of wear and tear suffered by athletes at any age—the muscle pulls and sprains, the traumas to tendons and ligaments, the erosion of overused joints. They must also be vulnerable to the medical problems associated with people of their advancing years: arthritis, failing eyesight, coronary risks, not to mention the simple fact that the body becomes more vulnerable to routine injury in the middle years, and its ability to heal itself declines.

A pulled muscle can happen more easily to a man of fifty than to a twenty-year-old. And while it may keep the younger player off the courts for a week or so, it can be a season-stopping catastrophe to the senior player.

The Grand Masters may have been subject to all these facts of life, but they seemed to have a remarkable ability to rise above the ills that ordinary flesh like yours and mine is heir to.

During a match in 1978, Frank Sedgman snapped an Achilles tendon, the crucial length of fiber along the back of the leg that anchors the calf muscle to the heel bone. It is as central to running as the lungs are to breathing. An Achilles injury is crippling as well as exceedingly painful. It could have been expected to take Sedgman out of competitive tennis once and for all. Instead, after surgery, he came back the next season to win both the singles and doubles championships.

There has been an even more dramatic recovery than that. Sven Davidson collapsed with a heart attack, survived medical "death," underwent multiple bypass surgery and was back on the tournament circuit several months later!

In the whole first decade of the Grand Masters, from 1973 to 1982—fifteen to twenty tournaments a year for a total of something like eighteen hundred individual matches—there were only five defaults because of illness or injury.

There are obvious incentives for a Grand Masters player to stay on the court or to get back into action after an enforced layoff. Unlike professional baseball or football, in which a player can spend the season on the disabled list and still draw his salary, tennis is strictly pay for play.

The pay is hardly lavish by the current inflationary standards of professional sport. During the first decade of Grand Masters competition, the tour leader usually came away with $50,000 to $75,000. Also-rans could finish with anywhere from $20,000 to $40,000 if they played regularly. That would mean spending fifteen to twenty long weekends (the tournaments last three or four days) in a form of activity which the competitors prefer to just about any other kind of work they've done in their lives. Seixas and Beppe Merlo, for instance, quit jobs as stockbrokers to tour in the Grand Masters. Sven Davidson was a fugitive from the computer business. Tom Brown took off from his California law office to play the tournaments. Gardnar Mulloy was a nonpracticing member of the Florida bar.

In what the Grand Masters sometimes refer to as "mainstream tennis"—the men's Grand Prix and the Women's Tennis Association tour—winner's prizes routinely run $25,000 to $50,000 for a single tournament. And it goes on up from there. Ivan Lendl and Hana Mandlikova collected $187,500 each for winning the 1985 U.S. Open.

The biggest prize offered for winning any Grand Masters tournament is $10,000, and sometimes the winner's purse is as little as $4,500. But even that is more than the old-timers ever competed for on the pro tours of the 1940s and 1950s. Furthermore, as I was to learn in the course of the tour, the prize money is only part of the financial story.

Grand Masters crowds are nothing like the numbers that sometimes flock to mainstream tennis—the thirty-eight thousand that have come through the gates of Wimbledon to watch a single day's schedule of matches; the twenty-one thousand at Roland Garros stadium in Paris for the French Open, the same number at the National Tennis Center in New York for the U.S. Open; the thirty thousand curiosity-seekers who gathered in the Houston Astrodome in 1973, when Bobby Riggs got dumped by Billie Jean King in their hyped-up "battle of the sexes."

Grand Masters crowds are far short of the audiences these same players were used to in their heyday. Nothing like the twenty-five thousand at White City Stadium in Sydney, Australia, who witnessed the victories of Seixas and Trabert over two Aussie whiz kids, Ken Rosewall and Lew Hoad, in the 1954 Davis Cup (still the record attendance for a single official tennis event). And far short of the fifteen thousand who slogged their way through the worst blizzard in New York's modern history, the day after Christmas, 1948, to see Riggs open the defense of his pro crown against the new flash from the amateur ranks, Jack Kramer, in the old Madison Square Garden. Weather be damned, that was only twenty-five hundred short of the capacity crowd that had watched Fred Perry and Ellsworth Vines open the 1937 tour.

But as far as the old pre-open-tennis pro tours were concerned, those huge Garden crowds were a rarity. Survivors of the tours can recall—all too painfully—facing tiny huddles of a hundred or so spectators at some ill-chosen waypoint on the itinerary.

The Grand Masters escape those low points, just as they miss out on the highs. Once in a while they play before mainstream-size crowds—when tournaments are held in conjunction with big events like Wimbledon and Jack Kramer's Pacific Southwest Open in Los Angeles. Over seven thousand fans turned out to see the Grand Masters on their own in Johannesburg, South Africa, in 1976—the Grand Masters record—and they drew five thousand plus to Pauley Pavilion on the UCLA campus that same year.

But most of the tournaments are intimate affairs, played in the chummy atmosphere of clubs built to hold no more than a couple of thousand spectators—an exhibition crowd. As in mainstream tennis, the gate is almost incidental because the purses are guaranteed by sponsors, mostly local banks and business firms. The overall tour is backed by a so-called primary sponsor. In the early years of the Grand Masters it was Almaden, a California winery owned by a national distillery. More recently the tour sponsor has been a life insurance company, Mutual Benefit of New Jersey. Which seems appropriate for a group that symbolizes long living rather than high living.

If there is any one player who more than any other epitomizes the Grand Masters, it is Frank Sedgman, one of the heroes of Australian tennis legend, a distinguished figure in world tennis history and a fixture on lists of the all-time greats.

Sedg—blue-eyed, with curly auburn hair and a shy grin that made him instantly likable to men and women both—was the first of an Australian wave that rolled over the tennis landscape in the early 1950s. It filled a power vacuum left when two great American champions defected to the professional game—first Jack Kramer and then Pancho Gonzalez. On came the Australians, and they kept right on coming for most of the next two decades.

Along with Sedgman came Ken McGregor, Mervyn Rose and Rex Hartwig; followed by Lew Hoad and Ken Rosewall, Neale Fraser, Ashley Cooper, Mal Anderson and on through Rod Laver and Roy Emerson, Fred Stolle and John Newcombe. The waves of tennis talent seemed practically endless, like troops coming ashore on D day, and just about as hard to fight off in their annual march toward the Davis Cup and most of the other major objectives in the sport.

In was Sedgman who led the way, winning the U.S. singles in 1951 and 1952, and Wimbledon in 1952; sweeping the Grand Slam doubles titles with McGregor; and powering the Aussies to three straight Davis Cup victories. When Sedgman turned pro in 1953 he proceeded to give Jack Kramer the closest run of any challenger in head-to-head competition on the tour.

In the Grand Masters, Sedgman took charge from the beginning, and he remained the dominant player from 1973 to 1979. That was not surprising for a fine athlete, distinguished by great speed, who had obviously kept himself in superb condition. Sedg's success was gratifying to me as a tennis fan, since I thought of him as a tennis player's tennis player—an all-court performer with all the requisite strokes, still beautifully executed. As a tactician, he had the forward instincts of a World

War I general. Besides, he hadn't lost any of his off-court charm. As he turned into his fifties, the cheery face was now weathered, sun-reddened, but the boyish manner was still there— modest, almost bashful.

The first time I met him, at a Grand Masters tournament party, I embarrassed him to the point of blushing by asking him to compare himself with some other great champions of the game. Another time I mentioned the match in which he'd won his second straight U.S. singles title—Forest Hills, 1952. It was a breezy, straight-set win which his opponent, Gardnar Mulloy, later described as one of the worst runaways in the history of the event.

"Ah, well," Sedgman said sympathetically, "Mulloy was a bit unfortunate, you know. He'd played Rosewall in a tough semifinal the day before. He'd had a tough quarterfinal, too. And I'd had an easy time of it. You've got to have a bit of luck going your way."

He forgot to mention that Mulloy was also thirty-eight years old at the time (Frank himself was just twenty-four). Maybe from the Grand Masters perspective, thirty-eight no longer seemed like such a remarkable age for a tennis player.

In those first seven years of the Grand Masters tour, Sedgman's strongest challenge came from Torben Ulrich, the bearded Dane. Every year but one it was either Sedgman or Ulrich who wound up at the head of the tour in total number of points awarded for wins in successive rounds of play, and also in total prize money. (The year they both missed, 1977, the leader was Rex Hartwig.) Every one of the first seven years, furthermore, Sedgman or Ulrich—one or the other, sometimes both—played in the final round of the season-ending playoff, the Grand Masters Championship Finals. Twice they met head-on for the championship, and Sedgman won both times. But not without a struggle.

All of which certainly *was* surprising, since it was hard to think of Torben Ulrich in the same company with the great Frank Sedgman. On the old amateur circuit Torben was more distinguished by his eccentricity and longevity than anything

else. Oh, he'd won some European tournaments in the 1950s—
the Danish and British hardcourts (meaning clay in the Europeans' perverse lexicon; to Americans, hardcourts mean paved
surfaces, cement or asphalt composition). He won the French
indoors and the Canadian doubles. As for the Big Four events,
Ulrich got no further than the semifinals at Wimbledon—twice,
in the doubles.

Torben's most notable achievements came late in his career
—in fact, after it appeared to be over. In the 1964 Wimbledon
he and his younger brother Jorgen stirred up some early-round
excitement, Torben especially by beating Tony Roche, the up-
and-coming young Australian. A British reporter at the time
described the win as "a fine scalp for a player [who] . . . was
thirty-five years old [and] . . . perhaps ten years or so past his
peak." Torben then proceeded to throw a scare into the Number 2 seed, Chuck McKinley, before going to the sidelines,
where he was joined by Jorgen, a victim of Germany's Wilhelm
Bungert.

But wait! as they say in the commercials. There's more!
Four years later, at the first U.S. Open, I saw Torben reach the
round of sixteen, eliminating fifteenth-seeded Marty Riessen
and then pushing the Number 4, John Newcombe, to the limit
before yielding the five sets. And the next year, 1969, he figured
in one of the most dramatic matches in that year's Open. It was
a third-round loss to Pancho Gonzalez—a titanic five-set battle
between a pair of forty-year-olds, foreshadowing their meetings
in the Grand Masters later on in the Seventies.

But overall, Ulrich's record in the big time was that of a
journeyman, and he entered the Grand Masters with none of
the prestige of the superstars. His success took some of the
other players by surprise, even those who were aware of his
religious training habits, his dedication to physical fitness.

He was even more of a surprise to the fans. Arriving as a
virtual unknown, he quickly established himself as a favorite.
His arresting looks and his highly individual style—inventive,
good-humored, sparkling with bits of theatre—invariably won
the crowd, including me. Even if his strokes still weren't overwhelming, they were beautifully tuned, and he seemed to have

added a variety of new spins to his repertoire since his circuit days. And it was always fun to watch an Ulrich performance to see what piece of bizarre strategy he'd come up with to deflect the other guy's power. Or what piece of comedy to break the tension or relieve the routine.

When I saw my first Grand Masters tournament, in 1978, the Sedgman-Ulrich hegemony was still perhaps at its most potent, and most of the players from the original nucleus were still active—Davidson, Gonzalez, Seixas, along with some lesser-knowns. Over the next five years of sporadic tournament going, I became aware of changes in the cast, as younger players began coming of age—forty-five, that is—and gradually displaced their seniors. But Sedgman and Ulrich remained fixed stars in the senior firmament. And for a while, even though the leadership was clearly passing, both of the old tigers continued to be factors in the race for laurels and prize money.

But when I caught up with the 1983 Grand Masters tour in a midsummer tournament at Orange Lawn Tennis Club in suburban South Orange, New Jersey, I realized that things were shifting underfoot. It was as if I had stumbled into some sort of chronological fault. Sedgman and Ulrich looked little changed with the years, but suddenly they were alone. And even they seemed vulnerable to the tremors of time.

All the other old familiar names were missing from the tournament draw. Gonzalez and Segura, Seixas and Rex Hartwig were long gone. Now Sven Davidson was the latest to join them on the sidelines—retired. Bobby Riggs was on the premises, but only as a bystander, watching from the VIP seats under the marquee. Gardnar Mulloy, the oldest of the *old* Old Guard, the World War II generation, was still winning senior tournaments somewhere as he entered his seventieth year. But not in this league. Not in the Grand Masters.

A whole new generation had taken over in the last few seasons. *Junior* seniors, you might call them. On the big scoreboard near the entrance to the clubby little stadium where the draw was posted, you could read the names of Neale Fraser, Mal Anderson, Ken Rosewall—all members of the Australian wave that had followed in Frank Sedgman's wake. Also in the field was Alejandro Olmedo, a transplanted Peruvian with a face like an Inca sculpture, who played under the United States flag on the winning Davis Cup team of 1958—one of just three interruptions in the Aussies' eighteen-year sway. The only American from that age of Australian dominance was Eugene Scott from New York, a Yale-educated, grass-court specialist of the 1960s, semifinalist in the 1967 U.S. Nationals. An exotic note was supplied by dark-skinned, jet-haired Ramanathan Krishnan, a former perennial champion of Asia and mainstay of India's pesky Davis Cup team from the mid-Fifties right through the late Sixties.

Here was the advance guard of the transition generation— players who bridged the gap between the old amateur sport, with its segregated code, and open tennis with its lavish prize money, its teenage professionals, its powerful agents brandishing rich endorsement contracts. Two of the players, Anderson and Rosewall, had even *won* major open tournaments. Rosewall, unlike all the Grand Masters ahead of him, had never even retired from competition, not even briefly. He had never tried his hand at any other occupation, tennis-related or otherwise. He had been a full-time tennis player before he was eighteen, that's what he was at twenty-eight and thirty-eight, and that's what he remained at forty-eight. He had simply moved from one circuit to another, from the mainstream to this gentle backwater.

The overwhelming fact about the newcomers was that they were a whole tennis generation younger than I. Fine players and solid citizens though they might be—ancient as they might seem to any fan brought up in the open era—they simply didn't qualify for the Golden Age of tennis.

The Grand Masters tournament at Orange got under way with an interesting match between Krishnan and Olmedo. At first the pudgy-looking forty-six-year-old pride of India was overpowered by the Inca chief's attacking game. Olmedo, a year older, still looked surprisingly quick, and his serve still came in with an authoritative thump.

But in the second set, Krishnan began taking Olmedo apart with deceptively wristy strokes. Krishnan's shots kept passing Olmedo as he moved in the wrong direction. The Indian beat the Peruvian going away.

Then Torben Ulrich came on, looking solemn and quirky in his plenitude of hair. A fifty-five-year-old relic of the original Grand Masters tour.

Ulrich was simply demolished by the forty-eight-year-old Rosewall, who ran him so far off the court with angled volleys and placements that he could never find a toehold in the match, or even a platform for his usual theatrics. Once, after winning a point on a dubious call, Ulrich was chased clear into the stands by a slashing Rosewall overhead. Returning to the court, he stopped to pick a flower from one of the courtside planting boxes and offered it to the beneficent linesman as if in gratitude for the previous point—perhaps as if to encourage another generous call. It was a wan gesture, although it delighted the audience.

The match ended soon afterwards, 6–1, 6–0, with the crowd cheering Ulrich as vigorously as they cheered the winner. Five or ten minutes later Torben was still sitting meditatively at courtside, flexing his hand as if trying to shake some sort of pain or stiffness.

Frank Sedgman's first-round match, against Gene Scott, paired the oldest (fifty-six) and youngest (forty-five) members of the troupe. Both, in their prime, had been distinguished by their speed, but Scott never had anything like Sedgman's weapons. The old Yalie's game had always seemed more cerebral than instinctive: He often played points with a certain overdeliberateness, as if asking himself as the ball came off his opponent's racquet, "Now, what's the proper response to *that*?"

That was pretty much the way Scott played the first set—playing with a slight limp—while Sedgman moved around the court with his usual fluidity, hitting approach shots that kept landing, heavy as cannon balls, within inches of the baseline. Scott had trouble getting his racquet under them, couldn't return them with any kind of force or depth. Point after point ended with Sedg just where he always liked to be—in command at the net.

In the second set, Sedgman's approaches started landing just a bit shorter (a sign of fatigue?) and Scott began figuring out what to do about them. He was getting his racquet back earlier, especially on the backhand, and he was hitting out— hitting beautiful topspin passing shots that dipped down into the court beyond reach of Sedgman's racquet. Topspin—most effectively and most easily hit on slow clay surfaces like that grandstand court at Orange—is a weapon not as often seen in the arsenal of older tennis stars, trained as they were on the faster grass courts, which favor the use of underspin on approach shots. Scott, like Sedgman, was a born-and-raised grass-court player, but he seemed to have added something to his game in his born-again phase.

The match went into a third set, in which Scott established an early lead with a service break. He looked fresher, and the age advantage was sure to widen with the match. But suddenly Sedgman righted his game, and the eleven-year age gap seemed to disappear. Now they were playing even, point after brilliant point.

Down 4–5, with Scott serving for the match, Sedgman surged pantherlike onto the attack, and quickly reached break point. It was the moment I had been anticipating: the old Wimbledon champ, the old champ of Forest Hills, asserting himself. What I did not anticipate was the thing that happened next: The old champ blew a routine overhead.

The four points that followed were a remarkable example of the serendipity, disguised as luck, that often decides sports contests. On three of those four points Scott hit solid, deep first serves, and each one of them bounced crazily off the taped service line, catching Sedgman off balance and eliciting weak returns. Suddenly, unexpectedly, it was Scott's match, by a score of 3–6, 6–1, 6–4. Sedgman, the longtime ruler of the Grand Masters, had not even made it through the first round.

One of the delightful things about Grand Masters tournaments, along with the good sportsmanship, is the intimacy of the little clubs in which they are played—a contrast to the remoteness of those huge stadiums whose crowds are required to support the macroeconomics of the Grand Prix circuit. The cozy quarters at clubs like Orange mean that the players are accessible to their fans. I was standing only a few feet from Sedgman and Scott after the match when Bobby Riggs came down from the marquee to congratulate both of them on what he described as "a beautiful game of tennis, really wonderful to watch."

Some of the spectators were still standing in their places, applauding. From just beyond the little jewel box of a grandstand you could make out the genteel sounds of club doubles being played on the old grass courts.

Riggs complimented Scott on his effective use of topspin— "overflow," he called it, as if deliberately misusing a phrase in some foreign language, the way some cutup in a French restaurant might order a "chocolate mouse."

Then Riggs turned to Sedgman, who was sitting with his reddened face buried in a towel. "That was nothing to be ashamed of," the 1941 U.S. Singles champion said consolingly to the 1951 U.S. Singles champion, the 1939 Wimbledon winner to the 1952 Wimbledon winner. "The match turned on three liners."

Sedgman barely looked up. "Aaagh," he said, "I'm just too old." He wasn't smiling. At fifty-six, he was exactly a year older than Torben Ulrich. Both of them had given the old enemy, time, a hell of a battle, but it was clear they were losing ground.

Surveying the wreckage of change around me, I was reminded of something I had been told by the founding father of the Grand Masters, Alvin Bunis. It was during a tour final, played some years earlier at Greenbrier, a toney old resort in the Blue Ridge mountains of West Virginia. With a nod in the direction of Sedgman and Sven Davidson, both then superb-looking specimens just past fifty, who were playing a spirited match on the court below us, Bunis told me he liked to think that the Grand Masters had revolutionized prevailing ideas about the aging process in relation to sports. Obviously athletes were capable of playing longer and better than the traditional wisdom used to allow.

"But," he added emphatically, "don't get the idea that the

Grand Masters is some kind of geriatric laboratory. It isn't. And it isn't a rest home for retired tennis players. Every player knows he's expected to maintain a professional level of skill and fitness. I underline *professional*. That means it has to be worth paying to watch. Fifty-five seems to be some sort of break point. After that age a player's game isn't apt to meet professional standards—it's no longer worth the price of a ticket."

"And then?" I asked.

Bunis nodded approvingly as Sedgman came in behind a chipped return of service and volleyed for the point. He answered without taking his eyes off the court. "When you're through, you're through."

Al Bunis is a convivial gent, five years older than Frank Sedgman, with sparse gray hair, a taste for London tailoring, and, by his own admission, a degenerating backhand. "It used to be my best shot," he announces mournfully, as he comes off the court after a couple of frustrating practice sets against one of the Grand Masters.

Bunis learned his strokes on the public courts, first in Kansas City, then in Cincinnati, where he grew up in comfortable circumstances, the son of a department store executive. Never a world-class player, he was good enough in his teens to hold a national ranking in the Boys 15s and the Juniors (16 to 18). And he was good enough at forty-five to be ranked again: Number 7 in that senior bracket—Number 2 in doubles. In between he won a Midwest regional doubles tournament (the Tri-State) with his older fellow-Cincinnatian Billy Talbert, played a few tournaments on the Eastern grass-court circuit, put in three years in the World War II Navy and came home to graduate from the University of Cincinnati before going into business as a scrap-metal broker. He did well enough at it to sell out profitably and retire at the age of forty-nine. Then, in the standard style of old tennis players, he sat down and figured out a way to get back into the game full time. In this case not as a player but as an entrepreneur—a tour promoter.

What led him to the idea of the Grand Masters was a combination of nostalgia and his own recent experience in some senior tournaments. He was impressed by the high level of play among his contemporaries and intrigued, as he put it, by "the experience of watching tennis minds at work." If the tennis was still that good among the lesser lights, then how good might it be among the stars!

He began to think seriously about tournaments for former world-class players. The trick was to find old champs who were still playing enough tennis to make a decent showing.

For his own amusement and experience Bunis staged a tournament in Cincinnati involving four solid U.S. seniors: Tony Vincent, Al Doyle, Lou Schopfer and Bunis himself. That was in November 1972. It drew a good crowd and a good press, with the result that Bunis got an inquiry from a club in Milwaukee: How about putting on a senior tournament for them the following summer, with some marquee names in the field?

Bunis went off on an exploratory tour in search of well-aged talent. His old Cincinnati compatriot, Billy Talbert, had a well-known history of going anywhere to help tennis or tennis players. As usual, Talbert agreed to participate. Bobby Riggs had a reputation for going anywhere for a buck. This time, after a strenuous negotiation, he agreed to forgo a guarantee. Other old players fell into line, including a couple of foreign contenders—Ulrich of Denmark and Torsten Johannson of Sweden.

Some of these old-timers were still hitting the ball well, and some were just dim shadows of their old reputations. Bunis figured he needed one towering figure to put him over the top —a superstar of recent enough vintage to be remembered, whose tennis was a reasonable approximation of the past.

He found the right man in the nick of time. Found him in a most appropriate place, Wimbledon, just a week or so before the Milwaukee tournament was scheduled to start.

"As a matter of fact," Bunis recalled some years later, "it was in the *locker room* at Wimbledon. There was Frank Sedgman. As I remember, he was playing in some sort of special veteran's tournament that was being held as a kind of sideshow to the big event.

"I told Frank about my Grand Masters project, about the tournament coming up in Milwaukee. He didn't seem to believe I was serious about this idea, so I told him, 'All right, meet me at my hotel tomorrow morning, and I'll show you how serious I am.' Well, he was curious enough so that he showed up in the lobby at Claridge's the next morning, and I walked him down to an airlines office and bought a ticket, London–Milwaukee, and handed it to him, and said, 'That's how serious I am.' Well, Frank showed up in Milwaukee."

In the very first Grand Masters match ever held, fifty-six-year-old Frank Parker beat sixty-year-old Bitsy Grant at the Town Tennis Club in Milwaukee, on the same court where they had met in a tournament forty years before. The very first Grand Masters tournament winner was forty-five-year-old Frank Sedgman. The prize was a thousand dollars, provided by local sponsors. Bunis himself financed the players' expenses. He came out with enough of a profit to convince him that he was onto something.

There were two more Grand Masters tournaments in 1973—in Memphis, Tennessee, and Richmond, Virginia. Sedgman won one, and Torben Ulrich the other.

The following year, 1974, the Grand Masters became an organized tennis circuit. The rest is history, officially recorded tour by annual tour in the United States Tennis Association yearbook, along with the results of the U.S. Open, Wimbledon, all the other mainstream tournaments and the dozens of national championships in different age groups on all kinds of surfaces.

By 1980 the Tennis Grand Masters (to use the organization's official copyright name) had become enough of a tennis phenomenon and enough of a financial success to attract the attention of the burgeoning tennis industry. Bunis got an irresistible offer and sold out to the huge sports conglomerate called IMG. The initials stand for International Management Group. Among its multiple, overlapping activities, IMG promotes tennis tournaments, packages them for television, and also serves as agents for the people who play in them. Tennis players tend to change agents the way they change racquets, but at one recent point IMG's list of talent included Bjorn Borg, Mats Wilander, Vitas Gerulaitis, John Newcombe, Peter Fleming and Tim Mayotte among the men—along with most of the current Grand Masters. Among the women it listed Chris Evert, Martina Navratilova, Billie Jean King, Virginia Wade, Kathy Jordan and Tracy Austin.

Selling out to IMG didn't end Al Bunis's connection with the Grand Masters. They still needed his paternal touch, because the sports management business is a young one, populated by yuppies—men and women both—whose personal knowledge of tennis goes back no further in time than the oversize racquet. Their idea of a tennis graybeard is Jimmy Connors, who they think has been playing forever but who won't in fact become eligible for the Grand Masters until 1997.

So Bunis continues to travel the circuit as a paid consultant —a link to history. He introduces the matches with little biographical sketches of the contestants over the public address system. He instructs and supervises the umpires and other officials, in effect serving the functions of referee and tournament director. He plays the role of Big Daddy to the whole entourage, which includes not only the players but also an IMG tour manager and often a representative from the executive suite of the tour sponsor, Mutual Benefit Life. Bunis describes the jurisdictions this way: The tour manager takes care of all business matters, while he himself takes care of tennis—he is there to see that the traditions and standards of the game are maintained.

What happens when a player no longer meets Bunis's standards, when, say, on reaching the fifty-five-year limit that Bunis once cited, his game no longer seems worth the price of admission?

It is pretty much like what happens to those thirty-five-year-old linebackers in the football training camps, bracing themselves for a visit from the Terrible Turk. That's the football pros' term for the team official, usually an assistant coach, assigned to the distasteful job of notifying players who have failed to make the cut.

In the compact, three-round format of Grand Masters tournaments (just two rounds of doubles) there is room for only eight players—the elite of their age group. There used to be a fairly big roster of fill-ins, when there were twenty or more tournaments a year, including several events abroad. But IMG streamlined the schedule, reducing the tour to two series of tournaments—one series in the spring and one in the fall, for a total of fifteen to eighteen events.

Now the same eight men play the whole tour with occasional substitutions from a bench or just two or three players. Fall below the rank of Number 10 or 11 among the world's forty-five-or-older tennis players and you've dropped right out of the Grand Masters.

Beyond it there is nothing but the so-called supersenior tournaments for fifty-five-year-olds, for sixty-year-olds, and so on, right up to eighty-year-old competitors. These are official, USTA-sanctioned events involving skilled and vigorous competition, but traditionally they used to be disdained by most world-class players. The early rounds are populated by old geezers in elbow braces and baseball caps, with dubious strokes. The later rounds are minefields packed with danger to the prestige and egos of old champions. It can be discomfiting to find yourself bracketed in the semifinals against, let's say, a former twenty-fifth-ranked player who has stayed in shape and worked on his strokes for twenty or thirty years, while you had no place to go but down.

The general feeling used to be that if you'd once won Forest Hills or played in the Davis Cup, then you had nothing to prove in an old geezers' tournament—and a lot to lose. As Vic Seixas, a nonparticipant, says, "Eventually somebody you shouldn't lose to will beat you, and then it's a big deal."

To a considerable degree, that feeling has loosened up. Gardnar Mulloy and Bobby Riggs, for example, are now fixtures in supersenior championships, along with a number of solid, if little-known former players. To old pros like Riggs and Mulloy, it's better than not having any championship to play for at all. To others, it is still the abyss.

By the summer of 1983, when I saw the Grand Masters tournament at the Orange club in New Jersey, Frank Sedgman and Torben Ulrich were the only players left from the original

Grand Masters, the only ones to have been spared by the tennis version of the Terrible Turk. And it looked as if he might be breathing down their necks as well. The ultimate winner at Orange was Ken Rosewall, who went on to wind up as overall winner of the 1983 tour. In the year-ending playoff tournament in Florida, he was unexpectedly beaten by the newest member of the Australian "youth corps"—forty-five-year-old Fred Stolle, who joined the circuit late in the year but came on with a flourish.

The runner-up to Rosewall in the point standings and prize money was Mal Anderson. Sedgman and Ulrich ended up near the bottom of the list.

By the time those results came out, I was already looking forward to next year's tour, my appetite whetted by a visit to the record books. I was checking the birth dates of former tennis stars, to see who might be turning forty-five in the coming months and therefore eligible for the Grand Masters, when one name leaped out of the pages. An Australian. Of course.

It was Rod Laver, by some lights the best tennis player of all time. In a couple of matches—one as an amateur at Forest Hills, one as a pro in Madison Square Garden—the best tennis player I'd ever seen.

Laver versus Rosewell again! The prospect of those revived glories couldn't fail to stir the blood of any tennis fan. It certainly stirred mine. Here was a chance to relive tennis history, and I was determined not to miss it.

Over the winter the Grand Masters would be scattering to their homes and offices—in Melbourne, Brisbane, Madras, New York. Some, including a couple of transplanted Australians, would go home to Southern California, the tennis heroes' Valhalla. Home to await the winter cut. Survivors and newly eligibles would reassemble in Nashville, Tennessee, in the early spring of next year: a troupe of middle-aged men ready to begin another season of combat as professional athletes. They would be joined by another—rather less fit but just as dedicated to the hacker-and-watcher's form of tennis as they were to the playing professional's. That would be me. I intended to follow the 1984 tour around the country, catching as many tournaments as I could, for as long as I continued to feel like watching good tennis.

I was in a position to do that because I had recently put a career behind me (a little too early to call it retirement) as a television journalist. I had also undergone the kind of medical crisis that stirs intimations of mortality and questions about the flight of years. Restored to the game with a lot of cautionary advice from my doctor, I was eager to make the best possible use of my time on the courts.

By paying close attention to the Laver-Rosewall replay (and the byplay among the lesser contestants), I thought I might get some insights into the elusive mysteries of tennis. I also thought I might get some insights about the limits and possibilities of age. The Grand Masters seemed worth watching on that score because they were stretching established boundaries. They were doing something difficult and doing it extraordinarily well for many years longer than people used to think it could be done.

Besides all this, I had a fan's curiosity about the special nature of champion athletes. What drove them to seek the heights of excellence? What kept them in the game, or sent them back to it long after their time had apparently passed?

Finally, I had sentimental motives. By my somber calculations, Frank Sedgman and Torben Ulrich, the last of my generation, had no more than a single year of competitive tennis left —*if* they made the next year's roster at all. Passing the fifty-five-year mark, they were still hugging Ulrich's curve of declining potential, but the curve itself seemed to have taken an abrupt dip. The 1984 tour was almost certain to be their last hurrah.

And if that was the case—if the revived Golden Age of tennis was about to go down the tubes, taking my revived youth with it—then I wanted to be there as a witness.

PART II

Reunion in Nashville

The Fit and the Fitter

THE MARYLAND FARMS RACQUET CLUB in Nashville, Tennessee, is a monument to flourishing suburbanism. It sits on the outskirts of the city in what used to be the pasture of a thoroughbred horse farm but is now a business park in an early stage of development. You reach the place by turning off a highway lined with large houses built in a style that might be called neo-plantation, which takes you out of downtown Nashville and deposits you in the community of Brentwood.

Brentwood is one of the city's tonier suburbs, retaining much of its original horsey aura. Locals sometimes refer to its residents as "the mink-and-manure set." The racquet club is where they go to indulge their penchant for indoor forms of strenuous leisure. The building echoes the traditional design of the surviving horse stables, but it is new and vast. Its interior is a complex of lounges furnished like country living rooms—deep sofas arranged around stone fireplaces—and carpeted hallways leading to a swimming pool, exercise rooms, and two separate clusters of tennis courts. When I checked the place out on a blustery late-winter afternoon, grandstands and boxes were still being constructed for the Grand Masters tournament that was scheduled to start that evening.

In the midst of the sawing and hammering, players were getting the feel of the hard paved surface and the rhythm of their strokes, rusted by months of relative inactivity. Ken Rosewall and Gene Scott, on one side of the net, were hitting against Neale Fraser and Ramanathan Krishnan, on the other side. While stroking balls to each other, Rosewall and Fraser kept up a kind of crosscourt exchange of news.

It was the day after the Presidential primary in New Hampshire—the traditional overture of the American political campaign. The papers I'd read on the plane from New York were full of Gary Hart's surprising victory over former Vice President Fritz Mondale at the Democratic party polls, along with the echoes of President Reagan's withdrawal of U.S. Marines from Lebanon, a couple of days earlier. But those issues probably couldn't have been expected to stir the interest of a couple of Australian visitors. Their news was of a much more personal sort. It was concerned with names and events from their separate home towns and their intersecting tennis circles back in Australia. Somebody had left one racquet company for a job with another. Somebody was opening a new condominium resort; they were having trouble with the financing. A new group was being organized to take over. Somebody would become the head tennis pro if the money problems got worked out.

Scott, whose interests are eclectic and rather cosmopolitan, interjected an occasional question or comment. Krishnan was silent and serious, concentrating on the depth of his backhand.

This was reunion time. For the last day and a half the Grand Masters had been straggling in to Nashville, most of them delayed by ferocious blizzards, which had shut down airports all over the eastern half of the United States. Krishnan had made a midnight arrival from India by way of New York. Fraser had come just as far in distance, and the transition had been even more complicated and more drastic. He had wrapped up his duties on the sidelines of a Davis Cup match as nonplaying captain of the Australian team. He had barely taken time to join in the celebration of his squad's victory over Yugoslavia before catching his flight to the States. The match had been held in the heat of the Southern Hemisphere's upside-down summer. It had been played in the city of Perth, in the far southwestern corner of Australia, which meant that Fraser had to fly a distance equal to New York–Los Angeles before he could even get out of his own country and begin the twenty-four-hour trip across the Pacific and the American continent. Talk about jet lag!

"It was a hundred and two bloody degrees in Perth!" Neale declaimed, with a gesture toward Nashville's wintry outdoors. "Yesterday! Or whenever in hell it was!"

He and Rosewall began to play practice games as the other two players left the court. From the effort Fraser put into every point, it looked as if he was trying to make up for the whole winter in a single practice session. "All right now, let's go!" he kept prodding himself, as if getting ready to serve match point in a tournament final. He blasted in another big serve.

The day before, at a welcoming lunch for the players, half the guests of honor were missing—victims of the weather. There was a table full of local media—the print press plus television, which would be carrying the semis and finals, and radio, which was busy lining up the few available stars for guest shots on talk shows. The rest of the room was filled with local sponsors and their guests, along with some other VIPs.

The tournament was a significant event on the civic calendar. Nashville sports and business interests were hoping to make their city one of the regular stops on the annual Grand Masters tour. Beyond that, they aspired to bring in a mainstream tournament as well—"maybe even something as big as Memphis," one booster told me. Memphis, a rival city, is the site of the National Indoor Championships—"an $800,000 to $1,000,000 package," my informant explained. The Grand Masters package was just one-tenth that size—somewhere between $80,000 and $100,000. So this tournament was to be a kind of low-budget pilot.

It was also a kind of microcosm of modern tennis economics.

The tournament was billed as the "$40,000 Third National Bank Grand Masters," but that simply referred to the players' purse. That and the bulk of the other costs—stadium rental, erecting and dismantling the stands, salaries for staff, expenses for advertising and promotion—were underwritten by the Third National Bank of Nashville and a group of lesser sponsors. At most tournaments Mutual Benefit Life is the primary sponsor, but in this case they would simply carry the players' hotel expenses plus some incidentals.

If the event drew capacity crowds all four days—a triumph beyond all reasonable expectations—then by my arithmetic that still wouldn't come close to paying the cost of the package, especially since half the gate receipts were earmarked for the benefit of a local cause, the Nashville Symphony Orchestra. The deficit would be covered by the sponsors in exchange for having their names and logos displayed around the premises and mentioned in the publicity. That's no different from mainstream tennis, in which even huge sellout events like the U.S. Open collect more from outside commercial interests than they get from the gate.

As individuals, some of the Grand Masters might be playing for reasons of ego, nostalgia or pure love of sport. But they wouldn't be here without some corporate benefactors picking up the tab.

At the VIP luncheon the duties of spokesman for the Grand Masters would normally have fallen to Al Bunis, but in his absence—he was one of the blizzard victims—the role was filled by one of the players, Roy Emerson. Emmo is almost as much of an old hand as Bunis at this sort of thing. On the old pro circuit he used to play a role comparable to that of a *tummler* on the Borscht Circuit—the comedian cum social director whose job it is to stir up activity and keep the guests entertained at those Catskill Mountain resorts north of New York. Emmo kept the locker rooms stirred up all right with his constant needling and his repertoire of songs. They ranged across international boundaries, from the old Australian anthem, "Waltzing Matilda," to "Ciao, Bambina."

Introducing his colleague Torben Ulrich to the Nashville luncheon crowd, Emmo paid tribute to the bearded, pigtailed veteran as a pioneer in the field of fitness. Torben, he said, was an exponent of aerobic exercise and health food back when most athletes were still swilling soft drinks and doing plain old-fashioned calisthenics.

"I'm starting with Torben," Emmo explained, "because he's the oldest. How old are you now, Torben? Sixty-five?"

"Eighty-five," said Ulrich. He looked somehow diminished in a jacket and tie, possibly the only ones he owned. I had rarely seen him in anything but tennis shirt and tight shorts or a mismatched sweatsuit. Once, after a Grand Masters tournament in the South, I happened to catch the same flight to New York that Ulrich was on. He made the entire trip, from his hotel lobby to LaGuardia Airport, barefooted—not a conventional mode of dress for middle-aged passengers. When our paths diverged at the terminal he was rummaging in his racquet bag for a pair of tennis shoes, which he felt sure he must own since he had just finished playing a tennis tournament.

After disposing of Ulrich, Emmo the emcee went down the Grand Masters roster. Every player, present or still awaited, was identified by some reference to his age or his agelessness. Presenting Rosewall, Emmo said in an admiring tone that Kenny was unchanged "since the first time I ever saw him play, back in 1953—he's still one of the meanest players on a tennis court." Krishnan was introduced as "a forty-six-year-old gentleman without a gray hair in his head." That prompted me to observe that Emmo, a year older, had a sprinkling of salt in his short, brown hair. And Ulrich seemed to have sprouted a few strands of white in his luxuriant dark beard since I saw him at South Orange. Was it something I had failed to notice, or had the winter been tough on these supposedly ageless heroes?

"Gene Scott," Emmo went on. "Now the only reason he'll be here is he's an American and a very famous college athlete. I've been told that he got ten letters from Yale, though I can't imagine why any one would even want to write to him."

The speaker concluded with a few historical observations. "If you want to know what's happened in tennis in the last twenty years, well, I signed my first professional contract for $75,000, and to earn that I had to play about 360 days in the year. The other day Jimmy Connors played one exhibition match and earned $75,000 in two and a half hours.

"Ten years ago," he went on, "I never realized that there

would be a professional competition for people of the age we've reached. What are you going to see when you come out to watch us in the next few days? I think our tennis is comparable to what you'll see from Connors and McEnroe." He said that with a straight face, but then he broke into a kind of impish grin. "Well . . . maybe we do take a little more time between points."

There was a brief interlude of business at the podium and then the public-address system burst into an explosion of disco music. Six or eight identically leggy young women began bopping down a runway through the banquet room, the only discernible difference among them being that some were tall and leggy while others were *small* and leggy. They had been recruited from the club's staff and membership to display sportswear fashions from the pro shop. I thought they did credit not just to the inventory but to the tradition of Southern womanhood.

Afterwards I noticed some of them, still fetchingly done up in their tiny skirts and form-fitting exercise suits, buzzing around the tennis players. The ladies seemed to be warming up their act for a cocktail party that was to be held for the visitors that evening. Emerson and Mal Anderson were getting the biggest play. Both are rangy, outdoor types—slightly overage Australian versions of the Marlboro man. They come by that look honestly. Mal grew up punching cows on his father's ranch in the Queensland range country. Emmo's family ran dairy herds, but the lifestyle was much the same.

As far as the local media were concerned, the stellar attraction wasn't the relatively youthful Aussies but ancient Torben Ulrich. The reporters clustered around him, plying him with questions about his diet, his conditioning routine, and his opinions on various issues not necessarily related to tennis.

In a kind of benign sing-song, like a Zen chant delivered with a Scandinavian accent, Torben observed that society was becoming increasingly depersonalized, commercialized, professionalized . . . that sports reflected these same trends . . . and that the Grand Masters itself was not immune. He said he missed the pioneering spirit of the original troupers. "We knew we were doing something special, you see. There wasn't all this aerobics and fitness in those days. Now of course you have eighty-year-old marathoners, you have Senior Olympics, old basketball players. We were the groundbreakers.

"There used to be more nostalgia in our tournaments. Gonzalez and Sedgman were legends. People came out to see if they really existed. But it's different now. They know that Laver and Rosewall are real, because Laver and Rosewall were never out of sight."

In the old days, he went on, the tour existed for the sake of the tennis and the comradeship. There was more of a fraternal feeling among the players, reunited after years of little or no contact with each other. Now, he observed, the Grand Masters was becoming more commercial, like tennis in general—like sports in general.

In what way?

"Oh . . . it's hard to say." He shrugged and went on to another question.

Torben's outlandish ways and his iconoclastic views have been savored by several generations of tennis players, but it's only in his most recent, or Grand Masters, incarnation that he has acquired much of a civilian audience. One of the earliest recorded Torbenisms dates back to the amateur era, when another player caught him just as he was leaving the court after a match and asked if he'd won. Torben seemed to have trouble remembering. "I don't think so," he said. "I simply played in my usual way, and the other guy lost."

Ulrich's disdain for winning has since become legendary. He was asked in an interview to recall his "greatest career win" —a question so standard that most tennis players travel with several answers at hand, like extra pairs of sweat socks. Not Torben. "I don't have any 'great wins,' " he said, putting audible quotation marks around the detested phrase. "So that takes care of that subject."

Another standard question: "When did you start playing tennis seriously?"

Ulrich: "I have never played tennis seriously, and I don't think I ever will."

Ulrich's answers are sometimes severe, but his tone is gentle. He addresses all questions thoughtfully, often fingering beads as he speaks, in a mild Scandinavian lilt and with the benign expression of a guru counseling a seeker after wisdom. If this suggests a self-effacing individual, then the impression is far from right. An interviewer once told him that he sounded like a man who preferred anonymity to fame. Torben seemed affronted.

"An eagle is not anonymous," he said, summoning up metaphors that hardly suggest humility. "An oak tree is not anonymous. But they do not *seek* fame."

Sometimes his answers are like little masterpieces of elusiveness—to a degree that makes you wonder if his preferred form of exercise isn't leg-pulling.

At South Orange, the previous summer, as he was leaving the court, I noticed him being cornered by a fan who insisted on knowing Ulrich's secret of fitness.

"Nothing special," Torben said vaguely, "I just look after myself."

The fan wasn't satisfied. "Do you run? Lift weights?"

"Oh," Torben replied, as if he had never actually thought about it before, "I do a little lifting, a little stretching, a little running." He shuffled his battery of oversized Prince Graphites together and began collecting the rest of his gear. The questioner thanked him and started to turn away, but Ulrich continued evenly: "Then I do a little *more* lifting, a little more stretching. Some more running. Some walking. Some standing still. All that sort of thing."

The fan backed off, but Ulrich was in measured pursuit. "A little standing up, a little sitting down. A little sleeping, a little fasting. Between meals, after meals . . . "

The last I saw of them, Ulrich had his arm around his questioner, who was nodding helplessly as he was eased toward the grandstand exit, still being regaled with the minutiae of Torben's routine.

All of which is the kind of stuff that makes good advance copy—the sort of material the boys from the *Nashville Banner* and the *Tennessean* would relish as a way of filling space on the big event at the Maryland Farms club before there were any actual scores to report.

"Where do you live?" I heard a reporter ask Torben while the Marlboro men were amusing their female fans.

"Here," he said matter-of-factly.

"Here in *Nashville*?" the reporter asked. His eyes lit up at the prospect of a local angle he hadn't anticipated.

"Of course. I *live* wherever I am. This week I am living in Nashville. Don't you think that's right—to be aware of your surroundings, to enjoy whatever is here?"

Seeing that he had flustered his interviewer, he abruptly shifted to a more conventional line. "If you want to know where my residence is, I'm spending some time in the Pacific Northwest these days."

That piece of information surprised me. The last I knew, Torben lived—that is, resided—in Southern California, with his wife and teenaged son. If at fifty-five he now seemed even more elusive and free-spirited than usual, there was a reason for it, which I later learned: He and his wife had recently separated. He had friends in Seattle—one particular friend, I suspected—and he was supporting himself there in the off-season by conducting tennis clinics. He was also conducting a seminar at an adult education center connected with the University of Washington. His subject: Sports and Gender. It dealt with "role playing as it's related to sports—you know, the question of what's truly male or truly female."

The reporter asked him if he had been doing anything special by way of conditioning in preparation for the Grand Masters tour.

"You do what you normally do," Torben said. "You can't suddenly start doing something different. When you get older you can't rush it, you know. You might hurt something."

"What about your diet?" the reporter asked. "Do you eat anything special?"

"No," he said negligently. "Some croissant, some frankfurter—whatever is there."

As the reporters drifted away and the luncheon crowd thinned out, I asked Torben if he had any plans beyond the

Grand Masters—if he'd given any thought to what he'd do after his playing days were finally over.

The beads stopped running through his fingers. He offered an evasive smile. "In Denmark they have a funny saying: 'It's always difficult to predict, especially about the future.'"

One of the last of the troupe to arrive on the tournament scene was the impresario, Al Bunis. He dragged in on a flight from London by way of New York, looking storm-tossed, like everybody else, but still somehow dapper in his rumpled Burberry. Inspired by recent visits to his outfitters in Savile Row and Jermyn Street, he was well prepared for one of the preliminary activities, which he was immediately flung into: the fitting of the players for new Grand Masters blazers, the prescribed uniform for tournament parties and other ceremonial events on the tour. A Cincinnati tailoring firm specializing in that particular item of clothing had despatched one of its experts to Nashville to perform those duties under the leader's exacting eye.

The fittings were done in a room at the motel where the players were staying, on a highway strip near the Nashville airport.

"Rosewall—waist thirty-two," announced the fitter, a genial blond man named Ed Hyman, as he whipped a tape measure around Kenny's beltline. He made some notations on a printed form.

"I'll bet Kenny hasn't changed an inch in all the years he's played tennis," Bunis said, for the benefit of a couple of bystanders.

"I was thinner when I played in the Juniors," Rosewall said, deadpan. He fingered the red piping on a gray sample blazer that lay displayed on a bed, remarking mildly that it looked like a band uniform.

The "team" blazers are an old bone of contention between the players and Bunis, who designs them. He defended the new model, like the old ones, on the grounds of "show business," which he considers to be an important element in professional sport.

Rosewall's voice rose about as much as it ever does, reaching a level of mild affront. "This is all right for you," he said to Bunis, poking at the jacket, "with your steamer trunks and your four suits. But some of us are traveling from Australia with a suitcase and a gear bag, you know. If I'm packing this bloody jacket, I'd like to be able to wear it to some civilized place."

Bunis stood by his standard defense, and Rosewall gave up.

"How would you like your name on the inside pocket?" Ed Hyman asked. "Kenny? Kenneth D.?"

Rosewall seemed surprised by the question. "Ken Rosewall sounds good enough," he said.

"Eugene L. Scott," was the firm choice of the old Yalie, who came in a moment later. His waistline measured thirty-four and a half inches—hardly excessive for a man tall enough to look like a basketball player. It was, Scott confessed, about an inch and a half more than when he earned those varsity letters—not in basketball but in tennis, hockey, soccer and track (his event was the high jump). "But," he added, with a touch of pride, "it's less than when I started playing the Grand Masters." He paused as he started to leave the room. "Does anyone happen to know if they've got a therapist at this club?"

Apparently I was the only one in the room to whom it occurred that Scott might be looking for the services of a headshrinker. I guess I'd been spending too much time with media people, who are notorious neurotics. What he wanted was a *physio*therapist. In New York Scott visits a physical conditioning specialist two or three times a week, for general muscle tone-up and treatment of an arthritic hip, the cause of that gimpy gait I'd noticed in his match at South Orange. In Nashville, he was told, he'd probably have to settle for a standard clubhouse masseur.

Not everybody came through the weigh-in as brilliantly as Scott and Rosewall. Neale Fraser showed the effects of his sedentary winter down under, watching other people play tennis. Normally burly, he now looked a bit puffy.

"What's your weight?" Hyman asked him, pencil poised over his tailor's pad.

"It's variable." While still in the fitter's grasp, he called over his shoulder, "Mike, I've got to get my room changed. It's even worse than this one."

The complaint was addressed to Mike Savit, a young mustachio not long out of Harvard who manages the Grand Masters tour for IMG. He handles logistics while Bunis takes care of policy issues like whether umpires should exercise the right to overrule linesmen (rarely, very discreetly) and whether the blazers should have red piping.

I sympathized with Fraser. I was staying at the same motel, and my own room was a cheerless cube at the end of a dim and forbidding corridor. The atmosphere of the establishment was somewhere between *film noir* and a Russian novel—not exactly the Lower Depths, maybe Middle Depths.

The fitter wasn't letting Fraser off the hook. "What's your weight right now?" he persisted.

"A hundred ninety-one," Neale said. "But going down." He flinched just a bit as the tape measure went around his middle.

"Waist—thirty-six and a half," Ed Hyman announced.

"If your weight is going down," said Roy Emerson, who had just come in, "how come your belt size keeps going up?"

Emerson himself was checking in about ten pounds lighter than last season, when he had been visibly out of shape, but conceded that he needed to drop ten more. Ramanathan Krishnan was another player who looked as if he might have blushed a little at the tale of the tape, but he merely shrugged. "I tend to be on the heavy side," he said, as if that took care of all questions about conditioning.

I asked Krishnan if there was anything he did to prepare himself for the tour. I knew that he spent the winter ensconced behind an office desk in Madras, where he owns a company that distributes household cooking gas. I wondered if the annual transition to strenuous activity didn't require some change of routine or lifestyle.

"Oh, yes. Change of diet," said Krish. He speaks with the clipped guttural accent typical of his country. "I am a rice eater back home, but here I won't eat it."

"Why is that?"

"Rice makes you thirsty. It makes you drink too many soft drinks. Makes you sluggish. Puts the weight on."

I asked him what happened to the butane gas business while he went off to play jock in the States.

His usually solemn dark face broke into a white smile, as if he were pleased to be reminded of home. "My wife looks after it," he said. He had the contented sound of a man who has left things in the hands of Allstate.

"I like your warm-up suit," Bunis said to Mal Anderson, who had just turned up wearing an elegant new designer model. "When did they start making them for heterosexuals? No, I mean *do* they make them for heterosexuals?"

They kicked that one around for a while in the style of locker-room banter that passes for a common language in the multinational troupe. Bunis is the grand master of the friendly insult, excelling even Roy Emerson. Anderson is not an easy target. Though he does have a certain tempting straight-arrow quality, he is so relentlessly good-humored that barbs tend to bounce off him without penetrating.

Mal had just turned forty-nine—he was pushing Rosewall in age—but he checked in at his old Davis Cup playing weight, looking as lean and fit as always at six feet one and 165 pounds.

Just as Ed Hyman was getting ready to pack up his stats and his samples, in came Torben Ulrich. Height: five feet ten. Waistline: an incredible thirty and a half.

It was now barely noon, and Torben does not favor the morning hours. He used to have a clause in his Grand Masters player's contract stipulating that he would not be required to take part in any activities—matches, clinics, exhibitions, interviews, fittings—before the hour of noon.

That was in the easygoing, pre-IMG era of the Grand Masters, when it was operated as just a friendly deal between Bunis and a bunch of old tennis players. Torben had objected to having a written contract at all—it seemed much too cold and impersonal—but if there had to be one, he said, then he wanted that guarantee written into it.

Bunis is a businessman but not a stickler, so he agreed. The signing of the contract was scheduled for a suitably late time of day. Torben showed up with a lawyer: Gene Scott, a member of the New York bar, but not yet a member of the Grand Masters. Torben also arrived with another item that he wanted written into the contract. It was a poem, translated from the original Tibetan, on the subject of human relationships. Torben felt it defined his obligations to Bunis better than any of the standard legalisms.

Bunis had it typed in, and the parties of the first and second parts duly signed.

On the Court

ON THE OPENING DAY of the Nashville tournament I drove out to the Maryland Farms club with Bunis. His standard early-round costume is a tweed jacket worn with gray flannels or tan chinos and a shirt with widespread London collar and carefully knotted tie. But this afternoon he was dressed for action, not style. He was wearing warm-ups over tennis shorts. He intended to get in a set or two with Krishnan before the matches started that evening. He needed to work out the kinks from his transatlantic trip, he said.

We started to talk about the problems of age on the tennis court, and I reminded Bunis of his dictum, some years earlier, that fifty-five was the break point for the Grand Masters—the age beyond which a tennis player simply couldn't hack it in professional competition.

Bunis frowned as if he'd never heard such a preposterous idea. "I'd say it's more like fifty," he said.

I pointed out that two members of the troupe, Sedgman and Ulrich, were well past that age—that both in fact were past the former milestone of fifty-five.

He nodded. "Both very unusual individuals. Unusual but not invulnerable. That's why you won't be seeing much of them on the tour this year. Because Sedg is Number 9 and Torben is Number 10 in an eight-man field. It pains me to see it happen, but that's life. The only reason Torben is here is that Fred Stolle had other commitments this week."

Stolle, having beaten Rosewall in the 1983 Championship playoff last November, was technically the current Grand Masters champion, even though Kenny's overall tour record was better. Fred would open his title defense a week later, in the second event of the tour. Meanwhile, Bunis explained, since Ulrich lived on the West Coast, he had gotten the call to fill in. "You can't fly Sedgman all the way over from Australia to play one weekend. We'll work Frank into a few tournaments later on in the schedule. But Torben will probably get to play a little more—now and then, here and there. Neither of them will be a factor as far as the Grand Masters championship is concerned, you can bet on that."

The reason for the downward revision in Bunis's Law of Tennis and Aging was the recent toughening of the Grand Masters competition. Ulrich and Sedgman were victims not only of time but also of the fitness trend, which was affecting athletes along with the general population. You might even say they were victims of their own example. Year by year, the players who joined the troupe were better conditioned than their predecessors. Increasingly they were men who had stayed in shape. And some, like Rosewall, had even kept a certain match-play edge.

"Let me tell you," Bunis said, "it's hard to stay in the match against a player five or ten years younger than you are. Last year when Sedgman had to go up against Stolle it looked like a reasonable contest. For about three or four games. But Stolle is only—what? Forty-six? No, still forty-five. And he coaches Grand Prix players. Kids in their twenties. He plays sets against them, doesn't do too badly. Fred began hitting out, and the placements were going right by Sedgman. He simply wasn't able to catch up with the ball. Stolle's hitting got sharper and sharper. Sedgman looked slower and slower, older and older. It turned into a blowout."

The picture of that match, which I was glad to have missed, was endlessly depressing. Sedgman and Ulrich, the last two survivors of my age group, were not only a dying breed, they were already anachronisms—a couple of dinosaurs somehow preserved past their time. Just *barely* preserved.

I asked Bunis if we were apt to see many of the old alumni of the Grand Masters in the course of the tour—Gonzalez,

Seixas, Davidson or the other retirees. I wondered if they came around to the tournaments or otherwise stayed in touch after dropping out.

"Not really," he said. "Not many of them. And I'll tell you why. For one thing, you don't drop out all at once. You start being called for fewer tournaments, and then one day you realize you're out of it. But another thing is, there's always a little resentment, because nobody ever leaves voluntarily. Everybody thinks: I can still play if I just get back in shape, maybe work a little more on my footwork. No matter when it happens, it's always too soon."

Ulrich had the honor of playing the opening match of the 1984 Grand Masters Tour. The bad news was: He was playing Rosewall.

In the introductory spiel over the PA system, Bunis summed up Torben's lengthy career: ". . . A world-class player for well over three decades . . . Participant in ninety-eight Davis Cup matches for Denmark over a span of twenty-one years. . . . In 1975 and 1976, the top-ranked senior tennis player in the world." That didn't cover all the many facets of the Ulrich persona. Bunis went on to suggest a few others: "Poet, philosopher, artist, musician—the Renaissance man of tennis."

While first and last a tennis player ever since his teens, Torben had also been a part-time portrait painter and an experimenter in the abstract-expressionist style; a jazz clarinetist, doubling on saxophone and occasionally flute; a jazz critic reviewing records and performances for Danish publications.

The Renaissance man came trotting onto the court through applause and appreciative laughter. The laughs were for a pot of geraniums which he picked up from the courtside display and solemnly presented to Bunis as if to thank him for the flowery introduction. It was a slight variation on the floral presentation schtick I'd seen him use before. The comedy routine was in midseason form; we'd have to see about the tennis. Torben *looked* serious about that, all right. He was in his combat mode—the beard tucked up and tied under his chin in some kind of streamlined arrangement.

When Rosewall's turn came, the scope of his achievements seemed almost too much for rhetoric. Bunis made a pass at it: ". . . Ageless, incomparable . . . the first citizen of tennis." He gave up and went on to the list of major championships, starting at the age of nineteen: the French, twice; the U.S., twice—fourteen years apart; multiple Australian titles over a span of seventeen years. Everything but Wimbledon, the championship that forever eluded him. Bunis concluded with the not incidental fact that Rosewall was currently the highest-ranking Grand Master, having accumulated the most points on the previous year's tour.

The grandstand erupted again in welcoming applause. Rosewall ran in from the players' entrance and, to the further delight of the crowd, handed Bunis a single flower. The gesture had the same marvelous economy as Rosewall's game. He was willing to carry a gag just so far, it said, and no further.

Then Rosewall stripped the cover off a standard-size graphite racquet—a Wilson Ultra—and got down to business.

Among his locker-room colleagues Rosewall has long been known by the nickname "Muscles"—a reference to his unimposing physique. In a sport in which many players overpower their opponents with big serves and rifle-shot ground strokes, he has always relied on consistency and accuracy. "Muscles makes you change your perspective of the tennis court," a longtime competitor once remarked in frustration. "He doesn't use any part except the lines."

In the very first point of the match Rosewall moved Ulrich back and forth, from sideline to sideline, until, most unexpectedly, from a defensive position, Torben pulled off a perfectly angled dropshot for a winner. It was a gutsy and imaginative way to start a match. The drop shot is a statement: It asserts confidence. It usually gets its effectiveness by the sudden change of rhythm after a pattern of play has been well established. And even the best players rarely try a stroke requiring such exquisite control of the racquet until they've had a chance to loosen up. The shot Torben made was also the kind of shot that ought to be banned from the view of club players, the way pornography is kept from teenagers, because they might be tempted to emulate it.

Rosewall quickly got the point back, and eventually the game, when Ulrich charged the net behind a pretty good approach shot but blew the volley.

They played evenly until, with Ulrich serving at 2–3, Muscles delicately shifted gears and ran off a brilliant string of five consecutive points. First a backhand placement down the line to Torben's left-handed backhand; then a heavily sliced crosscourt approach shot with a crisp follow-up volley; a couple of great crosscourt returns; and a backhand approach shot down the line, which forced an error from Ulrich. The next time Ulrich served, Kenny broke him again and put the first set in his pocket, 6–2.

Again, in the second set, Ulrich started off well, and this time it was he who got the first service break.

In the course of his remarkably long career on the amateur circuit, Torben showed a talent for springing to life just when he'd been given up for dead. It was twenty years since that Wimbledon victory over Tony Roche, when a reporter marveled at the performance of a player then considered ten years over the hill. But here he was, a survivor of his own obituaries, still hanging in against one of the world's best in any age group.

And not just hanging in. Ulrich didn't hesitate to charge the net in the face of Rosewall's deadly passing shots—though he did pick his spots carefully, and made sure to put his volleys away sharply, beyond the reach of Kenny's lethal counterpunch.

But there was no way Torben could keep it up. Right after the service break, Rosewall broke back. He took command of the net. Not easily but methodically, he ran out the set, 6–3, and with it, the match.

It was good tennis. Torben had given the Grand Masters leader a run for his first-round money—a much closer run than in the match I'd seen them play the summer before, in New Jersey. It just wasn't enough to get the old bearded patriarch through a draw filled with the new breed of younger, tougher senior players.

The other first-round contests were just as interesting, all for different reasons.

Mal Anderson started off his match against his old chum and doubles partner Neale Fraser with a kind of bravura that seemed at odds with Mal's placid temperament and his workmanlike manner. What's more, Anderson's fireworks came from his service, which historically has been Fraser's forte—one of the great services, in fact, in the annals of the sport.

Three times in the first game Fraser had a break point on Anderson, and all three times Mal evened the score by serving an ace—twice down the middle, the third time sharply angled off Neale's left-handed forehand. At deuce, still another ace, and then Anderson served out the game.

Later on in the set Anderson served three more aces in a single game. He also hit a beautiful series of touch shots, which kept Fraser continually off balance—so badly that on one point he stumbled and took a heavy fall.

When you see a fifty-year-old man land on his hip with the full weight of his rather bulky body, you hold your breath for a moment. Neale quickly shook it off, but after that he stopped running for drop shots. Mal won the set handily, 6–2.

Up to that point, Fraser's own service—or really, his battery of different services, all big but with varying spins and angles —had been effectively spiked by returns that sometimes caught him on the way in to the net. Now Fraser began to cut down on the velocity of his serve—I figured he was trying to give himself more time to get in. He began knocking off the volleys, and when he pulled even in the second set at 4–4, I turned to the expert in the seat next to me—Al Bunis—and asked if he thought Fraser could catch his opponent.

"No way," Bunis said. "Look at Neale—he's puffing. And Mal sees it."

Mal saw it, all right. He was making his old buddy run. A couple of times I even had the feeling that he prolonged a point when he had a chance to put it away, just to draw a little more effort out of the other guy.

Fraser stayed with him into a tiebreaker, but that was as good as he could do. Anderson won the set 7–6 and still looked fresh when the match ended. Fraser was visibly done in.

Anderson is the sort of super–good sport who offers alibis on behalf of a defeated opponent. "I haven't done nearly enough preparation for this tour myself," he said over a post-match beer, "but Neale had none at all, with his Davis Cup duties. Sitting in the sun for three hours at a time—that's hard on the nerves, too. All the chance he's had to practice was hitting this afternoon for an hour or so."

Mal, by contrast, had stayed in shape playing squash at the club that he, his wife, Daphne, and his older son, Gary, operate back home in Melbourne. He also found time for an hour and a half or so of tennis three times a week. His sparring partner was Gary, who is in his early twenties and plays the old man about even.

Aside from the impersonal, businesslike way it was executed, one thing struck me about Anderson's dispatch of Fraser: The two men seemed remarkably evenly matched—in mechanics and tactics, in approach to the game, as well as in age (at fifty-one, Neale was barely a year and a half older than Mal). So the results came down to practice and condition.

That would turn out to be a pretty good explanation of a lot of Grand Masters matches.

5

Echoes of Wimbledon

IF YOU PAID ATTENTION to the buzzing of the fans as they were taking their seats for the opening-round contests or as they stretched at the refreshment stand between matches, the name you heard most, by far, was Laver. His reign as the undisputed king of the game was just recent enough for some young fans to remember. At least they could recall seeing the name or hearing about him—Rod Laver and his incredible left-handed passing shots, characteristically hit on the run with a topspin that cracked like a bullwhip, leaving opponents stunned. Laver the holder of the rarest record in tennis—that double Grand Slam achieved by no other player; all four major championships, fast surface, slow surface. With each passing year in the current age of specialists—fast-court serve-and-volleyers, clay-court baseliners—it gets harder and harder to imagine Laver's achievement ever being duplicated. It towers above the landscape of tennis the way Cy Young's 507 pitching victories stand unchallenged in baseball.

Or the way Laver himself dominated his contemporaries—first in the amateur ranks and then, after he hurdled Rosewall, in the pros. The year Rod racked up his first Grand Slam, 1962, he also won three other significant titles—the Italian singles, the Irish, and the German. That made him champion of six different countries, a big slice of the tennis world. In 1971, as a thirty-three-year-old professional, he swept through a field containing eight of the best players in the world—Rosewall, Newcombe, Ashe, Roche, Emerson, Tom Okker, Dennis Ralston and Roger Taylor—in a running series of thirteen head-to-head matches over a period of ten weeks. He whipped them all without a single loss, copping $160,000 in prize money for his efforts. As a campaign of devastation it had the effect of Sherman's march through Georgia.

No wonder that, when the arguments started among middle-aged tennis fans at the tennis club bar, about who was the greatest of all time—Tilden? Budge? Kramer?—the one player from the 1960s generation who was bound to get a few votes was Rod Laver.

In the publicity, Laver was getting top billing as the tour "rookie" and the obvious challenger to Rosewall for the Number 1 ranking in the Grand Masters. If you were making book on this year's tour, you'd have to count Fred Stolle in as an outside choice, off his last year's finish. But Rod would be the favorite. And it was Laver's debut in the Grand Masters competition that made the opening round at Nashville an *event*. It hardly mattered who he was playing.

His opponent in the draw happened to be Krishnan, who gave me a crisp scouting report.

"Rocket is hitting very well," Krish said in his guttural staccato. "Last time I played him must be twenty years ago. Wimbledon 1962. That's twenty-*two* years. He used to hit with more topspin in those days. Now his wrist is not strong enough. My own wrists were always strong and supple, but I myself am a less wristier player than I used to be."

"Rocket" is one of those nicknames that seem to fit almost everything about the person—in Laver's case it is not just his red hair and the explosive force of his shots but also his speed of foot and his headlong style of play. It is also a reference to his home town of Rockhampton on the east coast of Australia, a railroad town and meatpacking center in the forty thousand population range, about midway between Yeppoon and Wowan, and not too far from Moura, Baralaba and Banana. In that sparsely settled corner of the world, everything else is pretty distant.

I hadn't yet seen much of the bantam superstar. He was one of the last arrivals in Nashville, and he wasn't staying at the airport motel with the enlisted men. He was being put up—

more auspiciously, I trusted—at a downtown hotel with which
he had a personal business connection. It was part of a chain
involved in the management of Laver's Tennis Resort, a Florida vacation place of which Rod was part owner.

The afternoon before his first-round match Rocket had loosened up by playing a practice set with his favorite opponent,
Ken Rosewall, but I only happened to catch the last few points.
It was enough to make me marvel at the boyish enthusiasm
those two old rivals still put into the game. Rosewall especially.
When he brought off a shot that pleased him, he would let out
a sort of teenager's yip of delight. He and Laver seemed to have
some special taste for each other's game. As they were toweling
off afterwards, Laver confided to his longtime antagonist, as if
to a coach or a concerned friend, "I feel like I was serving well,
but I keep making those silly little errors!"

Nineteen sixty-two, when Laver and Krishnan had last met
on a tennis court, was presumably memorable to Laver as the
year of his first Grand Slam. It was also an easy date for the
Indian to remember. That was the year he got to the semifinals
at Wimbledon (where Laver bumped him). It was enough of a
feat, when added to Krishnan's multiple Asian championships
and his ninety-seven Davis Cup matches, to have made him a
national hero, just slightly less known to schoolboys in Madras,
Calcutta, Bombay and Delhi than the martyred political leader,
Mahatma Gandhi. Ram—an earlier nickname—was the first Indian player, and so far the *only* Indian player, to be ranked in
the world's top ten, achieving that eminence four straight years,
1959–1962. He was recognized as one of the great "touch" players of all time, with subtle, seemingly effortless shots that baf-
fled opponents. I'd seen him baffle Alex Olmedo in the Grand
Masters at South Orange, New Jersey, two decades-plus after
his prime.

Now Krish—visibly slower with the added weight of his
forty-seven years, admittedly less supple of wrist than in his
youth—was going out to face the Rocket in his first outing of
the tour. I asked Krish what he thought he'd have to do to stay
in the match.

"That's it," he said agreeably. "Just stay in the match. Don't make errors. Keep the ball in play."

"Rock him to sleep," was the way my consulting expert, Al Bunis, put it, in a subtle bit of alliterative wordplay. *Rock the Rockhampton Rocket*, I interpolated. "Lull him into an exchange," said Bunis. "That's the only way Krish can hope to keep him close."

We were watching from a courtside box, to which Bunis had withdrawn after making the introductory announcements. Bunis is a tennis table-hopper, rarely sitting in one place for an entire match, especially in the early rounds. Once he's satisfied himself as to how the match is going, he often wanders off to chat with the players or to conduct business with the IMG tour manager or some other member of the entourage.

"Krish is a very deceptive player," Bunis said, as the Aussie and India's hero were finishing their warm-up rally. "People see this slightly overpadded guy with that funny walk—it's almost like a waddle. They see him hit his soft stuff, and they say, 'What's he doing here with these *tennis* players? Why, I could hit that well myself!'

"But Krish has a remarkable talent. I'd say it's a talent for hitting implausible shots from impossible positions. And you can't read him. He hits the ball with that little flick of the wrist, at the last possible moment, so you can't really anticipate where the ball's coming."

The rookie contender was not easily deceived. He ran up a quick lead, hitting everything with great depth and pace, finishing off the points before Krishnan could get into them.

It was only well along in the second set that Krish was able to put his game plan into effect—and then with uneven results. On one point he engaged Laver in an exchange of ten cross-court shots, with Laver returning measured topspin backhands each time. On the eleventh, Laver hit a severe, unreturnable slice that barely came up off the court.

Now Krish took a stand. With a curiously sliced puff-ball service, in which he barely seemed to stroke the fuzz with his racquet, he slowed down the pace so severely that Laver did go to sleep. At least he let his attention wander enough to permit Krishnan to come to the net behind fine, skimming approach shots. Krishnan took a few games, but then Laver dug into his repertoire: serve and volley, topspin placements, vicious overheads hit inside-out so they angled away from his opponent. Rocket briskly ran out the match, 6–1, 6–3.

Krishnan came off the court as exhilarated as if he'd been a winner. "He has so many good shots!" he said. "He's a *marvelous* player!" He sounded more like a Laver fan than a badly beaten opponent.

Krish confesses to sentimental feelings about his Grand Masters colleagues—sentiments that go back to his early years on the tennis circuit, in the fifties.

"The decision to be a tennis player, to play in a serious way, was a difficult one for me," he says. "I was only fifteen years old, and there was no competition in India, so to be a tennis player I had to travel. I had to go to England to play the Wimbledon juniors. [He won it after a couple of tries.] My mother was against it, she felt I was too young. My father was for it. He was a government official, a tennis player himself. He traveled with me the first couple of years, before I started to travel on my own.

"In those years I was shy. I didn't even want to ask any one to practice with me. So that was the worst problem I had—being lonesome.

"My first friends were the Australians. Roy Emerson—you know how friendly he is. The Australians traveled as a team, so if you made friends with one, you had a *bunch* of friends. It's good to see Emerson, Laver and the rest of them again. It's nice to be reminded of the days when we were playing championship tennis, but it's not quite the same, really. When you play against Laver now, and he misses a shot, you realize he's just a human being. In those days we didn't think so."

Krishnan's dark squarish face is practically seamless; the crown of jet-black hair is full and sleek, never ruffled by his exertions on the tennis court. I asked him what exactly were the changes that he felt had affected his game—what made the difference between championship tennis and the sort of game that he and his old friends now played.

"It's not just the muscles that decline," he said, "it's the eyes. Eyes and muscles are the big difference. It's harder to see the backline, especially if the lighting conditions are less than perfect. And of course the reflexes are a problem. You are not ready to hit the ball exactly as you should be. But there are compensations," he assured me.

Like what?

"Experience. Temperament. I think we're more ready for the ups and downs of the game."

Late Learner

FOR ANY ONE with a healthy interest in time and its effects, the match between Roy Emerson and Gene Scott was probably the most interesting event in the first round.

"It seemed to me," Scott told me the following day, "that there was a kind of blink or twitch in Emmo's service. I could see that there must be one synapse that had gone amuck."

What Scott called a faulty synapse, or loose connection in the nervous system, is what you and I might have called a mental block. "Emmo doesn't have the confidence he used to have that the ball is going in," Gene explained. "I suffer with him because right now I do have it—that confidence, that fluidity on my second serve. I just throw the ball up, and I know it's going in.

"When Emmo throws the ball up, I can tell where it's going, not by the direction of his racquet but by the nature of his worry. If he's hit a fault to my forehand, then the second ball's going to go to my forehand, too, because he wants to get something close to the same motion—he's searching for a rhythm. And I'm thinking: *The poor bastard! His serve used to be his bread and butter. All of a sudden the mechanism has gone. He doesn't have it.*"

I was waiting with Scott in his room down the hall at the Middle Depths Motel while he finished unpacking. His observations about Emerson sounded a lot more sympathetic than his treatment of Emmo the evening before, when he eliminated the cheery Australian in three sets of hard, thumping tennis, taking advantage of Roy's service problems and his apparent lack of conditioning. The ten pounds Emmo said he'd taken off over the winter had left him still a half-step slow to the ball and one stroke short on the rallies. The forty-seven-year-old *tummler*—just a year older than the sedate Scott—was still too far off the form of his years on the old circuit, when he was known as probably the best all-around athlete in the game. He was distinguished for his muscular strength and his speed, honed by hours of relentless training runs.

Scott also had a reputation for athleticism, but it was less awesome. He was known as a player who used speed and agility—plus intelligence—to make up for limited talent.

Terms like synapse and references to the nature of an opponent's worry are not part of your average postmatch analysis. But words come easy to Scott. He is, among many other things, a writer and a rather fancy one. It was an article by Gene Scott that acquainted me with the word *eidola* (sing. *eidolon*, from the Greek, meaning ghost or phantom). It was in a reference to "Wimbledon . . . redolent with the eidola of the past."

Scott is the author of several tennis books, but most of his writing nowadays appears in his own periodical, *Tennis Week*, an insidey publication (circulation: 40,000) which he founded in the mid-Seventies on the upslope of the tennis boom. He functions as publisher and editorialist. Printer's ink runs in his veins. He comes from a moneyed Long Island family, and the money comes from the printing industry.

Gene went on from Yale to another toney institution, University of Virginia Law School, playing Davis Cup while still a law student. In the light of his later career, maybe it's more appropriate to say that he studied law while playing Davis Cup. He put in three and a half years with a large New York law firm —an experience he found boring—then left to start his own practice, mainly representing tennis players. But eventually he sidetracked his legal career and took the plunge back into tennis himself. "Tennis," Scott says, "is the language I speak."

He speaks it in just about every form, not just as a writer, publisher and senior circuit player, but also a TV commentator, a promoter (the Volvo New Jersey Grand Prix tournament, the

Westchester World Invitation in Rye, New York, and a minor winter event in the Bahamas) and a tournament director (the 1986 Nabisco Masters at Madison Square Garden). "Some people like to pick one thing and do it well," Scott says. "I like to try everything."

When he filed one recent year's income tax return, he was pleased to find that he'd made almost exactly the same amount from his writing and publishing as he had from his tennis playing and promotions. Scott's income is a private matter between him, his accountant and the IRS, but the Grand Masters slice of the pie was around $30,000.

Gene Scott's patrician background contrasts sharply with the working-class origins of his Australian colleagues and with the middle-class suburban milieu that produced many of the 1980s generation of tennis players. Scott represents the old *old* tennis tradition, the tradition of the exclusive Eastern clubs that made up the American grass-court circuit.

As a player Scott felt right at home in that environment. Between 1963 and 1969 he was a winner or finalist in almost every one of the stops on that circuit: Newport, Merion (Philadelphia), Baltimore, Southampton and Nassau (Long Island) and Orange—right on up to, but not including, Forest Hills. The best he ever did there was the semifinals, in 1967, when he was trounced by the eventual trophy winner, John Newcombe.

Scott's highest ranking in the United States was Number 4, in 1963, behind Dennis Ralston, Chuck McKinley and Frank Froehling, all a few years younger. But his best year overall was probably 1964, when, though he slipped a notch nationally, he was ranked as the Number 11 amateur in the world, in the unofficial international listing. By his own account, his best win came that year when he beat Fred Stolle in the finals at Newport, 10–8 in the fifth set.

That was the year Stolle was a finalist at both Wimbledon and Forest Hills, and was beaten in both by the world's Number 1 amateur, Roy Emerson. By 1964 criteria, in a match against Emerson, Scott would be the decided underdog.

Watching the match between Gene and Emmo, in Nashville twenty years later, you could have said that Emmo's service was only an eidolon of its former self. In one early game he served no less than three double faults.

Emerson's service, with its relatively low toss and its energetic curlicue windup, was always distinctively his own (though it was imitated by slightly younger Australians like Tony Roche and Owen Davidson). As a senior player Emmo had cut down on the windup. Yet he still looked to me as if he was overserving—trying to put more force into the delivery than he could safely control.

No, said Scott, that wasn't the problem. "It's simply that he's become a little tentative in his footwork. He still serves big, but when he moves in to the T, there's a little bit of waffle. A moment of uncertainty. He doesn't take control of the net the way he used to."

Whatever the explanation, Scott was catching him coming in with some fine topspin returns, especially off the backhand, that tripped him up or passed him. Scott took an early lead.

Emmo tried to muscle his way back into the set by sheer intimidation. Once he came charging in on an approach shot hit crosscourt from behind his own baseline—requiring him to cover a long diagonal distance in order to reach the net position. Maybe he could have brought that off in his young and speedy heyday, but not now. Scott caught him with another backhand—an almost Laver-like topspin that simply exploded off Gene's oversize Prince Graphite racquet. He won the first set going away, 6–2.

Emmo hit some beautiful winners to take the second set and even the match. But in the third, Scott's recently found fluidity of service pulled him into the lead. He finished with three consecutive boomers—one an outright ace. The American was the winner, 6–2, 4–6, 6–3, in a match that was reported as the first upset of the 1984 Grand Masters tour—the former world's Number 1 beaten by the former Number 11.

But it was an upset only if you didn't take conditioning into account, and if you looked at the old records without factoring in things that may have happened in the intervening years. For Scott is another example of late maturity, like Torben Ulrich.

The former U.S. Number 4 became a perennial Number 1 when he reached the thirty-five-year-old category, in which he won national titles on grass and clay in 1973 and 1974. A decade later he did the same thing in the 45s. It wasn't just that the competition was thinning out as players retired from competition. For Scott was one of those rare players who actually seemed to advance his game as a senior. In some ways he has continued to do so, gaining ground on his higher-ranked contemporaries. He can be studied as an inspiration to those middle-aged hopefuls who ignore the twinges of time and keep working on their strokes, experimenting with changes of grip and backswing and follow-through as if they still had a shot at the draw for the U.S. Open—well, maybe a shot at their own club trophy.

"I probably volley better now than I did in my twenties," Scott told me. "On American grass, which was not very good, all you had to do was get the ball back over the net and it was probably a winner. But on clay or *good* grass, like Wimbledon or Australia, the ball would bounce higher. I didn't know how to volley the ball away, so I'd stay back and rely on my athletic ability, my speed, my ability to stay on the court all day, and try to out-compete the other guy. Now I know you don't *volley* the ball—you don't just block it or punch it—you *hit* it.

"I also had to learn how to hit topspin off my backhand. I used to be mechanically weak on that side. I just couldn't deliver a winning shot off the backhand. Topspin—backhand *and* forehand—were just not part of my repertoire. In last night's match there were maybe ten backhands I would have been delighted to hit twenty years ago. I even hit a winning topspin *lob* off my backhand for the first time."

Scott paused to extract a sweater from an open suitcase and stow it in the closet of his motel room. He moved with a little stiffness. Last night's match had obviously been hard on his arthritic hip. He continued to talk about his late-blooming backhand.

"I take a great deal of pride," he said, "in the fact that I did it without a coach. I never really *learned* topspin—that is, I was never *taught* it. I accumulated the knowledge visually while making a film for television on Ilie Nastase the year he won the U.S. Open. [That would have been 1972, when Scott was already approaching thirty-five.] I did it watching ten hours of film rushes of Nastase hitting his topspin backhand. I still have that image emblazoned on my mind—his foot positions, where his elbow is. I mean I just watched that goddamn film so many times the backhand I hit is still Nastase's backhand. Obviously I can't hit it with his talent and flair, but I can imitate it. That's how I learned to hit my best shot."

Scott put a couple of shirts into a dresser drawer. "Obviously," he said, a bit ruefully, "this knowledge came a little late in the game."

All things considered, I asked, how would the improved, late-model Gene Scott—the forty-six-year-old Grand Masters player—do against the Scott of twenty-six?

He thought about that, but not very long.

"I was bloody fast at twenty-six," he said, sounding like a Yank who had spent too much time hanging out with Aussies. "I probably hit the ball pretty close to as hard now as I did then, but that's a function of the equipment. At twenty-six I played with a primitive wood racquet. The oversize graphite really helps. I've also worked with the weights the last two years, and I can notice the difference in strength. My left arm, which used to be a straight pipe stem, now even has a little bulge in it.

"But," he went on, "there is an undeniable loss with age. Speed. Vision. You just don't pick up the ball as quickly as you used to, so you don't have the time to prepare. You don't have the time to run the ball down, to use the power you may have acquired. The message doesn't seem to travel from eye to brain to hands as quickly as it used to."

He reconsidered the question, and amended his answer. "Maybe the main problem is not that there's that much of an atrophy, just that you don't do things enough. You don't spend an hour a day any more working on your volley. You practice an hour *altogether*, three or four times a week, fitting it in with your job and your personal life, and you try to do a little bit of everything. You know you're going to hit a lot more ground strokes than volleys in a match, so that's what you work on mostly. That and a little bit of footwork.

"You try to stay in shape, and you try to deal with your physical problems on an ongoing basis. Everybody's got some chronic injury that requires ministering to. It's not that we're hypochondriacal, just that with time and experience we've become aware of our bodies and how to deal with them. It gets to be routine, like putting on your shirt every morning. You're not trying to overcome the problem in the sense that you're going to cure it. You're just trying to minimize its effects and to accommodate it."

In the case of his own arthritic hip, Scott said, he'd found that it took a particular form of skilled massage—applied in his regular, frequent visits to a therapist—to give him reasonable flexibility and reduce the chronic pain that came with movement on the court. Roy Emerson, he said, had an exercise routine that he was supposed to follow for a chronic knee problem. Sedgman ran and did calisthenics to keep his repaired Achilles tendons limber. And chronic injuries, Scott pointed out, become part of the game. Part of your own game *plan.*

"You have to learn how to accommodate them—yours and the other guy's. You compensate for loss of mobility by trying to anticipate where the ball is going. You're extraconscientious about making the move back to the middle of the court after each shot so the next charge to the ball will be a little shorter, a little easier.

"On the other side, you may not hit certain shots in certain situations. For example, one of the things I was doing against Emerson yesterday—that big topspin crosscourt backhand. It can be a lot of fun to hit, it can be my best shot, but as an approach it may be the wrong shot to hit against Emerson because it will bounce high to his backhand, and what he doesn't like is bending *low*—that's because of his knee. So it would be much more effective for me to do the less elegant *under*spin, which stays very low and, because of his injuries, makes it hard for him to get down there."

Scott had finished unpacking and he excused himself, explaining that he was going out to the tennis club to hit some balls with his fiancée. Scott is a bachelor, long divorced; at about six feet three, he looks something like an Ivy League Gary Cooper. The resemblance does not go unnoticed by women fans. Scott has long led what struck me as an interesting social life. Over the years I'd seen him at tournaments and other tennis events around New York, always in the company of some good-looking girl. His fiancée, who had flown down to Nashville from New York for the tournament, was in the Scott tradition—a pretty, long-haired blonde in her twenties with a bone structure as fine as a bird's. It disguised a potent forehand.

Before Scott went out to practice, he gave me a capsule forecast of the 1984 Grand Masters tour. It would be a three-way race, he said—Laver and Rosewall crowded by Fred Stolle. Those three players, he said, would be the regular semifinalists. "That leaves one semifinal spot open for the rest of us —Emmo, Krishnan, Fraser, Anderson and me. The five of us will be fighting to stay out of the bottom of the overall point standings. The first year I played, I was fighting every week to get to the finals. Now the guys have gotten better. No matter how much work I do, Laver, Rosewall and Stolle are going to do better than I, just on sheer ability. I figure I'm fighting to wind up in the middle of the pack."

Scott's analysis was based on the rigid, rather cruel format of the eight-man tournaments. A first-round winner, advancing to the semifinals, gets seeded in the next tournament. A first-round loser gets to play one of the winners again. There are no "lucky draws" to help you break out of the losers' column.

Mathematically—which also meant financially—Scott's win over Emerson could turn out to be an important factor in the final standings of the tour. "Getting to the semis just once," said Scott, "I may have put Fraser and Krishnan behind me for the rest of the tour. It could mean I've already clinched sixth place, maybe even fifth."

What Scott was saying was that in this year's toughened competition Neale and Krish might not get to the semifinals even *once*—might not win a single match all year. If true, it was a bleak prospect for a couple of former champions.

The next day, according to form, Scott was knocked out of the tournament by Laver, who hit every shot in the book. *His* book. A lot of them were shots nobody else owned. There were examples of Laver's patented whiplash placements, hit on the run, crosscourt and down the line; volleys sliced viciously into both corners; volleys off his shoetops; half-volleys miraculously converted in midstroke into elegant little drop shots. Once Rod hit a drop from his own baseline along the whole diagonal length of the court—a shot so chancey as to be almost foolhardy. He hit it with such clever disguise and such perfect touch that it worked. A twenty-six-year-old Gene Scott might have reached it, but the forty-six-year-old arthritic took one hobbling step and turned his back.

If an opponent's chronic injury was part of the game on this circuit, then the circuit's newest rookie was learning fast. The score was 6–1, 6–2, and it went just about as snappily as the score suggests, leaving me with an impression of Scott's backhand that was totally different from the revelation of the evening before. I could not recall that Gene had brought that big topspin—his newfound "best shot"—into play more than once or twice. Otherwise, all I could remember him hitting from that side was a cautious slice.

"He can't hit it if you don't let him, can he?" Laver said in the locker room. His shirt was scarcely damp.

I asked him if he was having any trouble getting back into the game at his age after being away from regular competition for so long. He had played some tournaments against over–35 competition with some pretty tough players in the draw—including Rosewall, Emerson and another former world Number 1, Stan Smith. But those appearances were sporadic.

"No trouble," Laver said. He has a pleasant baritone voice, but his phrasing often makes his answers seem brusque, even a little belligerent. Given a chance to expand on a statement, he tends to soften it a bit.

"The only thing is," he added after a moment, "I might get too ambitious sometimes. Try too many experimental shots. That's when I tend to make those silly little errors. But that's the way I like to play—I've always played. I don't like to hit the same shot in the same situation every time. I like to try different things. That's the way you stay keen. You don't do it for the crowd, you do it for yourself."

"Laver," said Al Bunis, "is so *creative* on a tennis court. If you like tennis, you have to like watching what Laver does."

"Laver is a genius," said Gene Scott, sounding almost as much like a fan as Krishnan had the round before. "There really ought to be some sort of computer that says, as soon as he steps onto the court: 'Well, this guy is entitled to two games a set just because he is clearly better than any one else in improvisational skills.' Otherwise, he'll sometimes get beaten by people who don't have his flair and skill and artistry. And that seems unjust."

On the strength of Laver's performance so far, it also seemed unlikely.

7

A Night at the Opry

IF IT WAS already a successful tournament for Gene Scott, then it became even more so when he and Roy Emerson teamed up to beat Fraser and Anderson in the doubles. Fraser-Anderson is a veteran combination. Scott-Emerson was a pickup team, put together in the absence of Emmo's regular partner, Fred Stolle.

At the end of one long rally in the first set, Scott smashed a short lob, and Fraser, instead of conceding the point, lunged for the ball and took his second bad spill of the tournament. This time he landed on his chest with his racquet handle under him. For the rest of the match he stroked like a man who was hurting.

The day's other doubles contest was a walkaway. Ulrich and Krishnan, demolished by the team of Laver and Rosewall, went to the sidelines without a win between them to show for the tournament. Even Torben, with his professed disinterest in victory, did not look pleased with the result.

I watched some of the day's action in the company of Ken Rosewall's wife, Wilma, who had accompanied him from Australia for the tour. This is something she was free to do now that their two sons were grown up and on their own. Glen, the older, now had his commercial pilot's license; Brett was on his way to qualifying as a chartered accountant—"what you Americans call a CPA," she explained.

Wilma is a world-class spectator, who knows how to pace herself for a tournament. All but ignoring the first-round matches, she concentrated on her knitting—she was making a sweater for herself—sometimes while sitting far above the court at a window in one of the lounges. From there she could glance down now and then to make sure she wasn't missing anything important.

For the semis, in which her husband was playing Mal Anderson, she was spending more time in the stands, gradually working her way into the tournament like a top seed honing his shots for the final. It was pretty much the same pace her husband was applying as he moved through the draw, gradually stepping up the frequency of his attacking shots and sharpening his remarkable angles. Tomorrow, I figured, I'd see them both in final-round form—Kenny on the court, Wilma fully concentrated on the match in a courtside box. Teamwork.

Wilma has a decent background in tennis. Like Ken, she was playing in the Australian juniors when they met in their early teens. They were married at twenty-one. It's about that long since she's played the game seriously. The Rosewalls, she told me, do play a little family doubles at home—Ken, Wilma and their two sons. Glen takes a casual approach to the game. Brett is more intense and competitive, like his father. He is also following in his father's early footsteps—not as a tennis prodigy but by studying bookkeeping, which was Kenny's field while he was in school.

"Ken is very patient with the rest of us," Wilma went on. "He's a good teacher, and he doesn't mind taking the trouble. We used to play some social tennis, too. Mixed doubles. Ken isn't above all that—he just likes to play tennis. But he's too kind to strangers, and that made it hard on me. When I played alongside him, he'd never try to win the point for our side. And when I'd play against him, on the other side of the net, he'd dropshot me, lob me, do all kinds of mean things to help his partner win. Either way, I wound up doing all the work."

It was the standard wifely complaint about mixed doubles: When you play *with* me, you're no help; when you play the other side, you pick on me. I murmured something insincere and turned my attention to the court.

In a match full of beautifully played points, Anderson was hanging right onto Rosewall's heels, but Kenny always seemed to pull away just as things started to look interesting. Once Mal hit a superb offensive lob just over Kenny's head on a flat path into the far backhand corner—so clearly a winner it wasn't worth chasing. Not only did Rosewall chase it and reach it, but he returned it with a sizzling crosscourt for the point. "Do you think he *meant* to do that?" Anderson wondered afterwards.

Anderson never seemed out of the match until abruptly it was over. The scores were 6–3, 7–5. Rosewall had broken him neatly, economically—once in each set. Wilma had never even wasted a worried look on the match. Probably pacing herself for tomorrow. Today, after all, had been only a scene setter for the event that the Nashville Grand Masters was all about: the renewal of the Laver-Rosewall competition in tomorrow's final.

Wilma Rosewall's tennis-watching technique seemed all the more admirable because mine was faltering. Concentration —that was my problem. During a particularly one-sided patch in the doubles, my attention wandered to the sponsors' banners that festooned the courtside boxes, particularly to the one that advertised a real estate development with the quaint name of Harpeth on the Green. The phrase was hard to put out of my mind. Instead of studying the volleying techniques and the tactical patterns being displayed on the court, as any serious student of the game should be doing, I found myself mentally playing a bar game from my old newspaper days. The idea was to make up a catchy headline and then make up a news event to justify it.

A winning headline shaped itself irresistibly in my brain:

HARPETH ON THE GREEN
SINKETH IN THE RED

What was the news event that could conceivably inspire such a surefire attention-grabber of a headline?

Obviously it would be the collapse of the Nashville real estate market. Not wishing the local developers any bad luck, mind you—it was only a game, a little walkabout for mental exercise during a lapse in the drama.

The problem appeared to be contagious. The matches that

day were over so briskly that players were left with time on their hands. All day long you'd come across them in clusters, discussing nothing more compelling than whether now was a good time to eat, whether it paid to drive all the way back to the motel, whether there was a movie worth watching on TV.

The threat of boredom was worsened by an empty space on the social calendar. This evening, for the first time since the troupe began to assemble, there was no scheduled party to entertain the players.

A party I'd gone to a couple of evenings before had been a great success. It was held at the Maryland Farms club, and featured a lavish buffet, about the width of a doubles court, prettily landscaped with every possible form of finger food known to civilized man, plus a few chafing dish delicacies requiring those dainty little plates that drip onto your sleeve. There were little golden chunks of chicken breast, spirals of cheese and ham, miniature quiches the size of chestnuts, skewered shrimp arrayed in battalions, midget pizzas and giant stuffed mushrooms.

The lifted lids of the huge chafing dishes revealed bubbling acres of little meatballs and neat furrows of seafood crepes and a volcano of fiery chili. Off to one side was a dessert table like a confectionery garden, with dense chocolate cakes surrounded by trays of petit fours. It didn't look much like an athletes' training table, but the athletes were going at it—in a moderate sort of way.

There was a brisk traffic at the bars that were set up at strategic points around the room. The taped music that issued from several speakers had a nice beat to it.

Emmo came away from one of the bars, shouldering his way carefully through the crowd. He was cradling three or four pints of Foster's Lager, a popular Australian elixir, in his hands. Foster's was the "official beer" of the Nashville tournament—presumably a salute to the Grand Masters' large Aussie contingent. Being the official beer meant that a distributor in the area was one of the tournament sponsors.

"Not all for me," Emmo said breezily, indicating his cargo of bottles and nodding in the direction of a round table where a couple of his compatriots had installed themselves with some female admirers in a companionable circle of arms around shoulders. I recognized the ladies as some of the talent from the opening day lunchtime floor show.

"How do you keep in such terrific shape?" a Farrah Fawcett–type blonde asked one of the players, as she poked at his deltoids. He might well have asked her the same question.

"You *are* going to help me with my serve, aren't you?" said a young Brentwood matron in a dazzling white jump suit.

"What are you going to help *me* with?" said her escort.

Torben Ulrich came by with a small plate of goodies in one hand and a fork in the other. A young woman announced that since Torben was defenseless she was going to do what she'd been dying to do—stroke his beard. Torben smiled benevolently, but then she decided that what she really wanted to do was to pat his muscular backside. Torben didn't protest.

The early Grand Masters had a reputation for what Jack Kramer, in his young-rowdy days on the amateur circuit, used to call "chasing dames." In his later, staider period he referred to it as "socializing." As you'd expect, there were plenty of opportunities for a group of jocks with a certain aura of glamor and a patina of worldly experience, who also looked a hell of a lot better than most of us civilians. The only competing extra-curricular activity on the tour was poker—modest stakes, late hours, mostly on getaway nights at the end of a tournament.

As far as I could tell, in the latter-day Grand Masters, poker was a declining sport.

With no organized entertainment on the schedule for semi-finals day at Maryland Farms, the Grand Masters were left to their own devices. There were consultations during the awkward break of several hours between the afternoon and evening matches. Somebody suggested an excursion to the Grand Ole Opry, the country-and-western vaudeville that runs continuously on weekends. It is to Nashville what Lincoln Center is to New York. More. A lot of people who might slip in and out of the Big Apple without catching so much as a matinee at the Met or the New York City Ballet wouldn't think of passing through Nashville without a visit to the Grand Ole Opry.

Gene Scott, a longtime fan of Willie Nelson, Kenny Rogers and other country music stars, urged prospective Opry goers to wait until later that evening and join his party. He'd made arrangements for some good seats, which, he warned, were hard to come by.

"Why not go now and get it over with," Neale Fraser said, showing, I thought, a healthy irreverence for the local institution.

I had no interest in the Grand Ole Opry myself. I'm not partial to music that is performed in overalls, and I am rarely moved by lyrics with the rhyme scheme of a beer commercial. I was spoiled by an early exposure to Cole Porter, and my favorite musical Rodgers has a "d" in his name—it's Richard, not Kenny. So when the action at the Maryland Farms club was over for the evening, I waved goodnight to the Opry goers, had a drink in the clubhouse bar, and headed back to the motel.

It was about 11:00 P.M. when I got there, and I was ravenous. Inspired or perhaps shamed by the company of grown men with schoolboy physiques, I had restrained myself beyond my normal endurance at the cocktail party buffet, and I had been spending mealtimes at various local salad bars. By now I was suffering from an overdose of alfalfa sprouts and a deficiency of everything else.

When I pulled into the parking lot at the Middle Depths Motel, my headlights caught a solitary figure making his way toward the lobby entrance. It was Krishnan, his curious rocking gait unmistakable even in the less-than-perfect lighting of the parking lot. In India, it occurred to me, there would be nothing funny about that long, flatfooted stride. It was the customary gait of a man wearing a dhoti, that sort of draped, wraparound garment—a combination of toga and trousers much favored in the Asian subcontinent. The movement just looked a little odd in a warm-up suit.

Krish, I found myself ruminating, had never really outlived his alien status. Nor had he overcome the solitary habits of his

early tennis career. Once or twice I had seen him chatting ani-
matedly with dark-haired, dark-skinned fans—obviously compatriots—in one of the lounges at Maryland Farms (as I later
would at other stops on the tour). But more often he seemed to
be alone, as he was tonight, while the convivial Aussies were
generally laughing it up in threes and fours over their Fosters.
His self-effacing style made it all too easy to lose track of him,
even in the intimate company of the Grand Masters. Al Bunis
had once described him as "a man who has taken an oath of
modesty."

This time Krish, solo, was obviously on his way in from
dinner at the restaurant that adjoined the motel—an establishment that gave food second billing to its disco bar. But Krish
had the satisfied air of a man who had just packed away a good
dinner, maybe even including rice.

*The hell with Ulrich and Rosewall, with their thirty-inch
waistlines,* I decided. *My model is Ramanathan Krishnan, at
least for tonight.*

I parked my car and made my way past the boogeying couples in the bar. Leaving restraint in the check room along with
my coat, I ordered a giant taco which—molded into a sort of
fluted bowl like the shell of an ocean clam—held a sizable pool
of chili, surfaced with onions *and* grated cheese *and* sour
cream. It was accompanied by a face cord of french fries, and it
required a couple of good glasses of beer to wash it down. I
followed it with a dish of "our own" ice cream topped with a
sauce of hot spiced apples—a nice touch, I thought, designed
to appeal to those of us who had to eschew fattening garnishes
like hot fudge and butterscotch.

The meal left me thinking about a line from the late A. J.
Liebling, the distinguished writer and eater. In a paean to one
of the hyperglyceride sauces of the classic French cuisine,
Liebling appealed for "enough Béarnaise to thrombose an entire platoon" of bike-riding cardiologists. My own specialist, a
tall, scrawny distance runner who conducted his practice between marathons, would have been felled in his Adidas pavement treads by a mere reading of my dinner menu.

The next morning—Sunday, the day of the finals—I thought

about trying to hustle a couple of sets of exercise for myself, but I felt incapable of stroking a tennis ball, let alone chasing it around a court. I don't think there was anything wrong with the food. I was just paralyzed with guilt.

I breakfasted at a fruit bar—the matutinal equivalent of a salad bar—in one of the franchise-food joints that litter the Nashville landscape. Then I headed for Brentwood to watch history being made. Or remade.

Shemozzle

IT WASN'T just us fans who had been looking forward to a Laver-Rosewall final. In the ranks of the players that day there was a kind of holiday mood undershot with tension—the atmosphere of a heavyweight title fight. Up till now, there had been tennis matches; this was an *event*.

At breakfast in the motel and later on in the clubhouse the conversation was about how well Rocket was serving and how sharp Muscles looked in the preliminary rounds. The players sounded pretty much like fans talking about their idols.

"They're not just the two best players in the world for their age," Neale Fraser reminded us, "but two of the best who ever played the game. I mean, history will record their deeds!"

History would certainly have a hell of a lot easier time with the *deeds* of these two taciturn heroes than with their words or their innermost thoughts and feelings.

There wasn't much color in their background. The working-class suburb on the outskirts of Sydney in which Rosewall grew up, behind his father's grocery store, was as drab as Laver's small town on the fringe of the cattle range. That same lower-middle-class background produced most of the postwar generation of Australian tennis players, but it turned them out in two basic flavors. There were the free-spirited, often boisterous extroverts like Emerson, Stolle and their younger compatriot John Newcombe. And then there were the withdrawn, concentrated types like Laver and Rosewall.

Rod has never been accused of being chatty, and Kenny

seemed to be saving his words for the letters he was forever writing home to Wilma and the two boys while the other players yakked it up after the matches, got dressed and went out to socialize.

"We never see Muscles after dark," John Newcombe said once when he was a relative newcomer on the pro tour and Rosewall was the senior citizen. That, Newk said, was probably why Kenny had lasted so long.

It was on the tennis court that the personalities of Rosewall and Laver really emerged—and then in stunning contrast.

Laver as a player was all flamboyance—experimental, creative, full of wild imagination, hitting shots that were spectacularly his own. The Laver topspin backhand was one of the most ferocious shots in the game. It was hit with an extraordinarily wristy motion that sped up the flight and bounce of the ball instead of slowing it down, as so-called natural topspin—the conventional high-finish follow through—is more apt to do.

It was not just *how* Laver hit those explosive shots but *where and when* he chose to hit them that made him such a terror. He was apt to launch his rocket attack from any part of the court, at any point in the match, even if you thought you had him backed into a corner. Cornering Laver was like cornering a cobra.

Laver is always dangerous, Pancho Gonzalez once observed, because he has a habit of hitting winners when you've got him way out of position.

Rosewall, by contrast, was all patience, precision, control—a classic hitter who rarely if ever came over the ball. His most effective shot was an *underspin* backhand—severely hit and beautifully placed—that was rated second only to Don Budge's boomer off that side.

The basis of Kenny's game was his return of service, so well placed and unerring that it all but neutralized the server's normal advantage. "Whenever I play Rosewall," Rod once said, "I reckon I need two breaks of service in a set, because he returns the ball so well and puts so much pressure on me I know I'll lose mine sooner or later."

If you set out to do a chronology of modern tennis—Historic Dates in the Open Era—you'd be astonished at how many of the early ones turn out to be Laver-Rosewall affairs.

First, by way of preliminaries, there was a 1967 event that tested the audience for professional tennis and made believers out of the British tennis establishment. It was the first pro tournament ever permitted on the sacrosanct premises of Wimbledon. In the finals of that one, Laver beat Rosewall. Straight sets.

The first *open* tournament ever held anywhere, mixing professionals in with the amateur majority, came the following year at Bournemouth, England. It is often remembered for the first official victory of an amateur over a pro—Mark Cox upsetting Pancho Gonzalez in the first round. Cox went on to beat another leading professional, Roy Emerson. It was Laver who put a stop to that insolence. And the final was another Laver-Rosewall event, the victory this time going to Kenny.

The two also met in the finals of the first French Open, that same year, and Kenny won again. Laver soon got back in a winning groove, however. In 1969, the year of Rod's second Grand Slam, they met six times, and Laver won all six.

But it was that first great televised tennis event, the 1972 WCT Finals in Dallas, that stands out in the memory of many fans as a high point of the early open era and the pinnacle of the Laver-Rosewall rivalry.

It's a match well worth remembering.

Dallas. May 14, 1972.

It was the climax of an eight-man tournament—the same three-round elimination format that is used in the Grand Masters. En route to the finals, Rosewall struggled past Bob Lutz in a five-setter, then beat Arthur Ashe in three. Laver, reversing that pattern, bounced John Newcombe in straight sets, then had his usual inexplicably tough time subduing Marty Riessen, losing the first two sets before sweeping the last three with the loss of only three games. The other two players in the field, Tom Okker and Cliff Drysdale, had been eliminated by Ashe and Riessen in the opening round.

When Laver and Rosewall met for the championship, in a

basketball arena on the campus of Southern Methodist University, the crowd of 7,800 included Texas society and a sprinkling of TV celebrities. The Laver-Rosewall rivalry was by then a decade old, and Laver, now thirty-three, held the upper hand over his thirty-seven-year-old opponent. Kenny had beaten him in the 1971 WCT playoffs, but that was considered a fluke. Rod was coming into this match as the big winner on the 1972 tour and the odds-on favorite. NBC Television was allocating a modest two hours for their broadcast: 3:00–5:00 P.M. Eastern Standard Time.

The old antagonists were playing for the biggest prize of their linked careers—the unprecedented winner's purse of $50,000—plus a trophy that had a certain sentimental meaning. It was an old pro tour winner's cup, from Rosewall's personal collection, which he had donated to the WCT as heir to that tradition.

The new order of things was symbolized by the colorful outfits of the contestants. The arrival of open tennis, four years before, had overturned the tradition of whites. In the new revolutionary spirit, and in the interests of the TV cameras, Rosewall appeared in a brilliant orange shirt. Laver, for contrast, came on in bright blue.

Technically it proved to be a match of uneven quality, patches of brilliance alternating with surprising failures on both sides. The lead swung abruptly from one to the other. The one consistent element was drama.

Laver came out firing, hitting the corners repeatedly in what one account described as "an awesome display of controlled power." One early rally ended with a characteristic piece of Laver bravura, when he dashed back to cover a perfect lob in the far corner of the deuce court, spun around behind it, and lashed a furious backhand down the line, passing Rosewall at the net. Laver won that set, repelling a Rosewall charge in the process, 6–4.

The next two sets were a complete reversal. Laver, as was to happen repeatedly throughout the match, simply lost his service rhythm. In one stretch of six games he averaged less than thirty-three percent of first serves in—an atrocious standard. Rosewall, meanwhile, had his precision game in gear. He closed out the second set 6–0 and the third 6–3.

Set four was distinguished by repeated rallies in which both players, trying to mount an attack, had to scramble the entire width of the net, covering passing shots. Both kept having to retreat—and then managed to chase the other guy back as well. Single rallies would include practically the whole repertoire of tennis shots—drives, volleys, dropshots, lobs—hit with varying degrees of spin. Laver hit one of the hardest, rarest shots in the book—a backhand smash—no less than four times for winners. After teetering on the edge of defeat in that set, he pulled himself into a tiebreaker, and then, on the verge of losing that, won seven straight points. Fourth set to Laver, 7–6.

By now the match had already run past its scheduled time, but the TV audience kept building—dial-spinners apparently drawn by the protracted drama.

The heat of the court, ablaze with television lighting, was taking its toll in fatigue. Rosewall started the fifth set feeling down. A break of Laver's service in the second game—he did it with a spectacular running backhand, a Laver-type shot—gave him a shot of adrenaline. But when Rod pulled even at 4–4, Kenny sagged again, his face gray with exhaustion, his thirty-seven-year-old feet dragging. Rarest of all, his usually troweled-down black hair was mussed as he braced for Laver's service.

Laver's service troubles were still dogging him. He stood at 4–5 and 30–40—match point against him. The next serve was an ace. The crowd went crazy with released tension. Laver rode the wave and won the game. The next two games went on service, and once again they stood at 6–all. The match would be decided by a tiebreaker. The fans were tight and tired, like the players.

At 3–2 in the tiebreaker, Laver double-faulted, but then went on a brief roll. In the course of four points the whole match suddenly turned upside down. Laver was leading 5–4, out front for the first time since the opening set, with a chance to serve out the match. The crowd was in a sweaty uproar.

Now Rosewall, instead of merely bracing for Laver's service, attacked it. The delivery came in deep to Rosewall's backhand—a deliberate effort to surprise Kenny by challenging his stronger side at a key moment. Muscles returned it with a sizzling underspin. Laver, trying to volley the shot crosscourt, hit it long over the baseline. Score: 5–5.

Laver now serving into the deuce court. He goes with his favorite serve: a sliced delivery down the middle, bouncing low. Rosewall, anticipating that shot, plotting his return, decides to go for it. He takes the ball early, hits a rifle shot right past the incoming server.

Now the roller coaster has done another complete loop. It's Rosewall back on top, 6–5, and he's the one who's serving for the match.

With his modest serve, Rosewall is not going to try to overpower the receiver, but at most to surprise him. The most likely shot would be down the middle, into the open space wide of Laver's lefty backhand. Instead he serves deep but well inside the service court, jamming the receiver. This time Laver goes for it. Instead of hitting a safe chip, he hits one of his lashing backhands. But the swing is slightly cramped, not enough lift. The ball hits the net just below the tape and falls back. It is Rosewall's point, Rosewall's tiebreaker 7–5, and Rosewall's match 4–6, 6–0, 6–3, 6–7, 7–6.

For a moment, nobody could quite believe it was over. Then the crowd stood up, yelling and hooting as if they'd just seen the Southern Methodist Mustangs beat rival Texas Christian.

Rosewall's victory left him so exhausted and so dazed that he forgot his $50,000 winner's check on a chair in the locker room and had to go back for it. The next morning he flew home to Wilma and the boys.

The drama of the match and its historical significance were instantly recognized. *Time* magazine compared it to the World Series and the Superbowl. One tennis official called it "the greatest tennis match I've ever seen." A British writer identified it, with dubious precision, as one of the three greatest matches in tennis history, the other two in his book being Gonzalez's win over Sedgman in the 1956 World Professional

Championship at Wembley (London) and the Australian Jack
Crawford's five-set triumph over the Yank Ellsworth Vines in
the 1933 Wimbledon final.

By the time NBC signed off in Dallas at 7:00 P.M.—two
hours late—after four thrilling hours of championship tennis,
the TV audience had built in the course of the match to a peak
of twenty million, and the tennis boom had been given a new
upward thrust. The tennis-playing public, reckoned at a mere
ten million or so Americans at the end of the 1960s, would grow
to a faddish peak of thirty-two million by the end of the Seventies before leveling off to twenty-five million active participants. That includes all of us, from casual players logging a
mere three times a month on the courts to four-or-five times a
week tennis nuts like me.

You couldn't help thinking about that famous 1972 event in
Dallas as you watched forty-five-year-old Rod Laver and forty-
nine-year-old Ken Rosewall come to grips again in the intimate
confines of the Nashville club twelve years later. Their Grand
Masters colleagues were watching attentively in the front
boxes. Even Al Bunis was rooted to his seat—no wandering
around during this one.

When Laver ran out the first set, 6–2, I reminded myself of
how suddenly and dramatically the momentum had kept shifting in their classic Dallas match. But I didn't see how it could
happen this time. The hard court, relatively fast, favored Laver's power over Rosewall's accuracy. Rocket also had his
sometimes elusive service well under control. And this was a
more conservative Laver than the player of a dozen years ago.
Instead of terrorizing his opponent with chancey shots brilliantly brought off, Rod seemed mostly content to run Kenny
around the court with a variety of chips, slices, lobs, all kinds
of touch shots. It was only when boredom threatened him or
when temptation became irresistible that the old Laver took
over, like a freckle-faced Mr. Hyde emerging from inside a
racquet-wielding Dr. Jekyll.

Once, for example, on a break point in his favor, Rod risked
one of those experimental shots of his—a ferociously topped

return of a first service instead of a safe chip or a flat return. The ball spun into the net. A moment later, out of sheer stubborn insistence, he tried the exact same shot. Made it. Got his service break.

There was one classic Grand Masters moment—a reminder of the good old days before bad manners became routine and umpire-baiting a regular part of the game, like new balls and changes of court. The moment came after a series of three indisputably bad calls, all against Laver and all by the same linesman, who was obviously having a tough afternoon.

With each of the calls a few whistles escaped from the crowd.

Laver walked over to the chair and quietly asked the umpire, "Can you overrule him?" The umpire said yes he could, but was reluctant to do so—he wasn't all that sure he'd seen the last ball well enough himself.

That was all there was to it. With no more of a demonstration than a rueful head shake, Rod went back to his position on the court and went on with the game.

In the second set Laver continued on a roll, and Rosewall seemed unable to make any headway. No matter how much he lifted his game, Rod always seemed to be playing a notch above him. In one lovely exchange Kenny hit an impeccable offensive lob, and Laver scrambled back and somehow returned it with a high defensive lob, which kept the point going. Now Laver worked his way in, only to have the pattern repeated: a beautiful offensive lob by Rosewall—an impossible, scrambling return by Laver. It fell short—a sitter. Rosewall camped under it, swung carefully, and batted it into the net like any hacker.

When the umpire in the elevated chair called out, "Four—one, Laver—he leads in the second set," I couldn't resist the idea that it was all over. Yet Wilma Rosewall, in the adjoining box seat, wasn't even breathing hard. You'd have figured she was saving herself for a third set.

Wilma must have known something because Laver suddenly suffered a letdown, breaking his own service with a double fault. Now Rosewall finally made his move. On almost every point he was pressing, charging. Trying to mount a counterattack, Rocket committed several of his silly little errors. He netted three ground strokes in succession, then was forced into some volleying errors by brilliant returns and passing shots.

Suddenly, here is Rosewall leading 6–5 and about to serve for the second set, and during the changeover Wilma Rosewall coolly begins telling Neale Fraser about last night's outing at the Opry.

"It was a shemozzle," she reported. "You boys didn't miss a thing," she added, including me among the lucky stay-aways.

"It was what?" I said.

"A shemozzle. Don't you have that word in the States? A *disaster*. We had to stand for hours. Then they gave us seats on stage, behind the performers. We could hardly hear a thing. They introduced Kenny from the stage, and he got a nice hand. I'm not sure they really knew who he was, though. It didn't look like a tennis crowd."

Gene Scott had a dissenting review of the performance. "Even when you can't hear," he said, "I'm always charmed by the pageant of the Grand Ole Opry." Aside from the music itself, he admired the slick showmanship and the all-around efficiency of the production—qualities that appealed to the tennis promoter side of Scott. "The timing of the acts is perfect. The concession stands are always neat. And those good old country boys really know how to fill a house. It's never like the early rounds of a tennis tournament, where you can see rows of empty seats."

On the court it was Rosewall's turn to serve.

The unrecognized cynosure of the Opry audience went before a hushed crowd of his own people with a chance to pull even. Laver promptly broke his service, and the second set went to 6–6. Just like Dallas, 1972. History recaptured! *This* was what the Grand Masters were all about!

Laver, serving first in the tiebreaker, takes the lead . . . loses it . . . gets it back again. Seven points will win, and at 6–5 Laver steps up to the server's position in a total hush. Around me his fellow players are as tense as the fans. I hear Neale Fraser whisper to one of his colleagues, "What's it now? Big serve and volley?"

Laver arches his back and uncoils, blasting the first serve in and just sort of skimming the court surface as he rushes the net. Fraser is so involved in the point that he can't help calling it aloud, shot by shot.

"Oh!" Neale gasps at the serve—a boomer. Rosewall sends it right back at a wicked angle. "Oh!" says Neale again. "*Hell* of a return!" And then: "*Hell* of a volley! . . . What a hell of a lob! . . . Hell of a return! . . . Oh! Hell of a *point!*"

That final, winning shot was Laver's, and so, at last, was the match, 6–2, 7–6.

The born-again rivalry between Rod Laver and Kenny Rosewall, on the 1984 Grand Masters circuit, was off to a hell of a start.

The winners check was presented with an appropriate touch of ceremony—but, I noticed, with no mention of the amount. First prize, for most of the tournaments this year, was generally understood to be $7,500—$4,500 for others—but IMG was curiously reticent about the precise figures, as if embarrassed by the obvious comparison with the astronomical amounts being raked in by young players on the men's and women's tours.

I wondered what the secrecy was about. I couldn't have cared less if Kenny and Rod were playing for meal money. I decided to ignore the money and enjoy the tennis.

"That *was* good tennis, wasn't it?" said Torben Ulrich on the way back to the motel.

"I've never seen either of those two guys play *bad* tennis," I said.

"Haven't you? You've never seen Rosewall in one of his unexplainable 'downs'? You know—when his shoulders slump and he hangs his head between points like some little boy because he's hitting everything into the net or out of the court?"

Torben was off on one of his little exercises in taking a sports-page cliché—about fame, anonymity, victory, stardom, whatever—and holding it up to the light of truth. "You remember Rosewall being crushed by Connors at Wimbledon and Forest Hills the same year? When was that—1974? It was hard to tell in those matches whether it was a Connors 'up' or a Rosewall 'down'—both are so dramatic."

Of course I remembered those spectacular defeats. Wimbledon went 6–1, 6–1, 6–4. Forest Hills was even worse: 6–1, 6–0, 6–1. A couple of real shemozzles, even worse than Gardnar Mulloy's 1952 wipeout by Frank Sedgman at Forest Hills. In both cases the losers were aging and worn down by tough lead-in matches. But Torben thought there might be something else to it than age or fatigue.

"I don't know why it happens to Kenny," he mused. "It doesn't seem to be mechanical—you can't see that he's doing anything particularly wrong in his stroking. Maybe it's chemical. Maybe it has something to do with the male cycle. Maybe with Rosewall and Connors the down and the up meshed and amplified each other, sort of. Don't you think that's possible?"

It was obviously a rhetorical question, and I let it stand. How would Torben analyze Laver's win over Rosewall this afternoon?

He meditated on that briefly. Watching the highway from behind the wheel of the car, I couldn't see whether or not he was fingering his beads. Then he said: "Fast court, big serve."

PART III

The Way It Was

Transitions

Roy Emerson is one of those people whom strangers just naturally gravitate to. They start talking to him on contact. It's as if they sense they'll get a friendly response from this muscular character with the thatch of short, faintly graying hair, gregarious habits and an incorrigibly cheery disposition. "I like to keep people happy," Roy explains.

At the Nashville airport, the morning after the Grand Masters tournament ended, a waitress at the coffee shop began telling Emerson about all the good things she had cooked for her family for Sunday dinner. He listened appreciatively and made appropriate comments. At the gate he struck up a conversation with a round-faced man named Bill, who promptly told Emerson his age (forty-seven, coincidentally the same as Emmo's) and his occupation (insurance agent), and described his current state of being. He was, he said, "a burn-out."

"Burn-out," Bill went on to explain, "is when you've got a deal and you can't get excited about it. I got a policy to write on a new condo development in Atlanta last month—the whole goddamn project. Didn't mean a thing to me." He nodded at Emmo's two Head equipment bags bulging with tennis racquets. "I see you're a tennis player," he said, clearly not realizing how much of a tennis player he was talking to. It was like being introduced to George S. Patton and asking him if he'd ever been in the service.

"I'm a golfer," Bill volunteered. "I've got a sister who plays tennis, though. Damn good at it. But the last time I played, I beat her."

Emmo stared at him for a moment. "Not much fun in that, is there?" he asked. He sounded as if he was actually curious about the experience.

The flight was called, Emmo hefted his racquet bags and trudged along the ramp—a somewhat broad-beamed man in blue jeans and a warm-up jacket. The gear and the casual costume seemed mismatched with the attaché case he was also carrying. From it, when he reached his seat, he extracted a pair of granny glasses and settled down to the Op-Ed page of *The New York Times*. He gave that up after a cursory run of the columns, turned to the Business Section, and checked out the stock options.

Emerson was on his way to the second tournament on the Grand Masters spring schedule, but like other members of the troupe he would be stopping en route to transact some personal business. Laver was visiting a tennis resort in North Carolina that had expressed interest in setting up a deal with him for personal appearances, use of his name and so on. (Eventually, he decided against it.) Scott was going back to New York for a few days on some *Tennis Week* business. Krishnan and Anderson conducted a tennis clinic, an important and profitable sideline for the players, about which I would learn more later on. And Emmo was in the midst of a significant career change.

Maybe it would be more accurate to say that Emmo's career was taking a late swerve in its course. He had recently negotiated a job as tennis director—the fancy tennis-boom term for head pro—at Williams Island, a new resort development that was just being built on the Florida east coast near Miami. That was only an hour or so from the next Grand Masters tournament site, near Boca Raton, so Emmo was going to stop off for a couple of days to do a little advance personnel work, interviewing people for his staff. That was one of several aspects of the job that would be new to him.

Being tennis director meant that Emerson would have to supervise a staff of assistant teaching pros plus the clerks behind the counter in the pro shop. He would be charged with organizing and running a complete tennis program for Williams Island, which was being planned as a condominium colony surrounding two hotels. The program would have to include activities like clinics and tournaments for the tennis club members and hotel guests, plus a strong junior program to keep the kids occupied and develop any outstanding talents that appeared among them. For promotional purposes, he'd have to stage an occasional exhibition; he might play in them himself, he might bring in another star.

Then there was the whole merchant side of the club-pro business. He would have to do the buying for the pro shop, with a little help from his wife, Joy. They'd stock a variety of racquets, a few lines of shoes, designer outfits and all the accessories of tennis that were now marketed—little bootie-style tennis socks for women, colorful wristlets and handbands, jocks and panties, cutely decorated towels and gifts with tennis themes, ranging from desk sets to cocktail glasses.

And finally, once he got things organized and under way, Emerson would do a little teaching himself. Maybe two or three hours a day at seventy-five dollars an hour. Eventually, he figured, he ought to raise his rate to one hundred dollars an hour, the same as Fred Stolle charged at his nearby club, Turnberry. Fred had a couple of years head start as club pro and a reputation as a tennis coach. You couldn't expect to start right out at a hundred an hour.

The Williams Island club would be Emmo's base for six months of the year—November through April. The job wouldn't keep him out of future Grand Masters tours, though it might knock out one or two tournament dates. But resorts that hire big-name pros usually want them to maintain an image as players for the prestige that goes with it.

Nevertheless, this represented a serious transition for Emerson. For one thing, it would separate him from his family by the width of the continent, at least for a while. Joy was going to maintain their home in Newport Beach, California, until their son and daughter finished college in Los Angeles, where they attended the University of Southern California.

The other big thing was the element of routine, something new and alien in Emerson's life.

Emmo was a free spirit, a product of the wide-open spaces

of the Australian outback. He belonged to a generation of Australian tennis players who grew up learning the game on their own family tennis courts. In Australia of the 1940s and 1950s a private court didn't indicate wealth, as it would have for American kids. It simply reflected the immense popularity of tennis in a remote and little known country that had made its international mark in the Davis Cup competition, the way the Swiss made theirs in banking and hotelkeeping.

Kenny Rosewall's father supplemented the family income by operating a commercial court in his backyard. Rod Laver's dad built a family court out of red dirt collected from anthills. Out in the sparsely populated areas of the range country a family court was a kind of refuge from the meager conditions of life.

"There was nothing for kids to do out there," as Fred Stolle, a city boy himself, once explained, "but screw around and watch the animals. Watching animals can go just so far, so their fathers built them tennis courts to keep them from screwing around too much."

Roy Emerson's boyhood milieu was the family dairy farm in Queensland, where his daily chores included helping to milk 160 cows. When the family moved into town, a submetropolis with the arresting name of Black Butt, he distinguished himself in high school as a hurdler on the track team—he'd had all that open country to run around in by way of practice. But with the encouragement of the Australian Lawn Tennis Association he gave up both track and schooling to concentrate on the national sport. And ever since then he had lived the freewheeling life of a player.

He thrived on the amateur tour, reaching the position of world's Number 1 in the mid-Sixties, after Rod Laver turned pro, leaving the field clear. For two years—1964–65—Emmo monopolized the major championships almost as Rocket had. Emmo never won the Grand Slam—never won the U.S., British, French and Australian championships in a single year— but in the course of his career he won each of those tournaments at least twice, singles and doubles both. Altogether he captured more of the Big Four titles, singles and doubles, than any one before or since. His total is an astonishing twenty-six.

From the time tennis went open, in 1968, Emmo had made his living traveling the world as a competitor—a player. Oh, he did some clinics every summer, as a kind of busman's holiday, conducting tennis weeks at a Swiss resort. And he did a spot of coaching, when, for instance, Tracy Austin was trying to develop a volley and came down to Newport Beach for daily workouts with Emerson. But he wasn't pinned down, the schedule was his own, and, most importantly, it didn't affect his identity. He remained what he always had been: a *player*.

But now, when the two new hotels on Williams Island were completed, early the next year, and the first tier of tennis courts was marked out under the Florida sun, Roy Emerson would take on a new identity, one that implied a change of lifestyle. Roy Emerson would be a club pro, checking in each morning at his desk in the pro shop.

"Nine to five?" he speculated. "I suspect I'll hate it at first." A grin, then he brightened the forecast. "It'll take some getting used to."

The transition from playing pro to club pro is one that most tennis players resist but have to face sooner or later if they want to stay in the game at all. The superstar elite—the Lavers and Rosewalls, the Borgs, McEnroes and Connorses—may be able to live indefinitely off their endorsements, investments and connections, playing exhibitions until their arms and their names wear out. The others simply try to fend off the pro shop as long as possible.

When it comes to fending, the tennis player's model is a Grand Masters alumnus, Gardnar Mulloy, a man best known for his durability, a kind of eternal youth expressed by both his tennis game and his good looks. No one in the annals of tennis has been more successful at prolonging life as a player and postponing the real world of nine to five. But even Mulloy eventually had to give in. Sort of.

It was Mulloy's home base, a club in Boca Raton, Florida,

that was to be the site of the second tournament on the Grand Masters circuit. And hearing about Emmo's career plans on the flight down to Florida prompted me to pay an advance call on Mulloy, to get the view from the pro shop.

Gardnar Mulloy is a player who counts his career not in years but in decades. He made the top ten, the upper bracket of the official USTA rankings in his midtwenties, before World War II. He was in his late thirties when he achieved the Number 1 ranking, in 1952. And he was still playing the tournament circuit well into his forties.

It was at the age of forty-three that Mulloy won his first Wimbledon title—the doubles, which he captured in 1957 with thirty-three-year-old Budge Patty as his partner. The team they beat in the finals was Lew Hoad and Neale Fraser. The score was 8–10, 6–4, 6–4, 6–4, and against that formidable pair of Aussies, then in their early twenties, the old man, Mulloy, never lost his service even once. The victory gave Gardnar a nice piece of British silverplate to go with the four U.S. National Doubles trophies he had won with Bill Talbert back in his salad days (1942, 1945, 1946, 1948).

All this time, except for four wartime years in the Navy, Mulloy's primary occupation was: tennis player. He had a law degree from the University of Miami, and he dabbled at a practice for a while. He also had a couple of swipes at a business career, but nothing took. He even had a shot at politics, running for mayor of Miami, but professed to be relieved when he lost. "Like commerce," he noted later in a published memoir, "public office would have interfered with my tennis."

Nothing really interfered with Mulloy's tennis. It wasn't until he reached the ripe old age of fifty-six that he really gave in to the nine-to-five routine that most ordinary mortals have to live with. He took a job as tennis director at a Florida resort hotel. But even then he didn't give up his preferred identity as a player. He played exhibitions, he played senior tournaments, and when the Grand Masters started up in 1973, Mulloy, although already sixty, well past the normal limit, became one of Al Bunis's bench, filling in for half a dozen seasons before playing his last tournament.

Now, in the spring of 1984, at the age of seventy, Mulloy had recently changed jobs, taking on the position of tennis director at a new residential sports community called Boca Grove Plantation, on the edge of Boca Raton. The place was *so* new that on the eve of the Grand Masters tournament I found bulldozers noisily patterning the landscape, while cement mixers poured the foundations of "luxurious villas, condos and town homes" —quoting from the literature I found in the pristine tennis clubhouse. It adjoined a nifty little exhibition court—claylike gray-green Hartru—set among prettily landscaped outer courts. The Boca Raton Grand Masters was to be a kind of baptismal event for the Plantation's tennis program, and Mulloy as host pro was running the tournament.

I spotted him out in the new grandstand, fiddling with some seating detail—a tall catlike figure in a warm-up suit, with a Hollywood face deeply tanned under a gray brush cut. It was not the face, the body or the stride of a seventy-year-old man, but more like a vigorous fifty.

The gray brush was longer than the Navy flyer's clip worn by Lt. (j.g.) Gardnar Mulloy when he and Billy Talbert won their first national doubles title, the year after Pearl Harbor. The slight change in hair style is one of Mulloy's few concessions to the passage of time. He firmly believes that newer or younger isn't necessarily better. In the age of graphite, boron, magnesium and other space-age materials, he insists on playing with wood. I asked him if he didn't agree with Gene Scott, among others, that the new synthetic materials helped older players make up for lost power. Mulloy looked pained.

"Why would you want anything more powerful than wood?" he said. His standard tone of voice is a kind of peevish drawl. "All you need to do is reach the baseline."

Mulloy happens to be in a minority on this issue. The racquet material clearly favored by Grand Masters players was graphite in any of its various composite forms. (Graphite itself is brittle; it gets its extraordinary strength when sandwiched with some flexible material like kevlar or fiberglass.) Six of the ten Grand Masters players, I'd noted, were using composite racquets, mostly midsize. One, Fred Stolle, was then playing with an aluminum model, the Prince Pro, but he too later switched to graphite.

Most of the players had deals with racquet manufacturers, paying them $10,000 to $15,000 a year to use their particular racquets. Compare that with the $100,000 Bjorn Borg is said to have been paid for displaying the Bancroft racquet logo during tournaments in the United States (and another $100,000 for using a European racquet *outside* this country).

Some players used certain racquets without any such persuasion, simply out of a personal preference, as Emerson did with his midsize graphite Head Edge or Scott with his Prince Graphite. In Gene's case it was because he didn't want to compromise his freedom, as a journalist, to report on any manufacturer's products.

Rod Laver and Neale Fraser shared Gardnar Mulloy's preference for good old wood. But all three were using it in big-head versions—Rod's Pro-Kennex, Neale's Slazenger, Mulloy's Prince Woodie—which meant that, whether they knew it or not, they were really using space-age weapons containing a substantial proportion of graphite in their laminations. An oversize wood racquet made the old-fashioned way would be too heavy to swing.

The only *real* woodsman in the Grand Masters was Frank Sedgman, with his old, standard-size Australian Oliver. Frank Parker still clings to his old, standard-size Wilson "Kramer" racquet, too.

Even with their clumsy old wooden weapons, Gardnar Mulloy insists, the tennis players of his day were by and large superior to the current crop.

"Of course," Mulloy told me the next morning, settling his unbelievably trim body into a chair in his office at the rear of the pro shop, "what you do have today is tremendous depth of field. If you set up a team match—players from the era of open tennis versus players from the preopen era—Tilden, Budge, Gonzalez, Laver, et cetera—our top ten versus their top ten . . . why we'd kill them. Their first two hundred against our top two hundred, we'd get swamped."

Mulloy didn't stay seated very long. He exudes an air of

languor, but his hostly duties kept him hopping throughout the tournament. I had to catch him from time to time in his office. Although the pro shop had just recently opened for business, Mulloy's little sanctum was already deep in the standard clutter that all tennis offices quickly accumulate—the unopened cartons of new racquet frames, the coils of gut, the samples and brochures from manufacturers of tennis paraphernalia. Mulloy would shove aside the day's accretion, prop his sneakered feet up on his desk, and talk about the past.

The vast span of his career is almost impossible to grasp. It makes meeting him a little like shaking the hand of an old vet who once shook the hand of Lincoln. Or like listening to a tennis version of Mel Brooks's "2,000-year-old man." Mulloy has played against Bill Tilden, who won the U.S. Singles in 1920; he has played against Don Budge, the 1937–38 champion; and, he also likes to point out, "in my heyday I took Rod Laver to thirteen-eleven in the final set of the South American championships. I beat Rosewall twice, once at Forest Hills and once at Wimbledon."

Both those wins over Rosewall were in 1952, when Kenny (then seventeen) pointed out that Mulloy (thirty-nine) was "older than my father." That was the year Gardnar reached the U.S. singles finals for the first time and achieved his Number 1 U.S. ranking.

It was only six years later that he played in his first senior tournament—or "veteran's tournament," as the over-45s were then called. Until that time, just about the only names of former top ten players you'd ever see in the draw of a veterans' tournament were Bitsy Grant, the splendid little retriever from Atlanta, and J. Gilbert Hall, no world-beater but a solid Eastern player who once was ranked Number 8 in the country. Their example was widely disdained, as Mulloy recalled. "Everybody said, 'What do you want to play veterans' tennis for? You were a star! You're degrading yourself!' But I never felt that way. I still had a desire to participate in tournaments."

Mulloy kept participating for the next twenty-five years, and he hasn't stopped yet. In the pages of the record books devoted to national championships on various surfaces you will find

Gardnar Mulloy's name on the list for every age level he has reached so far: 45s, 55s, 60s, 65s and 70s. In the seventy-year-old bracket, in 1984, he simply wiped out the competition, sweeping the titles on all four surfaces, singles and doubles. Senior players consider that kind of sweep their equivalent of the Grand Slam.

Mulloy's 1952 victory over Rosewall at Forest Hills was in the quarterfinals of what was otherwise practically an all-Australian show—Sedgman, Hoad, Ken McGregor, Mervyn Rose. The two top-ranked Americans, Seixas and Savitt, went to the sidelines. A sports page account credits Mulloy with "something of a miracle in snatching victory from . . . the seventeen-year-old boy wonder from down under."

Mulloy, "who was competing in this championship before his opponent was born," was down two sets to one and 4–1 in the fourth, when he began an astonishing comeback. The reporter ascribed it to a change of tactics. Instead of staying back, hitting his preferred forehand from the baseline, Mulloy began coming in behind heavy slices deep down the middle or angled to Kenny's backhand. He managed to pull out the set and went on to win 8–6, 3–6, 4–6, 7–5, 7–5, in a match that had the grandstand in an uproar, drowning out the sounds in the stadium, where Savitt was losing to Mervyn Rose.

As Mulloy likes to remember it, the *real* turning point in the fifth set came at one particular moment when Rosewall, leading 4–2, dropshotted him, and "I ran up, barely reached the ball and got it over. The umpire called it my point, but I told him, 'No, I hit the net with my racquet.' He hadn't seen it, Rosewall hadn't seen it, but I knew it. So they took the point away from me and gave it to Kenny—they had to."

The game went to Rosewall, but Mulloy thereupon went on a tear and won the match. "That point I gave away could have beaten me," Mulloy says, "but my conscience wouldn't let me keep it. That's the difference between the players of our generation and the players of today. Do you think McEnroe would do that?"

McEnroe does some things that Mulloy was famous for long

before Johnny Mac was born—and I'm not referring to the backhand volley, which was never Gardnar's favorite shot. Like McEnroe, Mulloy was one of the celebrated stack-blowers and line-call protesters of his generation. But he doesn't hesitate to condemn the manners of current players as inexcusable. He ascribes it to a lack of standards, not just in tennis but in society.

"There's no discipline," he declared. "No discipline on the court, no discipline at home. My father once defaulted me in a match because of bad behavior. I was fifteen years old, I was playing my first real tournament, the Dade County championship down here in Miami, and I was in the finals against the perennial champion. He was an older guy, must have been twenty-eight or twenty-nine. I began yelling at a bad line call, and my father took the racquet out of my hands and told me to go home. I said, 'Dad, I can win this match!' He said, 'I don't see how. You don't have a racquet.' And that settled it."

Gardnar's father, R. B. Mulloy, a Miami businessman, had more than a parental interest in tennis. He was an active participant, and he and Gar were later to win the national father-and-son doubles three times. His disciplinary act may have settled the Dade County championship of 1929, but it hardly put an end to his son's tempestuous behavior.

In the 1950 semifinals at Forest Hills, in a match he lost to Herb Flam, Mulloy protested a line call with such tenacity that the tournament referee had to be called onto the court. And one incident in a tournament at the Queens Club in London wound up in the British courts. What prompted it was a world's-record late call. Mulloy and his opponent, Rex Hartwig, had already changed courts—"Hell, I was already in position to serve"—when a linesman's decision on the previous point was announced, and what had appeared to be Mulloy's game became deuce. Mulloy argued the official's decision so furiously that a British newspaper account next morning accused him of "a disgusting disregard for the decencies and decorum of the game." Mulloy, blowing his stack again, this time at the reporter, sued for libel, lost and had to pay the defendant's legal costs.

In comparing his own less-than-impeccable behavior with the sort of thing he deplores in current players, Mulloy draws

the kind of line that would do credit to a Philadelphia lawyer if
not a Miami one. It's a boundary, however, that other players
of his era also recognize, including another well-known pussy-
cat, Pancho Gonzalez.

The difference between today's brats and yesterday's
gentlemen, as the old-timers explain it, is the difference between bad manners and the firm exercise of your rights under
the rules of tennis. As Mulloy explains, "I didn't raise my voice,
I didn't use profanity, and I didn't prolong it. Oh, we used to
belabor the linesmen, saying, 'You're blind!' or 'Wanna borrow
my glasses?' Things like that. But we never gave the finger to
the crowd or we'd have been suspended. And that's what they
need nowadays. They need to be penalized. Why aren't they?
Because the officials are afraid of them. Because commercialism has taken over, and the tournaments don't want to lose their
drawing card on a default or a suspension."

Mulloy happened to be an innocent party in one of the most
celebrated incidents of misbehavior in the history of tennis.
One that resulted in the only recorded suspension of a player
from the sport because of "unsportsmanlike conduct."

It was in the 1951 U.S. Singles at Forest Hills, when Mulloy
was playing Earl Cochell in a fourth-round match. Cochell was
a fine tennis player, for several years ranked in the top ten, but
one with a persistent tendency to self-destruct. After repeated
conflicts with tournament officials, he had been pointedly left
off the Davis Cup squad that year and had been "disinvited" to
the important Newport tournament.

In his Forest Hills match against Mulloy, Cochell won the
first set, 6–4, but then began to feel the pressure of Mulloy's
heavy forehand. Cochell's service came undone, and after losing it for the second time in the seventh game of the set, he
angrily banged a ball out of the court. Then, as the *New York
Times* reported, he completely antagonized the crowd by pro-
ceeding to throw the eighth game in a blatant fashion, "returning service with the racquet switched to his left hand."

In an episode surprisingly like incidents of a later decade,
involving Nastase and McEnroe, the crowd and the player got
into a running hassle, with the spectators booing every shot

Cochell made. He protested to the umpire but got no satisfaction, and began to harangue his critics in the stands. The third set, like the second, went quickly to Mulloy, who recalls the next scene of the drama, which was enacted off the court.

"We went into the locker room for intermission—you always took an intermission after the third set in those days—and one of the officials from the U.S. Lawn Tennis Association followed us in and started to lecture Earl. Earl swore at the official [it was the tournament referee, Dr. S. Ellsworth Davenport, Jr.] and the official warned him that he was looking for trouble.

"We finished the match—I beat him—and some time after the tournament the USLTA had a hearing and suspended him. I talked to Earl and told him to write a letter of apology. I'm sure they would have reinstated him. But Cochell was stubborn. He felt he'd been treated badly and he refused to apologize."

Actually, the USLTA didn't wait until after the tournament. The executive committee met right there at Forest Hills and suspended Cochell indefinitely for "actions detrimental to the welfare of the game." His name disappeared from the rankings. One of the myths of tennis is that stubborn Cochell and the rigid USLTA remained deadlocked and he was banned for life. According to Cochell, now living in retirement in Petaluma, California, he submitted a formal apology the next year and was reinstated—but restricted to tournaments west of the Mississippi. However—one more twist—when one of the USLTA's western sections refused him expenses, he dropped out of tennis. Ten years later, in 1962, he returned to play some West Coast events, but by then his career as a top 10 player was far behind him. Mulloy, by then, was just hitting his stride.

The 2,000-year-old man of tennis paused in his reminiscences, and I asked him at what point, and in what way, he had first begun to feel the effects of age. I probably should have said "if."

"You take a tennis player," Mulloy said after a moment, as if he were talking about somebody else. "When he goes to hit a tennis ball, he hits it here" (he indicated a spot about an arm's length in front of him) "or he hits it here" (he moved his hand back a mere inch or so). "There is very little margin of safety. If he hits it here it's a good shot. If he hits it back here, the ball goes out. It goes into the net or over the line. The margin of safety is only that fraction of a second.

"You miss that shot, and you don't know how it happened. It's a shot you've made in your sleep. But what's happened is that you're that fraction of a second late, and the ball gets by you. Oh, you don't *miss* it, but it gets by the exact spot where you should make contact to hit it the way it should be hit. Especially on your backhand. You may still be able to hit your forehand, but you can't get around on your backhand any more." Another comparison occurred to him, and he threw it in for the hell of it. "You can run forward without any trouble, but you can't back up."

Can you still run forward as *fast* as you used to?

As with the stroke, Mulloy answered, even a very slight loss of speed can make a lot of difference.

"Distances in tennis are short," he said. "A man runs the hundred-yard dash in eleven or twelve seconds. That's twenty-five feet per second. A tennis court is only seventy-eight feet long. Thirty-nine feet on your side. You can get to the net in two seconds—that's plenty of time to make your volley. But now, as you get older, it takes you two and a fraction. And in that fraction the ball drops. You can get your racquet on it, but not well enough to make the shot."

Mulloy had just come in from the courts, where I had watched him hitting with three women pros—sharpening his game, he said, for an exhibition match in which he and Bobby Riggs were going to play, on the day of the Grand Masters finals. The Mulloy forehand was still an enviable stroke—long, fluid, effortless. But what he was hitting mostly against the women was a variety of flukey spins and trick shots, all craft and disguise.

I asked the former Number 1 American—the present Number 1 seventy-year-old—how he felt about his game nowadays. He admitted that he was playing fairly well. In fact, he said, he would still be playing in the Grand Masters himself "if Al Bunis hadn't kicked me out a few years ago. I wouldn't win any tournaments, but I could still play a good match against these guys."

It was just what Bunis had told me about the old boys and their reluctance to call it quits. Mulloy was nearly sixty-seven years old when he was finally severed by the Terrible Turk. He was the oldest player ever to appear in a Grand Masters tournament. Older than Riggs or Segura. Older than most people are when they retire from *desk jobs*, for God's sake.

But it was still too soon.

19

Family Scene

FOR THE BOCA RATON WEEKEND the Grand Masters were installed at a resort hotel that had some sort of IMG connection, a half-hour's drive from the tournament site. I found quarters at a motel that was closer, just a few hundred yards down the highway from the sentry-guarded gatehouse of Mulloy's plantation. In atmosphere it was a whole climate zone sunnier than the Nashville place, and it offered some nearby amenities. Adjoining it was a cozy little commercial development containing a late-hours supermarket, a small Mom-and-Pop tennis club, and a building identifying itself as the Florida Habit Control Center.

The only habit I have any hope of controlling is a tendency to overhit the short forehand (also on occasion the deep forehand), so I put myself in the care of Mom and Pop. They were a civilized couple of New Jersey suburbanites, name of Yates, who had migrated south after retirement from corporate life to run a pro shop while their two sons worked the courts as teaching pros.

The boys set me up—if that's the term I want—with a young local, who proved vulnerable to a backhand down-the-line passing shot. Unfortunately I do not have a backhand down-the-line passing shot.

That afternoon at the Plantation I found the Grand Masters entourage swelled by several new arrivals. One was Fred Stolle, the dark-horse entry in this year's tour. Another was Mary Laver, who had flown in from California to join her husband, Rod. She got a big affectionate welcome from the Australian contingent. Her husband got the standard treatment.

"How come you're wearing these Stan Smith signature sunglasses?" Roy Emerson asked him, lifting the shades off and examining them critically. "Is it because he's such a nice guy?" Smith, the American ex-champion, is a mannerly gent with religious convictions. He has a reputation for niceness which the freewheeling Aussies seem to find cloying.

"It's because I'm so fond of Stan," Laver responded, "ever since he beat me two, four and one at Brussels. Want anything to eat?" he asked his wife. Mary shook her head no, and he disappeared in the direction of a food pavillion that was just setting up for business alongside the stadium court. I made a mental note to check the date of that Brussels match. It turned out to be 1973. Laver's memory was almost as tenacious as Mulloy's.

Rod came back from the refreshment stand with a couple of hot dogs.

"He can eat anything and never gain any weight," Mary said enviously as her husband went to join some of his mates on a practice court. He does no special conditioning or training, she told me. "He doesn't need to. He's so active. You'll never see Rod sitting still. Around the ranch he's always busy doing something, and he never just *walks*. It's always those same quick little steps he takes on the tennis court. When he's getting ready for a tournament, he starts moving even faster. Even if I didn't know his schedule I'd still know when he's got a tournament to play. Everything speeds up—his walk, his speech, everything."

Rod, she went on to say, is as impatient as he looks. His well-known perfectionism is limited to tennis—his finickiness about his strokes, his racquets, his tennis clothes. About everything else, Mary said, he just doesn't have the attention span. Business? He does what his agents (IMG) tell him.

The Lavers are a trans-Pacific couple—Australian married to Californian. They have a teenaged son (called Ricky by his mother, Rick by his father), and Mary also has a daughter by a previous marriage. Mary and Rod first met at a tennis benefit event in Palm Springs, but she professes to have known nothing about the game at the time. Since then, of course, it has become a dominant influence in her life. It explains, for example, why the ranch was now up for sale.

The Lavers had bought the ranch, a spread near the town of Solvang, California, in the Santa Barbara area, to occupy Rod for what they thought of as his retirement. They planned to devote those years to leisurely raising Charolais cattle. "But," Mary said, "I'm convinced that man is never going to retire from tennis. One time at the airport in Hawaii we ran into an old man carrying a bunch of tennis racquets. He looked to be about seventy. Turned out he was nearly eighty. He said he was on his way to Australia to play in a tennis tournament. Well, Rod's eyes lit up. You could tell he was imagining himself at the same age, going off some place in the world to play tennis. I think that's really the way he wants to spend the rest of his life."

Mary is an attractive, rather hearty woman who favors the unisex tennis costume—warm-up suits in various colors— when traveling the tournament circuit with her husband. She experienced just enough of the early days of open tennis to realize how swiftly and drastically it has changed, evolving into what she sees as the overcommercialized, depersonalized Grand Prix tour of the 1980s.

"You don't see the camaraderie there used to be," she said. "The players all used to help each other out—with their strokes, with problems on the court and their personal lives."

Cheryl Savit, the wife of the young IMG tour manager, pulled up a chair and turned it into the early spring sunshine. "The young pros on the circuit now wouldn't give each other a thing," she agreed. Cheryl, who had flown south to share the Florida weather with her husband, had more than a wifely knowledge of the tennis business. Like Mike, she was making a career in the young field of sports management, and had worked as a tour manager herself, though not for IMG. "The whole atmosphere of the professional circuit nowadays is so competitive!" she added. "They're downright hostile to each other. A lot of them won't even go to a movie together."

"Not Rod's generation," Mary said. "They're all good friends. But on the court, how they want to win! Isn't it interesting how they'll never let on when they're injured? They never want to give an opponent any kind of edge. Never give him anything he can take advantage of. They know that just as soon as you show some sign of being injured, the other guy will be all over you like . . . like some kind of animal, making you run for the ball when you're hurt, making you hit off your bad side."

"Would they do anything like that in the Grand Masters?" I asked, in a manner that I hoped would pass for innocent curiosity. I remembered Anderson maneuvering the wounded Fraser in Nashville, and Scott talking about the factor of an opponent's injury as part of your game plan. "Would they exploit their good friend's injury?"

"Rod would!" his wife said cheerily.

Visitors from the Past

"How do you think these Grand Masters would do against the players of today?"

The question, like many asked by Bobby Riggs, is one that he is fully prepared to answer himself. He has raised it only as a way of generating conversation, which is one of Bobby's many favorite sports—tennis, golf, baseball, bowling, various games of chance, anything that has an element of dispute or competition to it. Especially if it's something you can bet on.

"Most of these guys hit the ball as well as they ever did. Some maybe even a little better," Riggs went on, quickly running around the net to return his own conversational serve. "But you can't say that they *play* as well as they used to. Not overall. Could players their age stand up to the pace and pressures of today's professional competition?" He shook his head dubiously. "A tough assignment."

This time Bill Talbert gets in a shot. "Rosewall did it," he points out levelly. "Right up to the age of forty-two."

There is no bet riding on this particular issue. The conversation, being conducted on the sidelines of the Boca Raton court, has been prompted by an item in one of the local papers, quoting Gardnar Mulloy. The host pro and tournament director has never been reluctant to offer his opinions on controversial tennis subjects. This time he had stirred up a little media dust by declaring flatly that the top half of the Grand Masters—Laver, Rosewall, Stolle, Anderson, maybe Emerson—could still beat half the draw at Wimbledon. It sounded a little like that old schoolkids' playground challenge, "Let's you and him fight!" But it added a little spice to the proceedings that were about to get under way at Boca Grove Plantation, just as Vitas Gerulaitis's disparagement of women's tennis (Martina, the Number 1 woman, said Vitas, couldn't lick the hundredth-ranked man) enlivened the 1984 U.S. Open.

Nobody would think of matching even the best of the Grand Masters, aged forty-five to almost fifty, against any of the sixteen seeded players in a Grand Slam event—the McEnroes, Lendls, Connorses, or even the Johann Krieks or Tim Mayottes. But against the bottom half of the draw, players ranked, say, Number 40 or 50 and under on the pros' computer?

"I think we'd do pretty well," said Ken Rosewall. The problem that gave him pause was not the quality of the opposition but the length of the big tournaments. "We're not used to playing five or six rounds any more," he said, suggesting that he anticipated a little trouble pacing himself as he played his way toward the quarterfinals.

Gene Scott wasn't nearly so sanguine. He feared that he and his peers would find themselves overmatched in speed, mobility, strength—"all the significant attributes."

Bobby Riggs and Bill Talbert seemed to think the match-up was at least worth speculating about.

The presence of these two ancients summons up a whole fading era of tennis, one that predates the memory of most of the players in the Boca Raton tournament. In 1938, the year several of the current members of the Grand Masters were born, Riggs and Talbert were competing in the Big Time, on the old amateur circuit. Survivors of that white-flannel epoch, along with Gardnar Mulloy, they are also part-time neighbors of Mulloy in Florida. Talbert makes his home in New York, and Riggs in California, but both have winter places near Boca Raton.

Both are Grand Masters alumni. Talbert by reason of his one appearance in the premiere tournament, in 1973; Riggs as an occasional competitor as late as 1982. But they are here in response to an older allegiance, a call from their old comrade Mulloy to come and help baptize his new club's tennis program. They are being trotted out at the Grand Masters tournament the way old boxing champs are introduced from the ring before a title fight. They have also agreed to team up as commentators for a cable television broadcast of the finals on Sunday.

Riggs-Talbert is an interesting pairing. The Odd Couple. Although they share a common past, they came out of tennis with two divergent perspectives on the game, which is the way they went into it. They are like those siblings who grow up so different—in personal style, attitudes, even in memories—that they seem to have spent different childhoods in the same family.

Talbert expresses the cool elegance of the Philadelphia Main Line, the Long Island North Shore, Boston and Newport —the habitat of Eastern society and its tennis clubs, which set the tone of the sport in the prewar era. That was not Talbert's natural background but an adopted one. He grew up in Cincinnati in a family with, as he describes it, more manners than means. The Depression made things all the tougher in the Talberts' modest household. You can tell how enthusiastically young Billy took to the life of the eastern club circuit from a passage in one of Talbert's several books about tennis and his many years in the game.

There was something rich and heady in the atmosphere . . . The clubhouse, the lawns, the people themselves had that patina of security—the tone that comes with social position established and reinforced over a period of generations. It was that special tone of "Eastern casualness." In the mellow sunlight of Merion, the girls in their light skirts and cashmeres seemed gayer and prettier; the men in their dressed-down flannels and seersuckers seemed suave and knowing. There was a wonderful sense of leisure being used with good taste and decency. People seemed to have the time, the means and the ability to enjoy each other's company . . .

"Tennis week"—the week of a tournament at any of the old Eastern clubs—is usually the high point of the summer social season . . . Hostesses are apt to plan their most elaborate soirées for the time when the tennis players are on hand. As the players move along the tournament route, like strolling minstrels visiting the courts, the doors of the summer houses swing open, the guest rooms start to fill, the orchestras strike up that peculiarly thin music reminiscent of expensive hotels, and the terraces light up to full lantern power.

The players themselves are the lions of this society. The game is their cachet, admitting them to places they might never reach with any other credentials. The circuit is a fantastic kind of melting pot. It's where a young man whose parents speak broken English and who has never worn a tie at the dinner table could find himself seated . . . with the daughter of an Ambassador or a Supreme Court Justice and possibly near His Excellency or Mr. Justice himself. Or where a fellow working his way through school by baling wastepaper on a janitor's gang [as young Billy Talbert was doing at the University of Cincinnati] could find himself accepted . . .

Talbert was looking back on all this from the comfortable eminence he later achieved in the game. What he remembered somewhat less vividly was how tough and even cruel the circuit could be to kids just trying to find a toehold in the sport. How grateful you were to be given one of the cots jammed into a windowless squash court or an improvised attic dormitory at the club. How abandoned you felt when, after an early-round loss, you came back to find your suitcase out on the sidewalk, your bed given to some lucky survivor, while you were left wondering how to stay alive until the next tournament. Because when you got knocked out, the hospitality stopped.

Ranked players, of course, had the benefit of expense money, administered by the various regional sections of the United States Lawn Tennis Association and distributed to their old favorites or promising young talents among the players. The official limit was fifteen dollars a day (plus transportation). By 1968, when the gates of commercialism burst wide with the arrival of open tennis, the rate had zoomed all the way up to twenty-eight dollars a day. That was supposed to be the limit, equally applied regardless of a player's ranking.

But of course, as we'll see shortly, under the laws of amateur tennis, as in George Orwell's *Animal Farm,* some were more equal than others.

The social aspects of tennis had a special appeal to Talbert because of the hard times in his own family and also because as an adolescent he had been isolated from other people by chronic illness. He was—and is—severely diabetic, kept alive by twice-daily insulin injections. Until he insisted on becoming an athlete, diabetes had been treated as a disabling disease, and its victims confined as invalids. Talbert's pioneering experience has made him a model to several generations of young diabetics.

As if to make up for his restrictive childhood, young Talbert set a partygoing pace that perfectly healthy young players on the circuit had trouble keeping up with. Some didn't want to. Gardnar Mulloy used to marvel at the way his younger doubles partner would come in after a big night, catch a couple of hours in the sack—or even change directly from black tie to white flannel—and then, after giving himself his routine but vital insulin shot, go out and play a five-setter.

"Where do you think Mulloy was all that time?" an old colleague once said. "Not tucked into his own little bed, you can bet your sweet ass!"

Mulloy, an avowed fitness freak who frowned on smoking and drinking, had a big reputation as a ladies man.

All the time Talbert was playing the circuit, he felt the pressure of a converging dilemma—the choice between playing tennis and making a living. Unless you were a superstar—a Budge or Tilden, a Vines or Perry—the only tennis job you could aspire to was to be a club pro. And you were thereupon lost to the game forever, under the strict amateur rules.

Talbert never gave more than a fleeting thought to turning pro himself throughout his entire playing career, which included thirteen years in the top ten, two singles finals at Forest Hills besides his four national doubles titles with Mulloy and one more with his young Cincinnati protégé, Tony Trabert. When Talbert played in the Davis Cup and later captained the team, it was strictly an unpaid activity. There was no loot to be split up among winning and losing squads like a World Series pool, the way it's done in the postmodern 1980s version of the Davis Cup.

Playing tennis, to Bill Talbert, was not a profession. It was a wonderful preliminary, at most an entrée to a profession. He wished he could prolong it forever, and he managed to for quite a while. He was past thirty when he eased himself off the circuit and settled into a business career, turning up for no more than an occasional tournament before bugging out altogether. His last big win was at the age of thirty-six, when he beat the rising Australian teenager, Roy Emerson, at the Pacific Southwest in Los Angeles. "I did it with my return of serve," he still recalls.

To the very end, as long as Talbert played the game, he played it strictly for the sport.

Bobby Riggs, by contrast, was by his own account a feisty hustler with an eye out for the buck—even when he was playing as an amateur.

Riggs says he is not offended by the term "hustler." He takes it as a term of endearment. What it really means, he says, is that he is a habitual bettor. "The bigger the bet, the better I play."

It has become an accepted fact of Riggs's biography that he won $100,000 on himself as an amateur at Wimbledon in 1939 (when a hundred grand was a lifetime fortune, not runner-up money for a Tokyo round-robin). He claims he achieved that coup by going to a London bookmaker and putting down £100 (then about $500) on himself to win the singles, and parlaying his winnings on the doubles and mixed. Some of his old buddies suspect Riggs may have exaggerated the size of his coup. But they concede that he loved to bet and he never lacked confidence in himself. And it's a historical fact that he swept all three titles—a long shot that Don Budge had achieved the two previous years but that wasn't brought off again until Frank Sedgman did it in 1952.

Call it hustling or call it betting, Riggs has earned his reputation in a long career of wagers that are even more dazzling for their creative variety than for any amount of money involved.

With bets on the line, he has played tennis while leashed to a hyperactive poodle, or with chairs placed as fixed obstacles in his end of the court, or tethered to a partner in doubles, or sharing a single racquet with the other guy.

Riggs says that most of those weird bets were actually devised by stockbroker friends in New York—ardent tennis players and habitual bettors, as many stockbrokers seem to be. They constructed these Rube Goldberg wagers in sheer frustration at trying to beat Bobby in more conventional situations, like handicapping with points or games.

Once Riggs engaged Ken Rosewall, who seldom bet, in a week-long series of money matches on a commercial clay court in New York. Rosewall didn't know it at the time, but Riggs was making daily side bets on the games with one of his Wall Street buddies, Jack Dreyfus. Rosewall, then in his mid-thirties, was giving Riggs, nearly fifty, points and games in various complicated combinations, for $500 a set. At the end of the week Rosewall was $1,000 ahead. At that point Riggs persuaded Kenny to go double or nothing on a final "set" that started with Rosewall down 0–4, minus 30 to Riggs's plus 30. In other words, Rosewall had to win four straight points to get to deuce before Bobby got two to win the game. Also: Riggs was allowed to hit into the alleys, and Rosewall got only one serve.

The handicap proved too much for Kenny. Riggs won the set and got even.

Riggs's appetite for sports and for bets are equally inexhaustible. He may be the original model for all tennis-nut jokes. He spent the first day of his honeymoon (the first of his three marriages) playing fifteen sets of tennis—he got married during a tournament, and wound up playing a delayed semifinal plus the finals of all three events, singles, doubles and mixed. Even as a fifty-year-old senior, he once played fourteen sets of singles in one day—on a hard cement court in California.

Riggs and one of his New York tennis chums, the old baseball slugger, Hank Greenberg, once played a daylong series of contests—for money, of course—which began on a tennis court, moved on to a paddle-ball court, and wound up on a basketball court in a foul-shooting duel.

In Las Vegas, on a single day, Riggs engaged in a putting contest with Joe Louis, the old heavyweight champ; shot baskets against two NBA pros; played backgammon; pitched cards into a hat; and played a form of tennis against singers Steve Lawrence and Paul Anka, with eight chairs on Riggs's side of the court and Bobby required to carry a suitcase and receive serve sitting down. He wound up the day in a poker game.

A former associate of Bobby's once told me about a dinner party at the Riggs house at which Bobby greeted the guests at the front door with a small rubber ball and a challenge: Roll the ball down the cellar steps and hit every step on the way down—with a little bet to make it worth while. It proved harder than it looked—for everyone except the host, who had spent the afternoon giving himself an edge by practicing the game he had just invented.

Riggs's passion for gambling is a classic example of Freudian overcompensation. His father was a fundamentalist minister who deplored gambling and didn't even allow card playing in his house. Bobby began making up for that deprivation as soon as he was old enough to count a poker hand or flip a baseball card against a sidewalk curb.

He was a passionate baseball player as a kid and began to play tennis when he was twelve. He was one of a wave that came out of the blue-collar neighborhoods of Los Angeles (Kramer and Gonzalez were among the others) to dominate the game in America and eventually force a change in its rigid traditional standards.

If Bill Talbert's account of life on the prewar tennis circuit reads like a society-page story, then Riggs's reads like an IRS audit. Bobby claims to have made a good living as an amateur tennis player. He was a self-proclaimed beneficiary of the hypocritical system sometimes known as "shamateurism."

As the top-ranked tennis player in the country, and winner of Wimbledon and Forest Hills, Riggs got $500, he says, for appearing in lesser tournaments. Sometimes the payoff would be in the form of a can't-lose bet. The tournament committee chairman of the host club would take him out to a far court and bet him five hundred that he couldn't jump over the baseline. Riggs also collected expense money, he claims, when he was admittedly getting free room and board as some club member's guest, and also had a free ride to the tournament site. And he collected salaries from a series of phoney jobs arranged by various well-heeled patrons of the game. He was on the payroll of a Wall Street broker, and he was on the payroll of a college heavily endowed by another tennis patron.

Throughout his "shamateur" career, Riggs says, he never had any trouble supporting his wife and child while devoting his time to tennis. "I drove a snazzy Cord convertible. I stayed at the best hotels, and rarely saw a bill for room and board."

The Riggs version of life on the "amateur" circuit is corroborated by Jack Kramer. His autobiography even includes a kind of rate card for the period right after World War II: $400 for tournaments in Florida, $750 in Texas, as much as $1,200 in California.

Another key source of income was exhibitions, informal matches in which stars were invited to play at clubs in the area of some important tournament. Theoretically these events were played only to promote the interests of the game, or perhaps of some charitable cause, and the players were officially entitled to receive only the standard per diem plus transportation costs. In fact, according to insiders, the standard fee for playing an exhibition at any decent club was $500.

Perhaps the worst thing about the "shamateur" system was that it was not only hypocritical but also inequitable. While the stars were being paid handsomely under the table, lesser players often had a tough time just hanging in on the circuit. The money stayed at the top, like cream.

And perhaps the only thing to be said *on behalf* of shamateurism was that it wasn't universal, even where the stars were concerned.

Vic Seixas insists that "I never made any money playing as an amateur, and they'll never convince me that anybody played amateur tennis to make money." Expense account chiseling may have existed on the circuit, he concedes, as it does in business, in government and every other part of the economy, but "it couldn't have been more than a pittance."

Seixas calculates that in the twenty-nine times he played in the U.S. Singles championship (an incredible number of years, during which he won once and reached the finals twice), he had to find accommodations for himself covering almost 300 days of tournament play—and he never collected a dime in expense money. The only freebie he got in all those years, he says, was a hamburger for which a friend insisted on picking up the check.

I asked Bill Talbert if he could explain the discrepancy between those two versions of amateur tennis. Talbert shrugged. "I just don't believe what Bobby says about the money. Or Jake either. I don't say they made it all up. I mean that even if some of the facts and figures are accurate, the overall picture is exaggerated. I just don't think they made as much as they say they did, and I don't think it was all that widespread."

So much for Riggs and Kramer. What about Talbert himself?

"I was the Number 2 tennis player in the country—Number 1 in doubles," Talbert said, his blue eyes fixed in a rather stern expression. "You'd think somebody would have come to me some time and said, 'We'll give you a certain amount of money for playing our tournament.' They didn't."

As a matter of fact, Talbert was both Number 1 *and* Number 2 in doubles one year—on top as partner to young Tony Trabert, and second with Gar Mulloy. Talbert says that whatever the facts may have been about payoffs in Florida, Texas or California, he feels absolutely sure that there weren't any on the simon-pure Eastern circuit, including Forest Hills itself. Nor was there any money under the table at Wimbledon. And, he points out, even Kramer concedes that much.

None of which says that some of the top stars weren't picking up an occasional $500 playing exhibitions at clubs just off the Eastern tournament circuit.

But as far as the National Championships were concerned, in those days the chance to play at Forest Hills was apparently enough of an attraction. And for many players the lure of the circuit as a whole was the VIP treatment a tennis player got from people who were VIPs themselves. What tennis offered, as Talbert once said, was "something that probably beats money—a chance to live well without it. "

However good the dough may have been in amateur tennis, it wasn't enough to hold Bobby Riggs. After winning his second U.S. Singles title in 1941, he turned pro and was pitted in a series of challenge matches against the professional champion, Don Budge. Budge—tall, red-haired, powerful—was the latest in a line of reigning pros that extended from Bill Tilden to Fred Perry to Ellsworth Vines, all players of enormous talent. Budge may have been the best of all.

Budge repelled the Riggs challenge, and then was forced to rest on his laurels during a three-year wartime hiatus when the pro tour was suspended and champ and challenger were both in the service. But after the war Riggs came back with an aggressive new strategy, determined to add the professional crown to his amateur titles.

Riggs is one of those athletes who was born to be underrated. He has sometimes been described as "a live animated cartoon—he looks like Bugs Bunny and walks like Donald Duck." His physique is slight—at five feet seven, 145 pounds, he was the exact prototype of Ken Rosewall. That and his reputation as a scrapper and a scrambler, plus his latter-day fame as a kind of professional male chauvinist jock in the hyped-up televised "battles of the sexes" against Margaret Court and Billie Jean King in the Seventies, have made it hard to remember just how good a tennis player he was.

Mainly a baseliner and counterpuncher as an amateur, Riggs had relied on speed and accuracy to take him to the top of the tournament circuit. "At my size, I knew I was never going to overpower anybody," Riggs once explained. His amazing consistency and precision came from a classic compact stroke executed with very firm wrist—again, much like Rosewall. He was perhaps the greatest master of the lob in the history of the game.

All of which adds up to the standard equipment of the great defensive player, which Riggs was. But at the same time he also had extraordinary instincts for the volley and great quickness along the net. These were qualities that he had found to be critical under the pressures of the professional game. He set about developing them and exploiting them when the professional tour resumed after the war. An attacking game, he had determined, was the only way to spike Don Budge's big guns —his thundering backhand placements, his heavy forehand approach shots and crunch volleys.

Riggs caught Budge in 1946 at a vulnerable moment in his career. Don's intimidating serve had been softened by a shoulder injury, and the defending champ had turned conservative with age—he was all of thirty-one. Riggs wore him down with a nonstop attack, coming to the net behind his own modest first service, behind his second serve, behind his return of Budge's second serve—and, whenever he could, even against Budge's big first serve.

With these aggressive tactics Riggs wrested the pro tour championship from Budge in 1946, successfully defended it in 1947—only to lose it in 1948 to a challenger; fresh from the amateur ranks, who took Bobby's own game plan and escalated it still further.

The newcomer was Jack Kramer, whose Big Game is still widely regarded as the very model of power tennis. Yet Kramer himself gives little, underpowered Bobby Riggs a large measure of credit for its development. It was under pressure from Bobby's unrelenting attack, Kramer says, that he brought the Big Game to its ultimate peak. Kramer not only attacked relentlessly, but he attacked with force. Big Jake—a rangy six feet two inches—focused his game on two critical strokes: serve and return of serve. He used them both as "high ground" for his big artillery. Serve or return—either one was to Kramer a way to seize control of the net.

Though Riggs battled Kramer even for the first twenty-four matches of their tour, Bobby soon crumpled under the nightly barrage. The challenger went on to win by a wide margin, sixty-nine matches to twenty.

The defeat left Riggs with no place to go as a tennis player. That's the way it worked in the heartless world of the pro tour.

Once you were dethroned, you fell back into the pack of also-rans taking turns at the new champ in a continuous round-robin. Or else you made way for the newest hot shot from the amateurs, who picked up the role of contender and the fat contract that went with it. The others were then reduced to the role of supporting players, performing in the so-called animal acts —the preliminary matches.

The reduction in income was abrupt and drastic. Riggs had collected $100,000 to defend his title against Kramer. The animal acts were lucky to make one-third that much. And aside from the tour there were only three significant professional tournaments: the World Championships at Wembley (England), the U.S. Pro, usually at Longwood (Boston), and the French Pro in Paris. The winner's prize never exceeded a couple of thousand dollars.

The amateur hot shot who came up right behind Kramer in the pros was Richard (Pancho) Gonzalez. He took on the challenger's role in 1950. Riggs hung on in the tour for a couple of years, occasionally as a player but mainly as the promoter. Then he settled, in a manner of speaking, into his wife's family business (photo labs) and drifted away from tennis. He got his exercise—and did his betting—on the golf course.

Bill Talbert meanwhile had graduated from tennis into a business career based on his circuit contacts with Fords, du-Ponts and other inhabitants of the nation's clubhouses and board rooms. He became vice president of a company that prints stock and bond certificates for corporations.

During the 1950s and 1960s, when Jack Kramer was leading the forces lobbying for open tennis, Talbert was on board the tennis establishment pulling an oar for the same cause. His six years as Davis Cup captain gave him an effective platform, and he used it to advocate changes in the structure of the game which, he predicted, could turn tennis from a club pastime to a sport with immense popular appeal. And when the tennis world turned upside down in 1968, and the big tournaments were finally opened up to the professional players, Talbert emerged as one of the major figures in the new order, occupying the highly visible role of director of the biggest money tournament of all, the U.S. Open.

But he even does that in the old amateur spirit. For running that huge commercialized event on behalf of the United States Tennis Association—that annual New York tennis festival bringing in an estimated $50 million in ticket sales, concessions, broadcast rights and ancillary benefits—Talbert doesn't get paid a dime. "I never asked for it, never looked for it, never wanted it."

Talbert can afford to be a little cavalier about money. Tennis paid off well for both him and Riggs, though in totally different ways. Bobby's circus stunts against Margaret Court (he beat her) and Billie Jean (he lost) earned him something over $100,000 directly, and the subsidiary benefits have continued ever since.

Now, when Riggs and Talbert, the old tennis circuit chums and antagonists, meet at an event like the Grand Masters tournament in Boca Raton, you can read their divergent history at a glance. Talbert, erect and elegant at sixty-six, shows up in impeccably tailored blazer, country-club trousers and an open-collared shirt that is too tasteful to be called sporty. He looks as if he had just stepped off the golf course at nearby Palm Beach, which is exactly where he had just come from.

Riggs, the same age, appears in an iridescent tan warm-up suit emblazoned with the words *Sugar Daddy*—he wears it by contract, one of the continuing residuals of the Billie Jean match. His pockets are loaded with samples, which he distributes to kids in the crowd. Riggs at sixty-six is a live commercial for a lollipop.

12

Oddities

WATCHING A TENNIS MATCH with Bobby Riggs in the next seat is like watching it on television. Along with the game you get an entertaining stream of commentary, anecdote, autobiography, disquisition, gossip and—if there are any silences left unfilled—just plain chat. Riggs shares with old-time broadcasters a horror of what they call "dead air."

"The difference between these guys and the players they used to be isn't very much," Riggs said, pursuing a subject he had raised earlier. "They're just a half step late getting to the ball, just a little bit slow getting the racquet around. But," he went on, echoing what Mulloy had told me, "that's all it takes to make the difference between a shot and a bad shot. Now *that*," he said, "was a *shot!*"

The match we were watching was a semifinal between Laver and Anderson, and Rod—after a little initial difficulty—was starting to unload his arsenal. On two consecutive points he had just hit superb crosscourt passing shots for a break that gave him a 3–1 lead.

"They can still put on a hell of a match, can't they," Riggs observed. "They've got a few good years left in them, Laver and Anderson. The real deterioration doesn't set in until . . . oh, about fifty-five."

I was about to cite the recent downward revision of Bunis's Law to him when a fit-looking gentleman with silver hair turned around from his seat just in front of us. "The real decline sets in at seventy-two," he said definitively. "That's when things start to get you even when you're in good shape. Like your back."

"How old are you?" I asked him.

"Seventy-two. I'm having a bad season." He turned back to the match.

Riggs was having "a darned *good* season," he told me. Bobby's interest in tennis was revived when the game went open, in 1968, and professionals were welcomed back into the tournament draws. Since he had already reached the age of fifty, the tournaments open to Riggs were the senior events. He has been moving up through the age brackets ever since with expectable success, following in the footsteps of his older colleague Gardnar Mulloy. In 1983 Riggs had made a sweep of the sixty-five-year-olds' championships on all four surfaces—"a senior Grand Slam," he called it—to go with his sweep of the sixties, four years earlier. "And," he announced firmly, "I'm gonna do the same thing when I hit the seventies."

Occasionally the paths of the two old cronies cross on some tournament court when Mulloy plays down an age notch as he sometimes likes to do for the challenge of it. In 1984 Mulloy beat Riggs for the national 65s grass-court title, 6–1, 2–6, 7–5. It was the reverse of the 1983 result, and one of Mulloy's rare career wins over Bobby.

In one important respect the Riggs approach to senior tennis is no different from his approach to the amateur circuit and the pro tour. He is incorrigibly competitive. "I always was the best player in the world for my age," he says, "ever since I was twelve. I still am."

His basic advice to other senior players: "Lob, lob and lob. Especially lob into the sun. Don't get fooled into thinking you have to look good out there. The name of the game is winning."

He has no interest in testing himself against Grand Prix hot shots and other players he is unlikely to beat. "I *hate* playing good young players," he says. "I only want to play old guys and women."

Bobby's interest in women was not always competitive. He was another one of those tennis players with a reputation for liking to socialize. Time and a couple of failed marriages didn't diminish his appetite for the extracurricular sport. Playing in a senior tournament after achieving his mixed-singles fame, Riggs, then between marriages, was offered dates with his choice of three women at the host club. One was described as the prettiest in the club, another as the richest, and the third as the biggest swinger. Riggs of course picked the one who presented him, at fifty-five, with the greatest challenge.

Bobby never paid too much attention to conditioning as a young player—never had to—but he began to take it seriously when, as a middle-aged gent with the beginnings of a spare tire around the middle, he began preparing for his match against Margaret Court. He began dieting, jogging, swallowing vitamins and a variety of other food supplements—an incredible total of pills that sometimes reached four hundred in a single day. Although he professes to stay perpetually in tournament trim, he is no longer faithful to the old regimen.

"Bobby is a phenomenon," said his new wife, Miriam, a small woman with a child's face, who was sitting with us in the stands. She squeezed his arm affectionately. "You know, he never stretches, never warms up, he doesn't run or do exercises."

"I stay in shape," Bobby said defensively. "I take my vitamins. Hey! This is some point!" He craned toward the court where Laver and Anderson were engaged in one of those remarkable exchanges in which two good players run each other up and back with a sequence of touch shots interspersed with deep drives—neither quite able to hold a commanding position without being driven from it. Finally the rally ended, in Rod's favor.

"You want to know one of the greatest oddities in tennis?" Riggs asked during a changeover. "Laver versus Vijay Amritraj at Forest Hills. U.S. Open. Fifth set. Laver lost his service five straight times. Can you imagine that? It was drizzling, and Laver was wearing spikes. Vijay was slipping and sliding all over the place. Laver—the best player in the world on grass, maybe the best server on grass, and he's got the extra advantage of spikes. Yet he loses his service five straight times. Vijay can't hold either—a fine server himself. Nobody holding service on grass. Can you figure the odds on that?"

If Riggs was trying to hustle me for some kind of bet on Laver-Anderson (or, for all I could tell, on Laver-Amritraj) then I wasn't biting. I might have been tempted to take a flutter on Mal when he began to make a run at the first set, but then he failed to put away a couple of crucial volleys, the rally fell short, and Riggs resumed his disquisition on the inroads of age.

Riggs had once been asked to compare his game as a senior with the game he played in his prime. His response could have got by over the signature of Casey Stengel, baseball's late master of the nonstop non sequitur. "The only thing that I don't have," Riggs told the interviewer, "is I cannot cover the court and my backhand has deteriorated and my serve has gone away. I don't have the quickness, and I don't have the reach."

I thought he might be able to clarify that statement, and he was eager to oblige. There is no single thing that suddenly happens to a tennis player at a certain point, he told me—"just a general overall deterioration. Speed, strength, reactions, everything. I used to be all over the net—you couldn't pass me. I'd dare *anybody* to pass me. *Anybody.* I can't cover the net like that any more. When I get up there I feel like one outfielder trying to cover the whole outfield."

On the court below us, Anderson—down an early break in the second set—began to give Laver trouble again, with some smart, deliberate play on the slow clay. Then it began to look like Nashville all over again—like the match in which Anderson kept dogging Rosewall but seemed to tense up every time he got within range. Or was it Laver, like Rosewall, rising to the occasion?

"Wow! That was some kind of volley!" said Riggs, as Rocket launched himself into the air and, with his body almost parallel to the ground, knocked off a winning shot. It provoked, along with Bobby's admiration, another one of his historical oddities. "Would you guess," he asked, "that Laver was the first foreigner ever to win the U.S. Juniors?"

Answer, which I neither guessed nor bet on but later looked

up: No, it was a Mexican kid, Esteban Reyes, the year before him—1955.

One game away from defeat, and 5–4 in the second set, Anderson now played two brilliant points, and had Laver love–30 on Rod's service. "I thought I was about to get the break back," Mal said later, in the locker room. "I badly wanted it back. But then he hit a damn good serve—hit it to my forehand, and I lost it in the crowd."

The serve went for an ace. Laver kept serving that way until he closed out the game and the match, 6–3, 6–4.

"Well," Anderson said with a wince, recalling the crucial point, "that's what you're supposed to do, isn't it—come up with the big serve when you really need it?"

"That's Laver," said Bobby Riggs. "The big shot at the right moment! That's making your point!"

He was talking about tennis, but he could have been talking about a crap game.

13

The Age of Australia

On a pathway leading from the clubhouse to the practice courts at Boca Grove, Mal Anderson and Neale Fraser were holding an impromptu conference about their forthcoming doubles match. Both had been eliminated from the singles by Rod Laver—Anderson in the semis, Neale before that, in the opening round. But as a team they were still in the tournament, scheduled to face Roy Emerson and his partner, Fred Stolle.

Normally, you'd have figured that match as a toss-up— Bobby Riggs would probably have given you even money, pick 'em. Anderson-Fraser and Emerson-Stolle: two excellent, experienced pairs, both ranking among the best doubles combinations of recent decades. But if you'd seen the Laver-Fraser match, then you had to wonder about Neale's physical condition. He was hitting with very little pace, and often his strokes looked forced and unnatural.

"I'm okay hitting off my backhand," he told his partner, "but everything else hurts." It wasn't so much the spills he'd taken during the matches in Nashville—the soreness was gradually going away, he said, putting a hand to his bruised ribs. The real problem was his arm; he decided he'd overpracticed on that one day he had to get ready for the tournament. The muscles of his forearm were giving him pain, and it wasn't easing with practice.

Anderson put a comforting hand on his partner's shoulder as they headed back to the locker room.

Players pick their own doubles partners in the Grand Masters, and, except for special circumstances, the teams generally stick together as long as both members stay on the tour. But Fraser and Anderson would have been brought together by sheer logic, even if they were not old mates whose savvy games happen to mesh very well. If Riggs-Talbert was an unlikely combination, then Fraser-Anderson was a natural.

They were a couple of the most obscure champions from the era of the Australian raj. But champions they certainly were, representative of that period in which their country's dominion was almost unbroken. It lasted from 1951 to 1968. The path had been cleared for the Australians by the defection of Jack Kramer and Pancho Gonzalez to the professional ranks; it pretty much stayed that way until the beginning of open tennis.

In no less than twelve of those seventeen seasons the champion of the United States was an Australian—and in almost half the U.S. Singles Championships *both* of the finalists were Aussies. They also won Wimbledon ten of the seventeen times, and the Davis Cup fourteen of seventeen.

Fraser and Anderson happened to fall between giants. They were overshadowed at first by Hoad and Rosewall, and later on by Laver and Emerson. But between them Mal and Neale won four of the big singles championships. Neale in fact did a Bobby Riggs at Forest Hills—he swept singles, doubles and mixed. And he did that two years in a row!

Fraser-Anderson happened to be the Davis Cup doubles pair on one of the few *losing* Australian teams of that era. In 1958, when the United States briefly wrested the cup away from the Aussies, Neale and Mal were overtaken by the team of Alex Olmedo and Hamilton Richardson in one of those five-set marathons that the Davis Cup annals are full of. The American pair were behind 10–12, 3–6 when they started a remarkable comeback, winning the last three by scores of 16–14, 6–3, 7–5. The total of eighty-two games made that one of the longest doubles in Davis Cup history.

Anderson, incidentally, also played the singles that time, and won one of his two matches, beating Barry McKay in straight sets. But what sets! The scores were 7–5, 13–11, 11–9. Altogether, in his three matches, Mal played a total of 190 games—which made the average score of a set 9–7. Hard-nosed tennis!

The next year Australia took the cup back. The Aussies proceeded to win in eight of the next nine years—until open tennis arrived and shook up what had come to seem like the natural order of things in the tennis world.

If you have ever wondered what drove the Australians to the heights of success they achieved during that remarkable seventeen-year span, in those days before the invention of money, then listen to that old down under team of Anderson and Fraser, reminiscing over a clubhouse beer—which is the way Australians prefer to reminisce, or do most other things, for that matter. The explanation, as they tell it, lies in three facts. One was a simple fact of geography—Australia's distance from the rest of the tennis world. Another was the support—call it subsidy—which Australian tennis players got from the sporting goods industry. And the third was the traditional British educational system, which prevailed down under, in which most boys finished their schooling at fifteen and then took jobs or learned trades. The system was both a handicap and a spur.

"In the States," said Fraser, switching his glass from his normal lefty grip to the right hand in order to spare his aching muscles, "in the States tennis players had more options than we did. Most of them went to college. They could keep playing there, and then they could play the American circuit in the summer, after they finished the college term.

"In Australia, if you wanted to be a tennis player, you also had to play the American circuit, ending up at Forest Hills. You probably had to play the European circuit, too. Clay courts on the Continent, then Wimbledon and the other British grass courts. In other words, if you wanted to be a tennis player, you had to go overseas. That's where you got your experience and made a name for yourself.

"Well, the only way you could get overseas was to play well enough to get picked for the Australian squad. Every year the

Australian Lawn Tennis Association would take a group abroad for the tennis experience, and they would be the ones from which the Davis Cup team was picked.

"Financially, very few of us could afford to go off and play the circuit on our own. I mean, that's a hell of a distance to travel—most of you people don't realize how bloody far it is from Australia to this part of the world. It costs a lot of money to get out of Australia. Well, you didn't want to miss out on it, and once you'd tasted it, you didn't want to give it up—the tournament life, the social life."

Anderson interpolated: "When you were one of the top players, you had a chance to meet interesting people. Business people. Government people. Show business. You'd be invited to somebody's home. You were sought after. Entertained." He chuckled. "You can't knock entertainment, can you?"

For a kid like Anderson, after a boyhood on a remote cattle station in the empty range of Queensland, the social life of the tennis circuit must have been at least as dazzling as it was to the American city kid, Billy Talbert.

"We were all mates on the tour," Fraser went on. "We were not only mates with the other Australians but with the guys from other countries. You'd go out together at night, see the sights, have a lot of fun."

"More like the Grand Masters, you might say," Anderson put in. "The players on the tour nowadays don't have this kind of experience."

"You worked like hell to make the touring squad," Fraser said. "Then once you did, you began to get a little help. The sporting goods manufacturers would engage you to work for them; that is, they'd give you some nominal job, and they'd pay you a salary year-round, enough to pay your expenses. But you had to earn it on the tennis court."

"What you mostly did for them," Anderson explained, "was, you'd play exhibitions. The money wasn't big, but it was enough to get along on, especially for a kid. Slazenger's was probably the biggest in the program. They had me and Neale, and Rosewall and Don Candy, George Worthington. Some of those names may not ring, but they were good players. And there was Roy and then John Newcombe."

That kind of subsidy would have been frowned on under the American amateur tennis code, but it was considered kosher down under—all perfectly legit under the looser regulations of the Australian LTA. It was really just a more blatant, more highly developed form of shamateurism.

"There is no such thing as amateur tennis," Roy Emerson once declared flatly, at a time when he was the reigning amateur, in the mid-Sixties. He was then described as "the highest paid amateur tennis player in the world."

An observer of the Australian tennis scene in the preopen era defined the difference between amateurs and pros as simply "a difference . . . in the method of payment." The amateurs, he went on to explain, "get theirs from 'expenses,' which are really appearance fees. Sometimes patriotic individuals or business firms paid leading players substantial sums so they could afford to reject professional offers and stay available for the Davis Cup."

Rosewall, as a twenty-year-old amateur spending most of his time on the tournament circuit, had nominal jobs with two different companies: Slazenger's and Carnation Milk. Once, while playing a tournament in the United States, young Kenny was introduced to the president of Carnation (the parent firm being an American company). The boss, hearing that Rosewall was an employee of his Australian branch, asked him what he did for Carnation down there.

"Oh," said Kenny, "not much of anything."

Rosewall and Hoad did well enough as amateurs to turn down $45,000 each to turn pro. It was two years before they were sufficiently tempted to defect—for $65,000.

Emerson was on the payroll of another U.S. firm: Philip Morris, the tobacco company. He was paid $8,000 a year, nominally as a public relations functionary. Between this and other sources of income, he made enough to reject a professional contract for several years before succumbing to a $75,000 offer.

Before that, in 1951, an Australian newspaper raised $25,000 by public appeal as a wedding gift to Frank Sedgman's new bride—a bit of generosity for which Frank showed his appreciation by postponing his professional plans for another year, another Davis Cup campaign.

Australian players had a different outlook on the game than most of the Americans. As Neale Fraser put it: "Guys in this country—well, if they didn't make it on the tennis court, they could fall back on their college degrees. Like I said, they had more options than we did. If we didn't make it, we had nothing to fall back on. That's what my father warned me."

Fraser had been talking in his brisk style. He has the bluff, rather beefy face of a guy you might strike up a conversation with in a London pub. The face has experience on it that, you sense, was not limited to a tennis court. Now Fraser paused to take a sort of meditative pull at his glass.

"I come from a professional family," he said. "They're all doctors or lawyers—my father, my two brothers. My father said to me, 'If you're going to be a tennis player, then you'll wind up a bum.' It was enough to make me work like hell, to be good at the game so I'd avoid being just another bum."

The Australian players trained together in their own country, they traveled five months of the year, they always had one or two of the outstanding juniors accompanying them in a kind of internship, and—perhaps most significantly—they lived as a team.

"When you're sitting down at meals every day," said Anderson, "and listening to the best tennis talk from the world's best players, you've got to pick up something, We learned to play smart on every kind of surface, but especially on grass. We were better at what we used to call chip-and-charge: chipping your service return and coming in to attack the server. We learned how to slice the ball deep and low—that's the way you set up your volley. So that was the kind of advantage we had, and we kept passing it along. We kept producing players, and we kept passing it along."

Fraser: "You built up confidence. We reinforced each other. I knew I was never going to lose my serve—I *knew* it!—so I knew I was never going to lose a match, no matter who I played."

Anderson: "We learned to attack the ball. We were in control of it. When you're playing as much as we were every day, the ball becomes much larger, you know. We played every day, and that's all we did, for months and months at a time. *They* were going to college. *We* were playing tennis, for a certain number of hours every single day."

In the current age of individual superstars, it's hard to realize that tennis used to be a kind of team sport—in the sense that the Davis Cup, a team competition, was the apex of the game, and everything else merely a kind of qualifying event for it. Wimbledon and Forest Hills were certainly big deals, but they were only *national* championships, after all. The Davis Cup—that was for the championship of the *world*. Its importance was further magnified by the six-year interruption of World War II. In the minds of some tennis players, in fact, that was the major historical significance of the war between the Allies and the Axis.

Gardnar Mulloy, whose career spanned World War II (as well as many other events of modern times), recalls the war years as a period of terrible frustration. "I went into the Navy flight program," he recalls, "and all through the war I had one burning desire, like everyone in those days, to play in the Davis Cup. That's all we ever thought about—to make the Davis Cup, make the Davis Cup!"

In due time the war ended and Mulloy's single-mindedness was rewarded. He got to play the last singles match in the 5-0 win by which the United States recaptured the cup from Australia in 1946. Subbing for Ted Schroeder, he beat Dinny Pails in straight sets. Schroeder and Jack Kramer won the other four matches, individually and as a doubles team.

The Australians were every bit as intense about the Davis Cup as their American counterparts.

"It used to be enough for us just to be playing for Australia," said Mal Anderson, commenting on the modern, open-tennis version of Davis Cup competition, in which participants are paid fees of $50,000 or more (*if* they can fit the event into their schedule of exhibitions, rock concerts and paid appearances at shopping-mall openings).

"Why," said Mal, "we couldn't imagine anything bigger than seeing your name in the scores of a Davis Cup tie! "

If there is any single thread of continuity running through the Age of the Australians, it is the name of their Davis Cup captain, the late Harry Hopman. He served in that nonplaying capacity through the 1950s and 1960s, and he is widely credited as the mentor of several generations of champions—the source of inspiration from which Australian dominance flowed. But Australian players of that vintage will tell you that his role has been exaggerated.

The way they talk about Hopman now is not as a coach or teacher but as a trainer, a ringmaster who put them through the hoops with endless push-ups, sit-ups, double-jumps and two-on-one drills (two players on one side of the net, one on the other, forcing the solo man to react more quickly and hit more balls than he'd have to in a match). All this on top of a five-mile run before breakfast.

Frank Sedgman thinks some of the drills were pointless in more ways than one. "It didn't matter whether you hit the ball in or out," Sedgman, the first in Hopman's line of stars, once recalled, "as long as you convinced him you were working hard."

When they talk about Hopman, Australian players often sound the way adults often do when recollecting a strict childhood: Maybe it was good for you, but you can't help resenting the grown-ups who put you through it.

If Hopman's old boys sometimes sound like teenage rebels rejecting their parents, then it was Hopman, they insist, who disowned them first. They say it happened to them all, one by one, as they turned professional. Soon afterwards, Hopman would be quoted as saying that some new kid could beat the pants off old Sedgman. Or Rosewall. Or Anderson. Whoever was the latest to defect to the pros.

Rosewall recollects that Hopman tried to dissuade him from

turning pro by telling him he'd never make it in that league, that he just didn't have the stamina.

Though the memory of Hopman is far from beloved, the habits of fitness developed under him seem to have stuck with that whole generation of players. And they concede that he was a great motivator. "He sort of got across the idea that you had to work hard at the game," Sedgman acknowledges. "If you wanted to be a success, you had to put time in, and effort.

"But," Sedgman adds, "he didn't teach the mechanics of tennis—we had our strokes by the time he got us—and he wasn't a real good tactician. He couldn't tell you much about what your opponent was going to do or the way you could beat him."

Mal Anderson echoes that idea. "About all Harry Hopman told you during a match," Mal says, "was something like 'Hit close to the lines.' Well, you didn't need Harry Hopman to tell you that!"

The putdown of Hopman is almost unanimous among his old boys, but it sounds like an epidemic of sour grapes when you consider Hopman's record. As Davis Cup captain he managed no less than sixteen wins in twenty-six tries. And as a player he was a good enough tactician to get his name into the record books. A doubles specialist, he teamed with Jack Crawford, one of the legendary heroes of Australian tennis, to win the Australian title twice (1929–30) and the German Championships once (1932). Hop and his wife, Nell, were mixed doubles champions of Australia four times in the Thirties. And in 1952 Hopman won the U.S. Seniors, in singles as well as doubles. He recorded at least one other noteworthy singles victory: He eliminated Don Budge in the 1938 Pacific Coast Championships, just weeks after Budge completed history's first Grand Slam.

Either Hopman knew a little more about the game than just hitting close to the lines, or he certainly fooled a lot of Americans. Tony Trabert would be one of them. Trabert, the mainstay of the U.S. cup team in 1953, gave Hopman a substantial measure of credit when the Australians beat the United States with a pair of teenagers playing their first Davis Cup campaign. The kids were Rosewall and Hoad.

"We were beaten," said Trabert, "by two babies and a fox."

The Hopman era ended with the advent of open tennis. Within a year or so, in 1969, with his pool of talent drained by defections to the pros, the old captain left Australia and moved to the United States. Eventually he gravitated to Florida, running a tennis instructional center for youngsters. He died early in 1986.

I asked one of Hopman's critics, Mal Anderson, how he would explain the decline in Australia's tennis fortunes in the decade since Hopman left.

"Well, it's probably a mistake to talk about an Australian decline," Mal said. "Sure we've gone down, but only maybe this much"—he held his two palms close together—"while others countries have come up. The Swedes, the Czechs, the Argentines and Italy for a while. Even, to some degree, the U.S.

"What happened in Australia was, when open tennis came in, the sporting goods firms dropped out, because the players were never around—they were out chasing the dollar. All over the world. As professionals, the players were all traveling as individuals, so the association didn't have any control over them. The association couldn't develop any junior programs because they didn't have the support of the sporting goods firms."

As a result, I asked, had Australian tennis lost good young athletes to other sports; for example, to the popular form of soccer called Australian-rules football?

"I don't think so," Mal said. Then he gave a sort of resigned, generational chuckle. "I think we may have lost some of them to the automobiles. They don't want to put in the hours on the practice court any more, some of them. They want to be out on the highways with their girls. But," Mal added in his usual upbeat style, "now there are junior programs getting started again, and I think in three or four years you'll see the results."

One reason for Anderson's optimism about his country's

tennis prospects is the influence of his doubles partner, Fraser, who inherited the Davis Cup job in the early Seventies, after Hopman left. Neale is Anderson's idea of a *real* Davis Cup captain. "Neale will tell a player things he can use in the course of a match, like 'Try hooking him wide when you serve from the deuce court!' or 'Time to chip and charge!' "

On the subject of Harry Hopman, as on almost any other subject, sooner or later Anderson finds something conciliatory to say. "You've got to remember," he says, "that it was a whole different generation when Harry Hopman was in charge. He was dealing with players who were under his control for eight or nine months of the year."

"I wouldn't want them that long," Fraser said. "I'd go round the bend. I don't know whether I'm consciously doing things different than Hopman, but . . ." He threw up his hands as if he were having trouble expressing some painful memory. Then: "Look, we were robots! We just did what we were told. Now you've got a bunch of individuals, with individual styles, their own managers, et cetera. You just can't treat them the way we were treated!"

Fraser was once asked by a reporter if he could explain the extraordinary powers of concentration that seemed to characterize the Australian players of his generation. Simple, Fraser told the interviewer. It was no problem for the Australians to keep their minds on tennis, he said, because that's all they *had* on their minds. "We had no other interests to distract us. Tennis was all we knew."

Mal Anderson's interests never wandered very far from tennis. For several years he played the pro tour in the tough company of Gonzalez, Segura, Trabert, Hoad, Rosewall. He left it and settled down to domestic life in Melbourne—he had married Roy Emerson's sister, Daphne—and the routine of operating his squash and tennis club. But he kept up the old training habits: the running and even some of the old Hopman calisthenic drills. He also kept playing racquet sports. When open tennis came in, he was in shape to return to the tennis wars; he felt he was playing as well as ever, in fact, and felt "just as keen." At thirty-seven he reached the finals of a Grand Slam event—the Australian Championship—and a year later was once again picked for his country's Davis Cup team. That was like an old grad suiting up and playing for the varsity in the Homecoming Day game. He was more than ready for the Grand Masters competition when he reached the qualifying age of forty-five.

Fraser, meanwhile, had dropped out of tennis, taking up a straight occupation. For fifteen years he was in the insurance business. It must have comforted his father, although, he points out, "for part of that time I was *close* to tennis, being Davis Cup captain."

What was the toughest part of getting back into competition as a player after all those years on the sidelines?

Fraser thought about that for a moment. "The court's the same size," he said. "Unfortunately. Eyesight's a problem, especially in indoor lighting."

I was still looking for a middle-aged tennis player who would tell me that my first, star-struck impression of the Grand Masters was true—that he could hit as hard and run as fast as ever. I thought Anderson might be my man. But he responded to that proposition a bit dubiously. He *might,* he said, be able to hit any given serve as hard or move across the court in the same number of seconds, *but* . . . "the big difference is you can't keep that up for four or five sets." He conceded this much: "I'm probably hitting my serve as hard as I ever have."

"But we didn't put as much emphasis on hitting the ball hard in the old days," Fraser put in. "I believe it was a bit of a myth that I hit the ball hard. I had a *variety* of serves."

"You still do," Mal assured him. "I believe it gets down to a matter of practice. If Neale played as much as I did, he would still be hitting every bit as hard as he did."

As for speed . . . well, in the absolute sense (that is, if you timed them off a mark, running from one side of the court to the other) they both thought they were capable of matching their best time for that short distance. "But," Fraser said, clearly uncomfortable with the suggestion that he was anything like the player he once was, "you've got to consider concentration. Sometimes you'll get to the ball just as fast because you reacted quickly, but other times it's almost as if you have to remind yourself to move. Concentration and discipline. In my younger days a bomb could've gone off in the stands and I wouldn't hear it. Now I can hear two flies on the wall. I used to serve and volley automatically. Now I know I should go in behind my serve, and I just can't force myself to. It's not that my feet won't move as fast, but I don't have the discipline to move 'em."

I asked Fraser what had brought him back to competitive tennis after fifteen years in a line of work that presumably met his father's approval. "I missed *playing* the game," he said almost fiercely. "I missed going out and winning a match. Oh, I won a few prizes and trophies for selling the most insurance policies. But that's not the same thing, it just isn't the same."

Fraser's return to competition as a member of the Grand Masters coincided with another major transition in his life. "I've been divorced for five years, and I've been back to playing tennis five years," he said, finishing off his beer. He slapped the empty glass down on the table emphatically. "Best five years of my life!"

14

Late Entry

SINGLES can be a game of power, or it can be a game of finesse. Doubles—with its interplay of four people weaving intricate patterns of attack and defense—good doubles can also be a game of great ingenuity.

Against Emerson and Stolle, the team of Anderson and Fraser played an ingenious doubles match. They hit angles that set up returns to Neale's backhand volley, sparing his aching forehand. They switched sides of the court on lobs in order to give Mal a shot at overheads that his wounded partner might normally cover. Neale was also easing up on his service, as he'd done in Nashville. But it was not, I now realized, to give himself an extra beat of time to get in to the net. It was simply to minimize the strain on his arm.

Anderson and Fraser kept the match going for three hard sets, but they were only fighting off the inevitable. At the end it was 6–4, 1–6, 6–4 for the other guys.

Though the heroics were on Mal and Neale's side, it was Fred Stolle who was the revelation of that match. That is, he confirmed what he'd shown the day before in his opening-round singles match against Gene Scott.

Making his first appearance of the season after missing Nashville, Stolle crushed Scott in straight sets, and he did it in a way that brought a whole new element into the tour. At forty-five, barely a year Scott's junior, Stolle stood out from the crowd with his youthful, disciplined style of play.

Stolle is a tall, rather ungainly looking character with a wonderful mock-solemn manner, which he uses to great comic effect, both on and off the court. In a singles match, when a passing shot whizzes by him or a lob floats over his head, he is apt to call "Yours!" over his shoulder to a nonexistent partner. Hitting a drive long over the baseline, he shades his eyes and peers after it, as if watching it disappear over some distant horizon.

Stolle has the kind of reddish-blond hair that gets bleached almost white by the sun, so at first glance you're not sure whether you're watching a prematurely aged forty-year-old or a youthful fifty. You're inclined to guess the higher number when you see him trudge to his position on the court. He seems bone-weary. With his curious spraddle-legged stance, he looks like two-thirds of a tripod. You expect him to stay planted.

You're not surprised when this big man powers in a big first serve. But you're surprised that he keeps doing it point after point, game after game. And you can't help being startled at how persistently he drives himself onto the attack behind that serve, also point after point, like a California teenager. Most of all, you can't help being struck by the way he gets his big, aging body down to the volleys, his bent knee almost touching the court in textbook style—the kind of move that most senior players tend to finesse. It's tough, as Neale Fraser was suggesting, to force aging legs onto the attack. It's even tougher to force creaky knees to flex for that first, low volley. And it's not that much easier when you're one of the younger members of the senior group, like Stolle. Fred's game seemed to make less of a concession to age than that of any of the Grand Masters.

"Yeah, well, I try to keep fit," he said offhandedly, by way of explanation. But, he declared, he didn't spend nearly as much time on conditioning now as he did when he was one of Harry Hopman's charges. "Then we used to run three to five miles every day, and do all kinds of jumps and knee bends. I never did like running. The only time I run now is when I'm late for a plane. As far as the exercises, I wouldn't dare do knee jumps. Might hurt something."

His routine nowadays, he told me, consists of a daily half hour on a stationary bike, eighty to one hundred sit-ups, stretching and, most of all, playing tennis. Even under the Hopman regime, with all its drills and exercises, he said, the most important element in conditioning was playing matches. That, he said, is where the Australian players got their strength and stamina—from playing three to five intense hours against tough competition every day. Playing each other. The way Stolle gets in his playing time now, as Al Bunis had pointed out to me, is by playing sets against the young pros he coaches.

Stolle's "classroom" is a court at Turnberry, the Miami-area resort where he had recently taken on the head pro's job. He and his family are now Floridians. One of his three children is a student at the University of Florida, while another is a product of Harry Hopman's tennis academy. Stolle is one Aussie who retained a certain fondness for the old captain, even while letting some of the old Hopman training routines slide.

Fred's transition to the pro shop was a gradual one. He had served as a player-coach in that curious experiment called World Team Tennis. One of the transient phenomena of the Seventies, it was revived in the mid-Eighties by Billie Jean King, with doubtful results. Stolle is one of the few other people I know of besides Billie Jean who regretted its passing.

With franchises in various American cities (and, curiously, a team representing the Soviet Union), Team Tennis tried to inject some of the raucous partisanship of professional football, baseball and basketball into what had been a relatively genteel, individual game.

"Would've worked, too," Stolle insists, "if it'd had just one more year. Only reason it failed was greed. Even some of the women were asking for contracts for a hundred or two hundred thousand a year. And some of them were only playing doubles! That killed it off, pushed the franchises under. Until then it was catching on—one more year would've done it. I was sorry to see it go. I enjoyed team tennis. I liked the concept. I liked the competition."

He sounded like a man who missed the old team spirit of the Davis Cup.

I asked Fred what he would have done with his life if open tennis hadn't come along.

"Oh," he said cheerfully, "if I wasn't a tennis player, I'd be

Ken Rosewall's backhand, one of the game's classic strokes, was first displayed to the American tennis public in 1952, when Kenny was just 17. He was a U.S. Singles winner at 21 (in 1956) and again at 35 (1970), a finalist at 20 and again at 39—an unparalleled span of years at the top. (*International Tennis Hall of Fame, Newport, R.I.*)

Rosewall at 50. The face shows a few years but the strokes are still sound as Kenny meets his strongest challenge for the No. 1 ranking in the Tennis Grand Masters. The challenger: his old rival, Rod Laver. (*Tom Fontana*)

Rod Laver's wristy left-handed topspin took him to the head of the amateur class in 1961. The next year he won the first of his two Grand Slams. (*International Tennis Hall of Fame, Newport, R.I.*)

Laver, as a 45-year-old "rookie" on the Grand Masters circuit—still experimenting with shots. (*Mutual Benefit Grand Masters*)

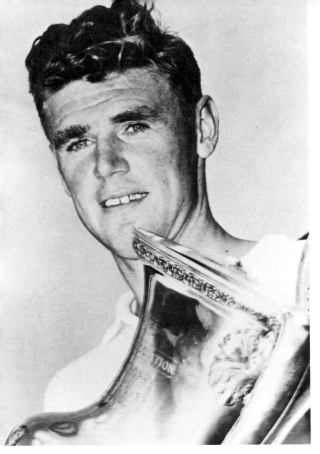

The Australian wave of the '50s began with Frank Sedgman, leading amateur trophy winner in 1951–52. Besides winning U.S. Singles twice and Wimbledon once, he swept the Grand Slam in doubles (with Ken McGregor) in '51 and came close to repeating the trick the following year. *(International Tennis Hall of Fame, Newport, R.I.)*

Aussie Davis Cup doubles team (1959–64) of Roy Emerson (left) and Neale Fraser were also Wimbledon champs in 1961. In Grand Masters doubles matches they are usually on opposite sides of the net. *(AP/Wide World Photo)*

Emerson, winner of more major championships than any player in tennis history, struggled against conditioning problems in the over-45 group. *(Tom Fontana)*

Now Australia's non-playing Davis Cup captain, Neale Fraser spends spring and fall competing again, though past the age of 50. *(Tom Fontana)*

Off-court cut-ups, Fred Stolle (left) and Roy Emerson played serious doubles for Australian Davis Cup teams in the mid-'60s, won the U.S. championship twice, and still team up on the Grand Masters tournament circuit. *(International Tennis Hall of Fame, Newport, R.I.)*

Flat, heavy ground strokes, a powerful serve and firm volley characterized Fred Stolle's game. As an amateur in the mid-'60s, he got time off from his bank clerk's job to play Davis Cup matches. In his first season on the Grand Masters circuit (1983), Stolle upset the tour leader, Ken Rosewall, his long-time nemesis. *(International Tennis Hall of Fame, Newport, R.I.)*

Known as a scrambler, Bobby Riggs also had solid ground strokes, a fine touch and a remarkable instinct at the net—qualities that established him as No. 1 amateur in 1939, when he won Wimbledon at age 21. "I always was the best player in the world for my age," Riggs says flatly. "I still am," he adds, pointing to his many titles in the super-senior age brackets. *(International Tennis Hall of Fame, Newport, R.I.)*

Veteran doubles team of Gardnar Mulloy (left) and Billy Talbert (second from left), four-time national champions, were dumped as Davis Cup tandem, considered over the hill by 1951, when Talbert was 33 and Mulloy 37. Talbert proceeded to win 15 straight doubles tournaments with another partner, Tony Trabert, and Mulloy won Wimbledon doubles six years later, at the age of 43, with Budge Patty. Mulloy and Talbert are seen here with Ted Schroeder (right) and Frank Parker. *(AP/Wide World Photo)*

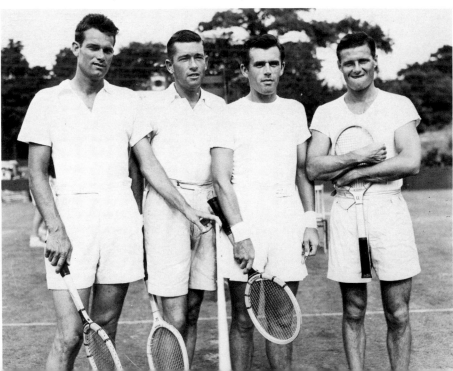

An anachronism at 45, Gardnar Mulloy still had enough left to win his third-round match in the 1959 Wimbledon singles, beating 18-year-old Earl Buchholz. Twenty-five years later, Mulloy was still winning tennis championships. *(AP/Wide World Photo)*

No. 1 player of the postwar decades, Jack Kramer holds winner's trophy at 1947 Wimbledon. For his 4th of July victory, Kramer received congratulations from Princess Margaret Rose, while her father, King George VI, and Queen Mother (Elizabeth) looked on. *(AP/Wide World Photo)*

Unconventional Torben Ulrich played exhibition match on New York's Lexington Avenue to help promote the 1969 U.S. Open, a tournament then in its experimental phase. *(UPI)*

Perfectionist Mal Anderson, a 1950s champion overshadowed by other heroes, is perennial challenger for honors—and prize money—on the Grand Masters tour. *(Tom Fontana)*

working in a bank in Australia. That's what I did in Sydney for
nine years before open tennis. I was a bank clerk when I played
Davis Cup. A bank is no place to make money, unless you own
it. I quit when I realized they weren't giving out any free samples to the employees."

Stolle versus Rosewall was the match that would round out
the semifinals at Boca Grove—the tournament was following
form. Even against the fearsome little mechanic, you had to like
Fred's chances, just on the basis of his early performance. And
there was more than that in his favor.

Stolle had the standard Australian credentials (the championships in Grand Slam tournaments, both singles and doubles, the Davis Cup experience) plus one special distinction:
He was, in the phrase of a *New York Times* writer, "sports' most
consistent runner-up." From 1963 through 1965, he was the
beaten finalist three times at Wimbledon, twice in the Australian championship, and once at Forest Hills (where he won the
U.S. Singles over John Newcombe in 1966).

Moving on to current events, Stolle had the most recent
mainstream experience of any of the Grand Masters, not ex-
cluding Rosewall. As late as 1981, at the age of forty-two, Fred
played in a semifinal at the U.S. Open. It was in the doubles,
in which he was partnered by thirty-seven-year-old John Newcombe. The creaky old Aussies hung in for five grueling sets
against McEnroe and Peter Fleming, the ultimate winners of
the championship, before bowing out.

Finally, I reminded myself, Stolle was officially the current
Grand Masters champion—so listed in the records of the USTA
—by reason of his upset victory over Rosewall in last year's
playoff.

It all turned out not to mean a damn thing at Boca Raton.

With an air of sheer proficiency, Rosewall took charge of the
semifinal match almost from the start. He played himself into
an early groove, going almost four full games in one stretch
without committing a single unforced error. In the face of Kenny's flawless stroking, Fred's game gradually broke down. As
Rosewall's service returns got sharper and sharper, Stolle's big

service went off. He became tentative, his footwork looked faulty, he wasn't making those admirably youthful low volleys. Finally, he was just Old Fred, another senior tennis player on Rosewall's list of victims.

Toward the end, almost insultingly, Rosewall took Stolle's own game away from him. Never known for potency of service himself, Rosewall came up to serve at 4–2 in the second set and proceeded to ace Stolle twice. (*One* ace is unusual on Kenny's modest delivery.) Then he broke Fred's service for the fourth time in the match, and it was over, 6–2, 6–2.

In line with the natural order of things, we would have another Laver-Rosewall final.

15

Good at Any Age

THE SUNDAY AFTERNOON CROWD gathered for the finals in sociable little clusters—gathered on the Plantation's clubhouse terrace well before match time with plastic glasses of white wine or Bloody Marys in hand.

The place had the tone and color of an Eastern club or an upper-class resort. I was struck, as I often am at tennis matches, by how many women were in the crowd. Unlike, say, a Cowboys-Redskins game or a battle of NBA basketball giants, tennis is one spectator sport that both sexes often approach with roughly equal enthusiasm and expertise.

Some of the usual dime-and-quarter betting was going on between couples, and there was no mistaking which of the two finalists was the betting favorite. Never mind that the slow clay court would favor Ken Rosewall's patient type of game, it was Laver who had impressed the crowd with his display of shotmaking in the early rounds. As usual throughout his career, Rosewall was being taken for granted and the other guy was getting the attention.

Ken Rosewall once described himself as "originally a counterpuncher—I used to make my play off the other guy's shot." In a sense the same thing was true of his image: Rosewall made his name off the other guy's brilliance. That wasn't his doing, it was just the way he was perceived by the tennis public. Even before he was famous as Rod Laver's opponent, he was best known as Lew Hoad's rival. It wasn't until his remarkable performance in his forties, when both of his antagonists had fallen by the wayside, that Rosewall's impeccable but unspectacular style of play became widely appreciated and he acquired an identity as a player in his own right. Until then he was playing in the shadow of two performers whom he often beat but whose style and court temperament were more charismatic.

Lew Hoad was blond, handsome, not much over average height but brawny. Cast in the same extrovert mold that produced Emerson and Newcombe, he was one of the most popular players of his generation—a crowd pleaser who was also a favorite among his peers. His strokes had the kind of power and flash that automatically command attention. He was a risk taker who often played with a kind of heedless abandon. Orthodox tennis minds despaired of his daredevil tactics, but he had the talent to beat the percentages.

Hoad had an extraordinarily potent serve, a punishing forehand hit with a lot of wrist, a superb volley, and aggressive instincts. A former player on the European circuit once recalled his first impression of Lew Hoad: "He hit everything on the rise. He played every shot like a half volley. He was a *bull*, even more of a bull than Jimmy Connors—always coming in, coming in, coming in at you."

Exactly the same age (their birthdays just three weeks apart), Lew Hoad and Kenny Rosewall were twin prodigies. They emerged onto the Australian tennis scene even before they were in their teens. At the age of seventeen they made their presence felt on the international circuit. That was in 1952, the year Rosewall was ousted by thirty-nine-year-old Gardnar Mulloy at both Wimbledon and Forest Hills. But that same year fuzzy-cheeked Rosewall had wins over both Mulloy and Vic Seixas, the Number 1 and 2 Americans; Hoad and Rosewall as a team reached the semifinals of the U.S. Doubles. Only a year later, at eighteen, Hoad and Rosewall began racking up titles in the Grand Slam tournaments and also led Australia to victory over the United States in the Davis Cup.

Rosewall was the first to mature as a player. When he won both the French and Australian championships at eighteen, he was the youngest ever to win either title. (Bjorn Borg was several months younger when he won at Paris in 1974.) And when Kenny and Lew teamed up to win three of the world's four major doubles crowns that year (only the U.S. title eluded them), they had racked up perhaps the most dazzling string of successes ever recorded by a pair of players their age.

They were good friends as well as effective doubles partners, as Laver and Rosewall later were. But when Kenny and Lew found themselves on opposite sides of the net they became almost pathologically competitive. As Davis Cup teammates, Kenny recalls, they couldn't practice together because what started out as a drill would inevitably wind up as a contest. They never got to work on their strokes. They simply couldn't help trying to put the ball past each other to win the "point" even when no score was being kept. It was impossible to shake the habits they had developed in competing against each other ever since the age of twelve.

Jack Kramer, who promoted a number of Hoad-Rosewall matches when, still in their early twenties, they became members of his professional tour, once said he liked watching those two play more than anybody because they always went at it as if it were a grudge match. He summed up the results: "Lew makes all the miraculous shots, and Kenny wins the matches."

Kenny did in fact hold the upper hand over his flashier rival early in their joint career. Even when Hoad emerged on top of the world of amateur tennis in 1956, winning Wimbledon, Paris and the Australian title, it was Rosewall who kept him from completing a Grand Slam, stopping him in a four-set final at Forest Hills. As if to prove that it was no fluke, Rosewall then won their next three straight encounters in tournaments later that year.

Hoad made the transition to the pros more easily than Rosewall. With his naturally aggressive style, Lew was better equipped to compete against the likes of Gonzalez and Tony Trabert. Like Bobby Riggs ahead of him, Rosewall had to teach himself the attacking game. By 1959, with Gonzalez aging and gradually phasing out of the pro tour, Hoad became king of the pros and was widely recognized as the best tennis player in the world.

His reign was unfortunately brief. Chronic back trouble and

a severe foot injury sapped his speed and power. Within a few years he was rendered *hors de combat*. Beginning with the 1960 tour, Ken Rosewall took over from his old rival, and reigned for the next five years, until he found himself engaged in another fierce rivalry in which he was overshadowed by another brilliant antagonist. The dramatic struggle of steady, precise Rosewall against spectacular Lew Hoad was over. The dramatic struggle of steady, precise Ken Rosewall against flamboyant Rod Laver had begun.

Unlike the gallery at Boca Grove Plantation, some of the Grand Masters players thought Rosewall had a good chance against Laver in their second final of the tour. Mal Anderson was one of them.

Mal was still brooding about his loss to Laver in the previous day's semifinal.

"I should have played him differently," Mal said, between bites of a sandwich from the refreshment kiosk alongside the exhibition court. "I should have played his forehand more. I can see that now. Of course, I hadn't played him in quite a while. But the main thing is, I didn't have enough confidence. I didn't have enough confidence to hit out when I had a chance to score.

"Now, Kenny," he went on, "he can play a different sort of match against Laver. Kenny can outwait him. He can beat Laver by keeping the ball in play."

The two featured antagonists hadn't yet emerged from the locker room; they were probably comparing notes on local restaurants. Or on the playing qualities of some new brand of gut they were trying in their racquets.

On my way toward my seat in the stands I ran into Rod's wife, Mary. She was chatting with a pro named Bob Neal—but not about the main event. They were talking about the exhibition match that was to follow the Grand Masters finals, singles and doubles. Bobby Riggs, after finishing his broadcasting duties with Talbert, was going to join Mulloy in what was becoming Bobby's standard number: a battle of the sexes, the two ancient Number 1's against a pair of young women pros.

"Bobby will just drop shot them to death," Neal said. "He's convinced women can't run forward. Or won't. They can move laterally okay, but not forward."

I remembered what Mulloy had told me about aging male players—that they have trouble moving *backwards*. I wondered if the women knew about that and were plotting their strategy accordingly, presumably planning to hit a lot of lobs. I didn't have to wonder too long. The female pair themselves appeared as if on cue—a couple of Amazons named Vicky Beggs and Bunny Smith.

"They're not going to beat us with power," said Bunny, as she joined the conversational circle. She gave a kind of snicker at the very idea of being outhit by two doddering old coots like Riggs and Mulloy. "They'll be trying to hit balls at our feet because we're tall. A lot of chips and drop shots." As for their own strategy: "We're going to play Bobby a lot. He says he's got a pulled groin muscle. Says he hasn't played in six months. He wants us to hit everything to his forehand."

"Is that what you're going to do?"

Beggs, a remarkably pretty blonde, laughed gently.

"Are you kidding?" said her partner. "We're going to hit lobs over him. Give him a lot of angles. Make him stretch as much as we possibly can."

They hefted their racquet bags and headed out to a practice court, chortling with anticipation.

It was a gorgeous day under the benign early-spring sun of Florida, the temperature just balmy, not the least bit cloying. The stands were full. A couple of thousand spectators, at a reasonable guess.

The match started with an air as gentle as the crowd and the weather. For most of the first set Rosewall was content to follow Mal Anderson's prescription: Keep the ball in play and wait for Laver to get overambitious. Rod, for his part, seemed willing to join in the waiting game—but for just so long. There would be long exchanges from the baseline, then suddenly Rod's whip-like backhand would flash out in a daring crosscourt placement. He moved out to a 4–2 lead. One service break.

"Laver," said Bobby Riggs, "has controlled aggressiveness. He has control of his shots, control of the match."

Riggs was talking to a cable television audience from an improvised broadcast booth—actually nothing more than a table lashed in place in the upper rows of the grandstand, where he and Bill Talbert were stationed.

Rosewall never panicked about his deficit, even as the set wound down toward what looked like an inevitable losing conclusion. Kenny stayed with his pattern, exchanging shots from the backcourt in a kind of lazy but irregular rhythm. He was varying his shots not so much in pace as in trajectory. They all came off his racquet equally hard (or equally soft), but sometimes they would bounce high and sometimes a little higher.

Abruptly, Muscles sliced a ball just over the net.

"That's a good time for a drop shot," Riggs observed. "Love-forty or forty-love—that's when you do it. It may not win the point for you in the first set, but it'll help you win one in the third. You've made him run, he'll pay for it later when he's tired."

That happens not to agree with Rosewall's own view of the drop shot, which he says he only plays when he thinks it will score a point for him outright. But I figured a former Wimbledon champion was entitled to his own opinion on strategy issues.

In the following game, with Laver one point away from a second service break and a headlock on the set, Rod tried a drop shot himself. But though the execution was nearly perfect, Rosewall read it, reached it, returned it deep for a winner. The next point was almost an exact duplicate—Laver seemed determined to bring that shot off—and Rosewall returned it again, this time for the point that put him back in the game.

Kenny won the game. He also won the next game and got his service break back, playing one beautiful point with a perfect offensive lob from an impossible defensive position. It skimmed right over Laver's outstretched racquet for a decisive point. The set was even again.

In the last few games of the set, it was Rosewall's consistency versus Laver's errors. Abruptly, the set belonged to Kenny, 7–5.

The second set followed much the same pattern: Laver taking command early, then Rosewall pulling even on a sudden break of service. The two small giants now played so closely that during one stretch I counted fourteen winners for Rosewall to thirteen for Laver, and eighteen errors against Rod's sixteen.

At 4–all Rosewall lost his service when a couple of forehands went awry, but then he broke right back, putting away the winning point by attacking the net and hitting an aggressive volley. Muscles then held serve, outlasting Laver in a couple of long rallies. Rod simply tried to end them too soon with too good a shot.

At 5–6, Laver serving—and pressing hard—Kenny hit a couple of lovely passing shots, one of them with his back to the wall. Laver's service was broken, and Rosewall had the match and the first-prize money. The scores were 7–5, 7–5.

The outcome, as Gene Scott analyzed it when he joined Riggs and Talbert at the broadcasting desk, was a matter of temperament and surface. Laver was too impatient to beat Rosewall on clay, Scott said. Laver "insists on winning his own way."

Off-camera, Scott elaborated on the peculiar psychology of the slow clay-court game. "Some players who are excellent in all mechanical aspects of the game," he said, "aren't able to shake the basic mindset of tennis, which tells you to end the point as quickly as possible. What you should be telling yourself on clay is to keep it going. The point of clay-court tennis is to rally, not to *end* the rally. Until you get rid of that, you're going to have trouble on clay."

Riggs and Talbert were full of admiration for both finalists. "The quality of tennis here," Talbert told his viewers, "was good by any standards. At any age."

After a trip to the showers, Laver and Rosewall came back on the court and teamed up to face Stolle and Emerson in the doubles final—a fine match, which went to three sets. Brilliant exchanges, with all four players at net, parrying each other's volleys, tricking each other with soft little dink shots. With Stolle serving for the match, twice in a row Laver lashed back with blazing topspin returns off his backhand and stopped the incoming server in his tracks. The third time Laver tried it, he netted the return, and Emerson-Stolle won the doubles, 6–2, 3–6, 6–3.

Oh, yes—the battle of the sexes.

Riggs played the same kind of game he had played in his television stunts against Margaret Court and Billie Jean. Every possible form of slice: dinks, chips, drop shots. Pittypat volleys. Billowy lobs. Serves that slid off his racquet without making a sound. Nothing you could recognize from descriptions of the Mad Attacker who had forced Jack Kramer to escalate his own serve-and-volley game.

Mulloy pretty much followed Bobby's example. Between the two of them I'm not sure there were as many as three shots in which the racquet was laid flat against the ball.

The women actually did a pretty good job of covering the short stuff, running forward almost as if totally heedless of their natural disability in that aspect of the game. It was a basic mechanical problem, I felt, that did them in. Or maybe it was overeagerness in trying to overpower their male victims. Anyway, what they did was make too many errors on what should have been putaway volleys.

The men, with their chintzy little game, finally scraped through, by a score that I failed to write down. I didn't think they'd done much for the cause of manhood, and they came pretty close to giving winning a bad name.

On my final morning in Florida, before breaking camp, I got in a few more licks of my own at the Yates family tennis grounds. A fit-looking couple in (I guessed) their late thirties, both with decent strokes, were hitting against a kid of sixteen or so. His name was Jason, and he asked me to fill in on his side for a couple of sets of doubles.

On the very first point Jason stepped up to the line and blasted a serve that dug a divot out of the clay and would surely have done the same to the poor lady on the receiving end if she hadn't sidestepped nimbly. It was long by at least a foot.

"Just spin your first serve in," I said, trying not to sound stuffy and patronizing. I was paraphrasing Bill Talbert's first law of doubles: Serve as if you're only allowed one fault instead of two. If you have to come in with a second serve, you're giving the receivers a chance to beat you to the net.

Jason brushed me off. "I always try to ace my mom," he said. "If you let her dig in against you, she'll start grooving her return." He wound up and fired a second cannonball, just about as hard as the first.

Jason held his service comfortably throughout the match. I had a lot of trouble whenever my turn came. Every time I laid my first serve in, the lady teed off and drove it back. When I put a little more stuff on it, she chipped it back wide and came right in to the net.

Jason was right. There are times when you just have to ignore the traditional wisdom, along with family ties, and take your chances.

The experience reminded me that I had been neglecting my own tennis education. The Laver-Rosewall issue seemed well in hand. It would be Rod over Ken on a fast surface, vice versa when they met on clay. Or so it appeared from the contrasting results at Nashville and Boca Raton.

Now I figured I ought to concentrate for a while on what the Grand Masters, by their example, had to tell us ordinary hackers about playing the game.

PART IV

Lessons from the
Masters

16

The Pros and the Ams

"WHAT'S THE REAL DIFFERENCE between the good club player and the tournament Tennis Player—capital T, capital P?" What is it, I wondered, that keeps even the most serious of us hackers from improving beyond a certain frustrating level?

My question was addressed to a leisurely group of Grand Masters during an afternoon practice. It had much the same effect as if I had shouted "Fire!" or "Stan Smith!" Everyone scattered in the direction of the courts, the locker room—any place where they would be safe from the unappetizing subject of . . . Christ! Club tennis!

Everyone except, of course, the obliging Mr. Anderson.

"The good club player keeps making the same mistakes we do," Mal said generously. "We make them less often, that's all. He takes his eye off the ball. Two, he swings late. And three, he fails to turn his shoulders on the backhand." Then he excused himself and hurried off to join Emmo, Krish and Fraser on the practice court.

The statement was hardly a revelation, but it was as much as I was going to get out of the old pros on that particular subject. Professional tennis players, like pros in any sport I know about, would really prefer to steer clear of amateurs altogether—steer clear of watching them, discussing them and above all, playing them. Pro versus amateur is at best a no-win proposition.

"There is just one thing that ticks off a good tennis player more than getting caught in a club game with some guy who couldn't have carried your racquets, and losing to him," Al

Bunis remarked one time in the course of a sociable luncheon in New York during a break in the tour. One of his companions at the lunch table was Bill Talbert, his fellow Cincinnatian. "The thing that's worse," Bunis continued, "is knowing that the guy is going to be bragging about it afterwards in the Cincinnati Tennis Club bar: 'I took a set off Bill Talbert!'"

"It never bothers me," said Talbert, who rarely admits that anything bothers him. "I tell myself I needed the exercise."

Gene Scott is admittedly bothered by the scalp-hunting practices of some of the better club players. What offends him most is the cheating they'll do, deliberately or otherwise, just to pick up a win over a name player.

"Footfaulting," Scott says, "is almost universal, and it's routine. I don't mean just edging your toe onto the line, I mean actually planting your whole body in the court. How fair is it when one player is allowed to get right on top of the net, practically in a volleying position, when he hits his service?

"And then, of course," Scott concludes, "there are the flagrantly bad line calls."

Don't get the idea that the Grand Masters never associate with ordinary racquet-swinging mortals like you and me. They couldn't avoid it if they wanted to. Every event on the tour began with a so-called pro-am tournament, a form of social doubles in which the pros played for a couple of hours in the company of club members, local sponsors and their guests, or media people—all of them, you may be sure, hackers of one degree of incompetence or another. The players were paired, one pro and one amateur on each team, and the individuals rotated after every few games so that every am got a shot at—and alongside —each pro. Or, as somebody put it, so the harm was evenly distributed.

The Grand Masters seemed to accept this brief association with the hackers as something that comes with the territory. They took the courts in a spirit of reasonable good humor and usually finished the same way. That doesn't mean they wouldn't rather have been doing something else.

In one pro-am that I watched (along with a handful of witnesses who had to be relatives and friends of the participants), an awkward gent who was one of the local sponsors crossed directly in front of Ken Rosewall to take an overhead that Rosewall had already drawn a bead on. Not only did the guy miss the ball completely, but he also managed to get in the way of his partner, so that Kenny—whose overhead is practically infallible—also whiffed. Kenny burst into laughter and consoled his chagrined teammate. Wouldn't you like to be able to brag that you once forced Ken Rosewall into an error? Nobody has to know that the two of you were on the same side of the net.

On another court a few minutes later, Roy Emerson counseled a partner who had just smashed an overhead into his own end of the court: "No, Bill, don't *bounce* them over!"

Bill was a lanky, pigeon-toed hitter in his fifties with pretty good strokes but a tendency to overplay them. Emmo maintained a kind of running commentary on his partner's game. When Bill blooped a service return into the air and misguidedly charged in behind it, Emmo called out, "Excellent lob approach!" A few points later, as Bill this time *strolled* to the net behind a return: "Ah, the old walking chip shot!"

The lob was purely accidental, and there is of course no such thing in tennis as a walking chip—that is, there shouldn't be.

Bill joined in the laughter from the sidelines, stepped up to serve, and hit a service winner against Rod Laver. Rod barely got his racquet on the ball, thereby providing a moment that has probably been mentioned more than once at the bar of Bill's tennis club. When the players changed partners a few moments later, Emerson took aim at Bill and aced him with a cannonball on a second serve—an obvious gesture of retaliation, one pro on behalf of the other. Laver couldn't stoop to do it, so Emmo did it for him.

I concentrated my attention on the club players at several pro-ams. Even the best of them did not provide a comforting picture of my own breed. In the first place, Scott was right: Almost everyone footfaulted—regularly. In the second place, Anderson was right, too: Almost without exception they committed Mal's trinity of mistakes: the wandering eye, the late swing, the incomplete turn. They also tended to commit another, closely related one—swinging from *below* the shoulder (with their wrists or their forearms) instead of getting their whole upper body into the stroke. They were hitting the ball as it reached them, or even got slightly past them, instead of moving into the ball with the swing and hitting it out in front. And the reason of course was lateness—lateness in getting the feet into position or in getting the racquet back, ready for the stroke.

Some players clearly *thought* they were getting their racquet back. And some of them were, but only partway. Then, as the ball approached, they would resume the backswing, pulling the racquet back the rest of the way, like a baseball batter with a hitch in his swing.

"Look at this guy," Bunis said, indicating a compact, fit-looking player of thirty or so, a reporter for a local TV station. "Now he's obviously played a lot of years. Got pretty good strokes, moves well. But he doesn't start his backswing until the ball bounces in his court. Every tennis player knows you're supposed to get that racquet back as soon as you see the ball come off your *opponent's* racquet. They know it, they think they do it, but they don't *do* it. Late preparation—without question that's the primary mistake of the club player."

He turned back to the court just in time to see the reporter with the late backswing hit a perfect forehand deep down the middle—a well-chosen shot in doubles—past Mal Anderson.

"Well," said Bunis, without changing the pitch of his voice, "at least no one got injured." He paused to applaud the shot. "The risk in pro-am tournaments," he went on, "is that people who don't really know tennis will think, *Why, these old guys aren't so much! I bet our club pro could handle them!* What some people don't realize is that these old guys are so good they can just lay the ball on the other guys' racquets. Which is all they're trying to do."

The main principle of social tennis is to keep laying the ball on the other guy's (or gal's) racquet, to keep the ball in play until an opening becomes irresistible, a point inevitable. When faced with the inevitable, I noticed, the pros would usually play each other. When a big overhead got hit, it was usually by one pro smashing it not at the amateur but at the feet of the other pro. The pattern of play struck me as a good model for the mixed doubles games that are a regular feature of tennis club life, in which partners are wildly mismatched, the men usually much stronger than the women.

First and Only All-Embracing Law of Social Mixed Doubles: *The object of the game is not to score points but only to keep the ball in play until a point is unavoidable.*

In the final game of one of these mini-matches, Emerson and Laver kept a rally going so long that even they got bored with it. But neither would yield to the temptation to kill it off. Finally, as a signal to put the point out of its misery, Emmo deliberately mis-hit the ball right to Laver. Rod, declining to take the point the easy way, deliberately mis-hit it back for a winner. It was some of the niftiest racquet work you'd want to see. Also some of the most remarkable self-restraint.

Emmo came off the court after the evening's schedule still wearing his warm-ups, not having broken a sweat. "Well," he said, "that was better than a kick in the ass, wasn't it?"

The Grand Masters never leave town—any town—without contributing to the improvement of local club tennis. They do this by holding a clinic on Saturday morning before the day's semifinal matches.

The clinics are run by Al Bunis with the help of two first-round losers. It's a paid assignment, but just barely: $150 per pro for a couple of hours of group instruction. There is no competition for the job. Torben Ulrich once remarked that there are three incentives for a player in any Grand Masters tournament: pride, money and the threat of the Saturday morning clinic.

In between tournaments the players sometimes go off on similar assignments, singly or in pairs, conducting clinics at corporate outings or conventions—the sort of affairs big companies like to stage at resorts or country clubs for key employees and favorite customers. Arranged for the players by their agent, IMG, these outings are the Grand Masters equivalent of

the exhibitions these same guys used to play during their amateur-circuit days. And like those events, they involve some
fairly important money.

For working a corporate outing a Grand Masters player gets
paid anywhere from $1,500 to $5,000 a day. And a player can get
one or more of these bookings practically every week of the
tour if he wants to keep busy. Which explains how a season on
the Grand Masters circuit can pay off even for a steady loser. It
also explains what Al Bunis means when he says, in commenting on a report that Frank Sedgman's earnings on one tour
exceeded $75,000, "I'm sure he made *substantially* more than
that."

Some corporate outings are elaborate productions, like an
event that Laver, Fraser and Anderson played at Palm Springs,
California, during a break in the 1984 tour. It was a four-day
show, which the players conducted on behalf of Nabisco, a
company whose cereal products Laver endorses. At Palm
Springs the players held instructional clinics for a group of
Nabisco executives and guests, ran and participated in a pro-
am tournament, and played some hit-and-giggle sets among
themselves.

More often these assignments are one-day affairs, like a
Laver-Rosewall program in Cocoa Beach, Florida. In that case
the sponsoring "company" was the local Chamber of Commerce. Rod and Kenny conducted instructional classes all afternoon, then played an exhibition match in the evening. It went
three sets before Rosewall pulled out a victory. Like Hoad versus Rosewall, Laver versus Rosewall is always a contest.
Against each other they are simply incapable of just fooling
around.

When the spring tour hit the Pacific Northwest, I caught a
couple of Grand Masters players in action at an abbreviated
version of the standard corporate outing. It was staged by the
tour sponsor, the Mutual Benefit Life Insurance Company, for
some of their key agents, VIP clients and star prospects in the
Seattle area. The site was a vast, elegant country club in Bellevue, Washington, a beachy suburb of Seattle.

The players were Neale Fraser and Torben Ulrich. Since Al Bunis is a paid consultant to Mutual Benefit as well as to IMG, he was also on hand to serve as a kind of emcee for the obligatory clinic. Standing in no-man's-land, between the service line and baseline, on one of the Bellevue club's immaculate indoor courts, Bunis addressed a group of about twenty men and women in tennis clothes facing him across the net, racquets in hand. An equal number of meeker souls, unarmed and in civvies, were ranged along the sidelines.

Flanked by his two tigers, both in warm-up suits, Bunis ran briskly through the catalogue of basic tennis strokes, offering some piece of unarguable wisdom about each. On the subject of service he told the class:

"In singles you should get two-thirds of your first serves in. If you don't, then you're hitting too hard, so slow your service down. For doubles raise your quota to seventy or seventy-five percent."

"Eighty percent," Fraser corrected him.

Relax when you serve, the class was advised. You can't serve properly if you're all tensed up. Keep your motion simple. An elaborate windup or lots of body English doesn't do anything for your power and only increases the chances of hitting faults. If you're consistently hitting your service into the net, you're probably pulling your head down as you swing, taking your eye off the ball too soon. If, on the other hand, you're consistently hitting long, you need to apply less force, more spin.

No news for the average tennis player in any of this, but no harm in the reminder, especially when some of it is coming from such a recognized expert on service as Neale Fraser. In any historical discussion of great servers, Fraser's name will usually come up, not far behind Gonzalez, Vines, Tilden, Kramer, Budge. Fraser's doubles partner, Mal Anderson, says of his partner's serve: "It's tougher than anybody's. I mean of our age bracket. Maybe some other age brackets as well. It's tougher than Laver's." He stops himself, realizing he might have said something offensive. "Don't get me wrong, Rod's got a fine service—anybody'd be happy to have that service. But

Neale's is *so* tough. He can do so many things with it. And all with the same motion. Oh, there's no finer service than Neale's."

Fraser, who declines to put himself in the same company with big servers like Gonzalez, considers disguise rather than power to be the key to a successful service. When the clinic splits into two groups, one working with each pro, Neale explains this.

The secret of disguising your intentions and keeping the receiver off balance, he tells the class, is to learn to hit all three basic forms of service (flat, slice, twist) consistently *and to hit them all off the same toss*. Don't throw the ball up to different spots—to your right or your left—as you're sometimes advised.

The difference between your services, Fraser demonstrates, making it look easy, should come from the wrist: from the kind and degree of spin imparted by the snap of the wrist on impact with the ball.

He pauses and hits three exemplary serves, all deep—one kicking to the forehand, one to the backhand, the last skidding low and fast.

"Another thing," Fraser throws in by way of a little bonus. "Notice how I finish my service motion. As I end my follow-through"—he demonstrates in slow motion—"I am stepping across the baseline into the court, ready to come in behind my serve."

Ulrich meanwhile is characteristically teaching tennis less in terms of mechanics than of mental attitude. He is urging his students to adopt a kind of "forward mindset," an attitude of always moving *into* the ball. It is, he suggests, not only a way of getting depth and force into your shots and advancing toward a commanding position at the net, but it also helps you *defensively*. It enables you to cut off the angles of your opponent's shots.

Torben's little lecture reminds me of a match I saw him play in a Grand Masters tournament about five years before, when he methodically broke down his opponent's formidable serve by continually moving forward to receive it—moving in so close that he was sometimes actually taking it on the service line, taking the ball on the rise and hitting a half-volley return. I'm talking about return of *first* serve. Torben kept charging in behind that return, of course, to take the net away from the server.

Torben's opponent in that match: Neale Fraser, then an intimidating new forty-five-year-old presence on the tour. Ulrich was fifty—just past his Grand Masters peak but still winning matches.

After about an hour of lectures and drills, in which the patients in the clinic ran around the court in continuous queues, hitting ground strokes against the pros, a doubles round-robin was organized. The two pros kept themselves moving between two courts, each playing a couple of games with as many different partners as possible.

In the standard outing format, the two pros would then have squared off against each other, probably for an eight- or ten-game pro set. If a Grand Masters player happened to be making a solo appearance, he'd probably have played a set against a local club pro. But the Bellevue program was running late. The proceedings had started around 10:00 A.M., it was now past noon, and Bunis and the players had to get on to the Grand Masters tournament site, way on the other side of Seattle. Besides, there was one more event on the Bellevue schedule that wouldn't hold. It was a vast, ornate brunch, lavish enough to make the substantial buffet at Maryland Farms in Nashville seem like a delicatessen takeout order by comparison.

The stars ate decorously, chatted up the Mutual Benefit agents and their customers, and joined in the applause as small red duffel bags decorated with the Grand Masters logo and stuffed with souvenirs were handed out to all the guests. Then, still in their warm-ups, Bunis and Fraser piled into a waiting limo and headed toward the main event, while Ulrich sailed off on his own.

Al Bunis sank back against the cushions of the limo and pronounced himself satisfied with the morning's work. It was, he said, a successful outing and an illustration of what he has concluded to be the ultimate value of over-forty-five championship-level professional tennis. It is valuable, he said, not so much as a sport, not as a geriatric experiment, but as a marketing device.

"What we have," Bunis went on, "is a group of experienced gentlemen as representatives of a product, a service, a company. They inspire confidence, they are associated with quality performance. They are especially effective in connecton with a financial service, like life insurance. In effect, you are being influenced on ways to invest your money by the likes of Neale Fraser, O.B.E., a solid citizen of fifty. I do not need to tell you that O.B.E. means 'Order of the British Empire.' That is not like being given financial advice by Jimmy Connors or John McEnroe or some other brash kid."

If Neale Fraser, solid citizen, ex-champion and former insurance agent himself, had any objection to the idea of tennis as a marketing device, then he didn't express it. But if Torben Ulrich had been in the car, I'm sure he would have winced and muttered some protest through his beard. Whatever influencing may have gone on at the Bellevue club that morning was certainly soft sell—I hadn't heard life insurance mentioned once, and certainly not by the players. Even at the luncheon tables, the talk was tennis. But to Torben, tennis at any age level is not a marketing device. He is one of those sentimentalists, like me, who persist in thinking of it as a competitive sport, with all the poetry of technique and the drama of a contest played out purely for its own sake.

It's both, of course—sport *and* commerce. Like any professional sport. As long as athletes have a following, sponsors will inevitably be willing to pay them to be identified with some particular racquet or tennis shoes, some resort or breakfast food.

There is nothing new about lavish endorsement deals. Jack Kramer regularly made a quarter of a million dollars a year for his autograph on the Wilson racquet. (An estimated nine million of those classic wood frames were sold before production was shut down in favor of a new graphite Kramer model, in 1985.) But the first of the really hot commercial properties was

Rod Laver. In the early 1970s, when his tournament earnings approached $300,000 a year—more than any other professional athlete had made up to that time—he was also endorsing the products of twenty-nine different companies, not all of them related to tennis.

In the years since then commercialism has sometimes been carried to a point of ludicrous excess, when players walk onto the court festooned with sponsors' logos, looking as graffiti-ridden as a New York subway car. That's been toned down by edicts restricting the size and obviousness of the "billboards." But even where it persists, rampant commercialism doesn't seem to have affected the game itself in any significant way. If anything, it has probably improved the quality of competition, since the big endorsement contracts naturally tend to go to the big winners.

The same thing was probably true of the Grand Masters, I figured. If, as Torben once said, the over-45s circuit was becoming increasingly commercial, then that was one of the reasons it was also becoming a tougher league to survive in. Money, like power, may corrupt. But a little *more* money often inspires.

The only really harmful effect of commercialism in tennis that I can see is a subtle one: the psychological impact on the fans. The emergence of megabuck sponsors is probably a factor in the loutish behavior of some of the spectators.

For it isn't just the unreal earnings of the stars that arouses resentment. I suspect it's also an awareness, conscious or not, that the fans are being crowded out of the players' feelings by the big boys who pay them the big numbers. It used to be a two-way relationship: hero and hero-worshipper. But the individual ticket-buyer no longer commands the players' loyalty because he or she is no longer paying the freight.

So the fan sitting in the upper reaches of the promenade at the U.S. Open, peering down at the distant court beyond the box seats monopolized by sponsoring corporations and other business firms, feels like an outsider. He senses that his idols are no longer performing for *him* but for purveyors of racquets, shoes, automobiles, breakfast foods, financial services. When that fan acts up, he is acting *out* his feelings of rejection, like the many alienated groups in modern society.

That's an explanation, not an excuse. I don't expect the situation to improve. Like many unpleasant aspects of contemporary life, it seems to be the price of progress.

17

Do Like They Do

THERE ARE two different ways of learning any art from the masters, including the Tennis Grand Masters. One way is to listen to them and try to follow their instructions; the other is to watch them and try to imitate them. As the old GI saying goes, you can do like they say, or you can do like they do—that is, you can try. The trick is to find the right instructor to listen to or the right model to emulate.

"If you really want to improve your tennis," Al Bunis once advised the great community of club players, "don't bother to watch McEnroe or Connors or Lendl. You'll never be able to do what they do. Watch Mal Anderson."

What you see when you keep your eye on Anderson is a textbook illustration of tennis mechanics—how to do the things your club pro always told you. On the service, total relaxation and no wasted motion. "All his energy," as Bunis said, "is concentrated on that little yellow ball." On the ground strokes, perfect preparation—the racquet back in position, gently cradled in the "off" hand, the ball taken early in the bounce while it is still on the rise.

"Hitting it early," Mal himself explains, "you might say that's the key to the whole thing. That's the way you'll hit deep and the way you'll hit with pace, because you're taking the ball before it's lost its velocity. You're turning the other guy's power back on him."

Anderson meets the ball well out ahead of his body, especially on the backhand, the body weight shifting onto the front foot with the forward stroke, the wrist firm as the racquet meets the ball. Finally there is a long, unhurried follow-through that lets the racquet head move smoothly in the direction in which the ball is aimed. It looks just the way it's supposed to.

That follow-through, as I watched it in match after match, reinforced something basic about the tennis stroke that had lodged in my mind ever since I heard Gloria Connors tell it to her son Jimmy. That was when he had barely graduated from the status of boy wonder and was still young enough to take instruction from his mother. He was practicing ground strokes for the benefit of a television camera crew that I was directing, and Gloria kept urging him, "Don't swing hard, Jimmy. Swing *long!*"

Swinging *too* hard is the fault that Ken Rosewall identifies as perhaps *the* major defect among club players. They also use too much wrist, he says, and they don't follow through ("Swing *long!*"). All these mistakes affect control, the quality Rosewall exemplifies above the others.

When you watch Rosewall hit his long, fluid backhand, and watch the same stroke executed by Anderson, Stolle and most of their compatriots, then you begin to understand one of the factors in the superiority of Australian players of the Fifties and Sixties. That was the backhand I recalled from so many frustrating semifinals at Forest Hills during that period—frustrating to American tennis fans because the winners (and thus the next day's finalists) so often turned out to be Australians.

With the ball taken early, hit with the full body weight behind it, landing deep in the court and skidding heavily off the grass . . . with all this it was the perfect approach shot, behind which the universally strong Australian volley would be brought into play. The Americans, by contrast (Seixas, Ralston, Graebner, Richey are some of the names that come to mind), seemed to be merely *floating* their backhands into the opponent's court.

Rosewall's backhand of course is not just the quintessential Australian stroke but one of the monuments of the game. When he is on the court you'll notice appreciative spectators concentrating on it the way London tourists stare up at Big Ben, waiting for it to strike.

Kenny himself describes the shot as hit with a grip shifted only slightly from his forehand. The racquet never swings free on the backstroke. It's always *pulled* back with the off hand. The wrist is rock-firm on contact. The head of the racquet is always cocked higher than his wrist, in contrast to the Bjorn Borg style widely taught nowadays, in which the racquet handle is held against the hip, with the head pointing toward the ground, ready to sweep upward to impart topspin to the ball.

Rosewall's backhand is almost never hit with topspin. Occasionally it's hit flat, but usually it's sliced so heavily, so severely and so early that the ball sometimes comes off the racquet with the same explosive sound as topspin.

No wonder there were so many Australian finalists on the grass of Forest Hills.

As even casual students of tennis can tell you, the difference between one player and another at any level of the game often has nothing to do with strokes. Knowing how to hit a shot is basic; being able to hit it consistently takes you up to the second level of the game. Knowing *when* to hit that shot and *where* to hit it . . . ah, now we're getting into *tennis*. We are in the fascinating province of shot selection and tactics.

Watch Rosewall hit a drop shot. He will save that deceptive little stroke for a moment when he's got an opening down the line. Hitting it crosscourt would mean the ball is in the air longer, giving the opponent more time to read and cover it.

Bobby Riggs offers another rule of thumb on the drop shot: Don't chance it unless you're a yard inside your baseline and your opponent is a yard *behind* his.

Watch Rod Laver exchanging ground strokes in a rally, and you'll see him hitting crosscourt until he's ready to approach the net. When the other player is on the attack, and Rod is looking to pass him at the net, he'll go down the line if he possibly can. That leaves the other guy less time to read the passing shot than if Rod went crosscourt.

Some of the tactical pointers you pick up by watching the Grand Masters or listening to them are familiar to any one who has lasted beyond the basic grip-and-swing lessons with his or her club pro:

- The best general rule on where to aim a tennis ball at any given time is to follow Laver's example: Unless or until you've got an opening, hit crosscourt. That way you're giving yourself the widest possible margin of error because you're hitting across the lowest part of the net—the middle —and you're hitting along the longest axis of the court—the diagonal. So . . . *rally crosscourt!*
- Conversely, when hitting an approach shot, hit down the line, except as an occasional surprise. Approaching crosscourt means you've given yourself the longest possible distance to travel in order to get to a volleying position. The Grand Masters confound me by approaching crosscourt as often as they do—and by getting away with it as often as they do. But maybe that's one of the things that make them Grand Masters and the rest of us not. *Approach down the line!*
- When at the net, facing a possible passing shot, anticipate that the return will come at you down the line, and be sure you cover that side of the court. That is, if you've hit a backhand approach shot (presumably to a right-handed opponent's forehand corner), position yourself for a return to your backhand side. Approach on your own forehand. Then crowd the forehand alley. What you're doing is forcing your opponent to try to hit crosscourt in order to pass you. It's going to be tougher for him to get his racquet around for that shot, and if he does, then the trajectory of his shot will give you more time to read it and reach it. Obviously, while covering down the line, you've got to stay alert for the crosscourt shot you're trying to provoke. In other words, *cover down the line, and scramble crosscourt!*
- Above all, when in doubt as to where the ball is coming at you—on the forehand side or the backhand, crosscourt or down the line—don't just stand there wondering. Take a guess, take a chance. Move! It was not unthinkable to see Kenny Rosewall caught moving the wrong way, but it was

rare indeed to see him not moving at all. What happened most often, of course, was that he moved to the right place. *Guess and move!*

Elementary, right?

Most tennis tactics, after all, are matters of simple geometry: the dimensions and angles of the court. Others are matters of common sense, which seem obvious once they are pointed out and underlined, as Vic Seixas did in a book based on his Grand Masters experience.

Seixas says that most club players misunderstand a basic principle of serve-and-volley. They try to hit an ace *and* come in behind it—a redundancy to begin with. If you ace the guy, you've got nothing to volley. But more important, it's also a combination almost guaranteed to result in a fault because you're trying to concentrate on two different things at once. The sensible tactic is to choose one objective or the other. Either go for an outright winner *or* come in behind a well-placed serve to volley away the ineffectual return. By definition, "well-placed" means you've hit it moderately enough to allow you to control the location.

Big servers like Laver and Stolle, I noticed, would routinely come in behind serves hit at ordinary (for them) velocity. When they cranked up the big boomer, they often stayed planted at the baseline. If they came in behind it, they might be passed by a return zipping past them before they could reach the service line.

Seixas also explains something about approach shots that had never occurred to me before. The reason to hit underspin rather than topspin when trying to get to the net is not just that you don't want the ball to bounce high (thereby giving your opponent time to set himself for a passing shot). Another reason is that the topspin stroke pulls you *away* from the ball, whereas underspin moves you *toward* it, giving you momentum toward the net.

And then there is the aspect of tennis for which there are no known lessons. It's the psychological side of a sport that probably has a larger emotional component than any game this side of marriage.

Whenever Ken Rosewall was involved in a tight game there seemed to be some point on which he would seize control almost imperceptibly. Mechanically. Methodically. By sheer stubborn resolve. Or by the force of his perfectionist temperament. Or by some other quality that you will never see diagrammed in a book on tactics or stroke production. Excellent shots by the other player would be returned by better ones from Rosewall—his angles growing sharper and sharper, the distance to the lines gradually shrinking—until finally you could almost hear the other guy saying to himself in despair, "That's the best I can do, and he's got an answer for it!"

I once overheard two old pros exchanging recollections of matches they'd played against Rosewall. The players were from two different generations, but the frustrations they described were similar.

"Everybody's got a Rosewall story," Cliff Richey said, and proceeded to tell one about a match they'd played in Texas, some years earlier, when Richey was not yet out of his twenties and Rosewall was past forty. "It was about two hundred degrees on the court—no bull. Hottest court I ever played. Kenny had played a match that morning; it went to 7–6 in the third set. Then he played doubles. Now he plays me. He keeps dropping his racquet in disgust every other shot. You'd think I was murdering him. When it was over, I'd lost love and one."

Gene Scott responded with an account of a match he and Rosewall had just played: a non–Grand Masters event at some small out-of-the-way club. "Early in the match," Gene said, "I hurt my ankle and asked for some tape. They brought me three rolls. One was black, for electric cords and hockey sticks. Another was masking tape, for painting window frames. And the third was scotch tape. By the time they brought the right stuff my ankle was all swelled up. I got killed, two and one."

"Tough," said Richey.

"Yeah," said Scott. "Up to that point I felt I'd been doing

well. I was winning everything but games. If not for the injury, I might have carried him to two and two."

As somebody once said, "Laver mauls you, but Rosewall breaks your heart."

Not that Laver's psychological weapons were any less effective. If anything, Rod's way of asserting himself—of reminding the other guy who he was up against when it counted—was more dramatic. At some important stage in the match, Laver—apparently caught out of position—would summon up the imagination and the nerve to hit the most difficult conceivable shot, the one you'd least expect in the circumstances. When anybody else, running full tilt after an angled placement, might gladly settle for a high defensive lob, Laver might hit a slashing crosscourt. Hit it for a winner. Or he'd pop a deft little topspin looper over the other player's head, leaving him helpless in the forecourt.

Again, Laver would step up to the line to serve at a moment when the current of the match was running against him (perhaps when he'd been having a hard time holding service) and he'd abruptly turn things around with an ace or a service winner, the way he did against Anderson at Boca Raton.

After one of these moments in a Laver or Rosewall match the victim, whether of mutilation or heartbreak, would often hit a routine volley into the net. Or he'd guess wrong on the direction of the next serve or placement. Or his own service would suddenly desert him.

If you watched Rosewall long enough you began to notice things that explained his success. The main thing was his inexhaustible enthusiasm for the game. "Kenny loves to play tennis," one of his colleagues said simply, and you could see that when you watched him practicing against Laver. Kenny would be hitting and running, whooping and yelling with the exuberance of a teenager. Silent, sober Kenny Rosewall? None other. If at any moment of the day you wanted to find Rosewall, try the tennis court. Approaching the age of fifty, a full-time tennis player for thirty-five years, he still spent more time practicing than any other player.

Laver's special quality was harder to define, and he wasn't much help himself. He is reticent and impatient, hard to pin down for more than a few minutes at a time.

But during the Seattle tournament I managed to catch him at a vulnerable moment. So did an old rival. It wasn't Rosewall.

13

Sweats

THE SITE of the Seattle Grand Masters was the Pacific West Sports and Racquet Club, a complex of mustard-colored hangars in a suburb called Federal Way. The peculiar name of the community celebrates the completion, back in 1929, of a highway the government cut through the lake and fir country bordering Puget Sound.

Just as Maryland Farms was dedicated to the spirit of active leisure, Pac West (the club's affectionate nickname for itself) was devoted to the interests of physical fitness. And if you have trouble with that distinction, it's the difference between designer warm-ups and a sweat suit. Sweats—those shapeless, wash-faded, two-piece outfits in which differences of class and sex, even physical condition, tend to disappear—sweats were the uniform of Pac West. In the parking lot you would see mothers disembark from station wagons with their toddlers, all dressed for exercise class. They would pass middle-aged men on their way out, carrying attaché cases and wearing sweats.

I took a look behind a door in one of the hangars at Pac West one day, and found myself confronted by about a half acre of Nautilus machines, most of them in use even at that early hour of a midweek morning. The bulletin boards in the corridors were filled with announcements of classes in martial arts, strenuous dance, and various ritual forms of exercise with names sounding like Oriental cults or sexual practices.

The whole surrounding community seemed to share the enthusiasm for physical well-being. In the shopping malls lining the route that gave Federal Way its name you would see whole families dressed as if J.C. Penney and the supermarket were only incidental stops on the way to the weight room or the running track.

Just after dawn one morning, torn from sleep by jet lag, I looked out my motel-room window and saw the pavements already clotted with early exercisers. Among them I noticed a familiar figure. It was Mal Anderson, just coming into the entrance drive of the motel at a pace suggesting that he was cooling down from a morning run.

It was not a normal sight. Running and other forms of conditioning are generally off-day—or even off-*week* or off-*tour*—activities. While a tournament is in progress, tennis is the only form of exercise most players have time, energy or inclination for.

Anderson's good example—as I thought of it—lodged in my mind. After breakfast, when I was out exploring the coastal countryside by car and found myself at an attractive stretch of hiking trail overlooking Puget Sound, I got out and ran for a half hour, until overcome by pine fumes, a surfeit of fresh air and impatience with a sport that has no score in it.

I am one of your city runners, accustomed to what has been described as "air you can sink your teeth into." But I am not a *voluntary* runner—not one of those enthusiasts you see plying the parks in nylon trunks and mesh singlets, logging their daily ten kilometers with eye on the stop watch and mind on the next marathon. In fact I don't really run; I only *jog*, and then only by doctor's prescription. It's the consequence of one of those classic episodes that began with chest pains and aching arms in the middle of the night. I spent the ensuing few weeks in the coronary care unit of a hospital, and several months after that in a state of invalidism, having suffered the occurrence inelegantly defined as a "myocardial infarction": a heart attack resulting in permanent damage to the organ.

A stress test (measuring the amount of effort my damaged heart could sustain) and then a discomfiting procedure called an angiogram (in which the arteries are probed with a tiny catheter inserted through the groin) indicated the immediate cause of the problem: a couple of blocked areas in the coronary artery. Bypass surgery was considered and then bypassed in favor of medication plus a program of cardiac rehabilitation consisting mostly of jogging graduated distances.

I began at a scant hundred yards. It was more than a year before I was allowed to go for a mile, and then only at my relaxed jogger's pace, before stopping to check my pulse and move on to a few sit-ups, step-ups and so on.

Eventually I worked my way up to a routine of two and a half miles—the major part of a half-hour's exercise program. The moderate, regular rhythm of jogging makes even considerable distances less of a burden on the heart than the abrupt stop-and-go action of strenuous tennis. It was boring as hell. But it was the price of getting back on the courts eventually. And now it was also a habit, one that I fell back on for exercise on off-days. Frequent medical checkups showed that it had restored my heart function and even improved my stamina. The thing it could not cure was a persistent hankering for tennis. The Puget Sound run had no more of a curbing effect on my appetite for a game than the olive in a martini would have on your interest in dinner.

Carrying racquets and gear, I headed for the courts at Pac West and encountered Laver and Fraser heading toward the same objective.

"Hey, Big John," said Laver. "Looking for somebody to hit with?"

"Sure," I said, trying not to sound overeager.

"Hope you find someone," Rod said sympathetically, holding the door open and motioning me through. He and Neale trudged on down the corridor, chatting confidentially about Brisbane, Melbourne and old Davis Cup buddies.

Hitting with Rod Laver, Ken Rosewall or any of the other old champions was a hacker's fantasy I had nourished from the first day of the tour. To actually face that Laver topspin bouncing up into your eyes, to try to dig out the heavy slice delivered by Rosewall or Anderson or Stolle—these were experiences that I often imagined as I watched them from the stands. I entertained no illusions about my chances of taking a game off any of them, no thought of displaying a famous scalp in the clubhouse bar. But I knew how to hit a tennis ball, felt I could rally with the ex-champs, maybe play a few points.

I also knew that I was not ever going to get invited to do any such thing, even if I hung around the practice courts like a kid with his nose pressed against the candy store window. Because even though I was by now a fixture on the tour, I was in no way part of it. I did not belong to the great and exclusive fraternity of *players*. I was an outsider. Among the pros, I was just another "am."

I have noticed that world-class athletes (not just tennis players but professional jocks in general) don't divide people into the same categories that most of us use: rich/poor, middle class/working class or whatever.

The way tennis players see the world, first of all there are *the stars:* athletes in various sports, show biz celebrities, political leaders if they are real headliners like Presidents and Prime Ministers, possibly cabinet members.

Next comes *the establishment:* influential tennis patrons, . sponsors, officials, agents.

At the bottom of the social pyramid are *the fans:* the undistinguished and indistinguishable multitudes who fill the seats, make noise and ask for autographs.

Somewhere off to the side, maybe slightly above the fans but not much, are *the media:* reporters, writers, photographers, TV and radio broadcasters.

Sponsors, officials and other members of the establishment are tolerated as a necessary evil. Al Bunis once remarked that he liked to stay active on the court, taking his daily beatings from Krishnan, because it maintains his image as a player and obscures his image as a mere tennis promoter. "The prestige of a promoter is just about this high," he said, indicating something unspeakable at about shoetop level.

If promoters are low-caste, then fans are the untouchables, to be avoided if at all possible. Media people cannot be avoided, must be tolerated. But they are mistrusted. For understandable reasons. Sports journalists, like critics in any field, have a license to insult, demean, inpugn and second-guess, even though they could not possibly do it any better themselves, and most of them do not really understand how it's done. They also misquote. Or they quote all too accurately. Anyway, talking to a journalist is not like talking to a friend.

The only people stars really feel comfortable with are other stars.

I did not find it surprising that Grand Masters seemed to prefer each others' company to that of any outsiders. Nor did I find it surprising that what these grown-up athletes mostly talked about was sports. In that respect, after all, they don't differ all that much from the male population as a whole. In my own field of television journalism, inhabited by well-informed individuals with inquisitive minds, the lunch table conversation is apt to focus on the recent performance of some preeminent linebacker or quarterback. If the President has just held a news conference on economic policy, or if the Marines have been pulled out of the Middle East, the discussion is less likely to be about the issue itself than what question gave Mr. Reagan the most difficulty or how the pullout will affect the political campaign and the media coverage.

Shop talk, in other words.

Most male conversation seems to be made up of those two elements: sports and shop talk. And among professional athletes, sports *is* shop talk.

Athletes, in fact, may be the greatest sports fans of all, and their interest ranges over more fields of athletic competition than does that of the average spectator and sports-page reader. Athletes also have a strong sense of being special, and they identify with each other more than people in any other field I know. Some years ago, when I was collaborating on a book with Bill Talbert, a citizen of considerable experience at high levels of the business world, I became aware that most of his heroes were athletes like himself, but they were by no means all tennis players. As an example of excellence he was just as apt to cite some major league first baseman he had admired as a kid in Cincinnati, or a cricketer he had watched in Australia, or a golfer or a jockey, his favorite rider being Eddie Arcaro. It startled me to hear a mobile, well-muscled racquet swinger like Talbert refer to a tiny man whose basic feat was to steer a speeding animal as "a great athlete." The two forms of activity seemed as different from each other as, say, farming and steel-rolling.

By coincidence, not long afterwards, I happened to find myself a member of a wedding in which Eddie Arcaro served as best man. Over a glass of nuptial champagne, I brought up Talbert's name, and then quickly started to explain, "You know, Billy Talbert, the ten——"

"Sure I know Talbert," said the jockey. "Fine athlete."

One afternoon when I was prowling the court at Pac West in Seattle, envying the Grand Masters their camaraderie and looking for a hit at some lower level of the game, I discovered that I was not the only member of the entourage hankering for exercise.

"I'm so tired of sitting in airplanes and grandstands!" exclaimed Wilma Rosewall as she unzipped the cover from a racquet and trotted onto the court. Unfortunately for me, she had already found another tennis player to hit with. It was her husband Kenny, who had a free afternoon and at that moment was meticulously checking the height of the net as if he were about to compete for prize money.

I contented myself with watching the Rosewalls for a while, admiring the attentive way Muscles returned his wife's modest strokes. If he had any temptation to correct her mistakes, he resisted it, limiting himself to encouraging sounds like an occasional "Bull's-eye!" when she hit a line, in keeping with Rosewall standards. It looked like a rare and exemplary case of a marriage accommodating itself to tennis—not always an easy adjustment.

I also noticed that against his wife, as against Rod Laver or the elderly hackers in the pro-am, Kenny never gave in to normal laziness, but kept moving toward the ball, never allowing it to bounce twice. His racquet was always ready, as if he were preparing to return one of Laver's ferocious topspins instead of Wilma's gentle slice.

Kenny finished off that afternoon of leisure by playing a set or two with the manager of the Pac West club, a former touring pro named Jody Rush. The local player, a friendly compact fellow in his thirties, made it surprisingly close, putting a lot of effort into every point. He had to because Rosewall was playing him much the same way he would have played a tournament match. Wasting little motion himself, he was moving Jody from side to side with his careful, line-nicking shots.

Discipline. Enthusiasm. An afternoon away from the office for Kenny Rosewall.

Laver, meanwhile, was being even more withdrawn and elusive then usual, responding to questions from the local press in a manner that was not just normally brusque but downright testy. One reporter expressed surprise that a player of his age and stature would still be running around a tennis court for pay. Rod turned away shaking his head.

"What did he expect me to do at forty-five?" Laver said to no one in particular. "Crawl off and die?"

A TV reporter, after watching Laver practice for a while, ventured the opinion that Rod didn't seem to hit as hard as he used to.

"I've been sick," Rod explained. "For years."

In fact he had been feeling miserable, if not for years then at least for a week or two. After Boca Raton, along with a few of the other players, Laver had flown north to compete in a tournament in Connecticut involving a group of what might be called *future* Grand Masters—former champions still in their late thirties. Laver woke up in his hotel room on the morning of his scheduled first-round match with a terrible case of the flu. The match was postponed for a day and a half to give Rod a chance to recuperate. He never did, but not wanting to disappoint the fans, he finally crawled out of bed and went on the court with a raging fever, losing to Roy Emerson.

Laver had come on to Seattle as scheduled, but his hollow-eyed pallor and the hoarseness of his normally pleasant baritone suggested that he was far from over his malady. While his resistance was low, I got him to sit down and talk.

19

Rocket

OF ALL THE MATCHES in the history of the Laver-Rosewall rivalry, the dramatic 1972 WCT final won by Rosewall is probably the most famous. But, not surprisingly, it isn't Laver's favorite.

"Kenny and I played a lot of matches in different places over the years," Rod recollected in his flu-hoarsened voice, "but there was one in Los Angeles—the Pacific Southwest tournament—when I played the best tennis I can remember. I won 4–6, 6–0, 6–0, but the score doesn't tell the story because it was close all the way. It was deuce-ad, deuce-ad, deuce-ad. But every game I'd come up with the shot that made it 2–love, then 3–love, 4–love.

"My returns of service and my passing shots were the things I felt most comfortable about when I was playing Kenny, but in that match I was able to get more impact than usual on my returns of serve. It was a seesaw match all the way, only after a while he just didn't win any games."

The place where Laver and I were talking was a kind of public lounge on a balcony overlooking the court where the Seattle Grand Masters tournament was just about to get under way. A painting of Laver and Rosewall in action in—what else? —the 1972 WCT final was on display nearby, a tribute arranged by the host club. Fans were starting to arrive for the day's matches, and as some of them drifted through the lounge they invariably did a double take, glancing from the brightly colored art to the live original in his tan warm-ups, with a battery of midsize Pro-Kennex racquets on the floor beside his chair.

I don't know what was going through their minds, but what struck me was how much the forty-five-year-old Laver sitting there resembled the blurry figure painted in the impressionistic style of the sports artist, LeRoy Neiman. It wasn't just that the rather slight body and the roosterlike face under its thinning red coxcomb were so recognizable. It was also because, even sitting down, he seemed to be in brisk motion as he was in Neiman's action portrait. As his wife had said, Rod is a man who never sits still. And he talks in the same restless manner, as if anxious to get on to the next subject. The next subject was tennis as a career: How did this ordinary-looking individual, endowed with no special physical qualities, grow up to be one of the greatest players in the history of the sport?

To begin with, Rod Laver was one of those Australians who grew up learning to play tennis as a family sport on a family court—the one his father built out of red soil collected from anthills.

"My father and mother both played tennis," Rod recalled. "My two older brothers played. My parents had a cattle station way out in the country about a hundred miles from the town of Rockhampton—my father was a cattle grazier—but then they moved into town in order to give their kids an education. Rockhampton was where I went to school.

"I couldn't tell you how or when I started my career as a tennis player. It just sort of happened gradually. I played tennis after school, and weekends I played tournaments. When I was fifteen I left Rockhampton and went to work for the Dunlop sporting goods company in Brisbane, with a chance to play weekends. All the tournaments were down there in the Brisbane area, within about a hundred miles. Dunlop would drive us—a team of players—to the tournaments. We were an asset to them because we used Dunlop racquets, and the tournaments would be played with Dunlop balls. But during the week I worked full time for Dunlop. I worked in the department where we'd write up the orders that came in for the various products and made sure that those orders went through and got delivered. Twice a week, like on Tuesdays and Thursdays, I got an extra hour off at lunchtime to go out to the tennis courts and practice.

"I went overseas with the Australian squad for the first time when I was seventeen, and maybe that's where you'd say I began my career, but I don't remember thinking of it that way at the time."

A middle-aged man leading a small boy paused on his way through the lounge, stared at Laver and made a gesture of recognition. Rod gave the briefest of nods—a greeting without encouragement.

"I don't know that I have anything to regret about it," Rod said, resuming the account of his early start in the game, "but it was a lonely life. I mean, I left home at fifteen, and I never came back. If you had your druthers you'd like to think you could be around your family a little more. But it turned out that I went to Brisbane, and then I went overseas for six or seven months at a time. I got home and played the southern circuit in Australia, which was another maybe two months. I'd go home for a little bit of time, but then I'd go back to my job at Dunlop. This was the way it worked.

"Without trying to pinpoint what other life you might have had, this was the one I chose. I enjoyed tennis, and in order to get better at it, then you had to stay in the system. That's what I did, and I felt good about it.

"I suppose we'd all like to think we'd do it a little differently. I guess I'd like to have gone to school for another four or five years, but it wasn't really needed back then in getting a job. Opportunities were a dime a dozen out there. If you were athletically inclined, there were so many things you could get into. And tennis players were well known. People respected the sport, they respected *you*.

"Twenty-five or thirty years ago, maybe an education wasn't so critical here in the States, either. Now, if you don't have a Masters or a Ph.D., opportunities don't pop up so quickly. If my son Rick ever wanted to have a career as a professional athlete, I'd like to see him combine it in some way with his schooling. At the moment there's nothing to worry about. He's fifteen, and he's working like hell in school to get the benefit of a good education."

Laver was one of Australia's most promising juniors, but for several years he played in the shadow of established stars like Hoad and Rosewall, Rex Hartwig, Mervyn Rose, Ashley Cooper, Neale Fraser and Mal Anderson. Laver's career really took off when he won the Australian Championship in 1960, at the age of twenty-one. The boost to his ego, he says, was tremendous.

Gene Scott, discussing the psychological component of tennis, once observed that "Jimmy Connors started winning because he was so confident, and Laver became confident because he started winning."

Laver's own explanation is not at all that different. "Up to that time," he recalled, speaking of his first major championship, "I'd been in quarters and semis. But all of a sudden I won that one—probably shouldn't have, though I played well. Anyway, that gave me the confidence you need to think, 'Well, I've got a shot at winning every time I play, no matter who I'm playing.' I think that was the forerunner of really doing well. It happens a few times, and all of a sudden you really start believing in yourself. If you get into trouble, don't worry, you'll get out of it. If it hadn't happened just then, I guess I would have thought, 'Well, I'm a quarterfinals player—that's as good as I am.' But because I won, I believed I was capable of winning.

"I had those two or three good years, and then pro tennis. That was a real transition. That's where I learned my tennis. Hoad, Gonzalez, Rosewall, Andres Gimeno—what an eye-opener that was, to find out how well they played against what I'd been playing. They hit the ball harder, they were also more accurate. They didn't miss! And when they had a chance to win a match, they never let it get away from them.

"Among all your amateur shots, you used to hit one haymaker that'd go in, to the surprise of the crowd. Well, these guys didn't play that way. They wanted their chances to be better than the one out of ten that'd go in. They liked their chances to be seven or eight out of ten when they went for it. Anything less than that, they'd give you a great big high lob and wait for the next opportunity."

By comparison with the other pros, Laver remained something of a risk taker, still inclined to go for the big wristy shot, though he learned to control it better than he had as an amateur and even learned to resist the temptation sometimes. He also developed the incredible variety of shots that came to characterize his game. And of course he soon broke out of the pack here as he had in the amateurs, to become *the* dominant player of his time.

When, in 1971, Laver swept through those thirteen consecutive matches against most of the world's best in the Tennis Champions Classic, one observer called it "one of the greatest of all performances in any sport—and certainly the greatest ever in the sport of tennis."

Laver in his prime inspired that kind of hyperbole.

If Rod at forty-five couldn't quite remember the decision that started him on his tennis career, then he could not only remember but could also explain his decision to end it—his decision to bow out of competition in the mid-Seventies, after his competition with Rosewall had tapered off and injuries had taken him off the courts for a while.

"I was facing the fact that I couldn't go out and win Wimbledon or the U.S. Open any more," Laver said. "I needed time to assimilate that idea. I couldn't accept the idea of entering events knowing I was going to get beaten, so I decided not to enter. It was almost relaxing not to have to go out there and win.

"But I got over that. I'm here, aren't I?"

I asked him to spell out the difference between a Laver-Rosewall Grand Masters match and one of their encounters back in the Sixties or early Seventies. He responded by ticking off the superior qualities of the younger Rod Laver.

"A little more speed, more accuracy, a little more bite to all the shots. I volleyed a whole lot better then, when it comes to picking up low volleys and being more aggressive. There's a

definite difference that happens with time. It's partly that
you're not picking up the ball visually—not from any physical
decline but the fact that you're not playing as many matches.
You lose the match-play sharpness. You used to make certain
shots automatically. Now you have to hesitate and think about
how to play them. Speed and strength come from playing all
the time. You're going to pick up the ball quicker, too."

Well . . . maybe. Maybe speed and strength did come from
playing all the time, but they also came from something else:
from *youth*. Even in the best conditioned of players there was
some physical decline with age. And even I—reluctant as I was
to recognize any change in the old heroes—was becoming
aware that their shots had less pace than they had fifteen or
twenty years earlier. And there was an undeniable loss of mobility. When Laver was forced to go wide for a shot, he might
reach it with a remarkable burst of speed, but he simply wasn't
recovering as quickly as he once might have. The next ball,
which in the old days he might have scrambled back for, was
apt to go by him into the open court for a winner. Like the other
ex-champs, Laver wanted to make sure you realized how much
better he used to be in his prime. At the same time, he gave the
impression of a man who was inwardly holding on to a certain
indelible image of himself. He almost seemed to be saying that
he could still do it all if he really wanted to. A little more match
play, a little more practice on the footwork . . .

As if confirming my own thoughts, Rod said, "On certain
days I can still make any shot I ever could. But on some days I
don't hit the half volley, or I don't make an approach shot that
I feel I should. A lot of that is footwork. When you're not playing all the time, your feet get lazy. And you feel like you're not
getting down to the ball the way you should."

He stopped, fished in his pocket for a handkerchief, and
honked the prominent Laver break.

"But I don't play the game now that I used to," he went on
with an air of something like bravado in the face of plain facts.
"I play safer now, rather than going out and going after the
point. You saw the match in Boca Raton—I was just getting the
ball back. Before, I used to like to crash the return of service.

I'd just tee off and hit it down the line for a winner. Second serve, I'd roll over the top of it and come in."

"Rolling over," of course, describes the wristy form of top-spin that Rod favors, as against so-called natural topspin, the long stroke that travels from low to high, finishing above shoulder level. I asked Laver if he felt that age had any effect on the mental side of his game. "Sure," he said. "Concentration. Before, you'd never let your mind get off your tennis. Now, you're thinking about other things. Business ventures. Family matters." He nodded solemnly. "Family definitely assumes the Number one position."

I mentioned his wife's prediction that he'd still be playing tennis in his eighties—her growing conviction that this was really the way he wanted to spend the rest of his life.

He considered the question. Yes, he decided, he'd like to play as an eighty-year-old. But, he added with perfect seriousness, only socially. He wasn't sure that at that advanced age he'd still be capable of winning a match. "I guess I'm competitive," he said almost apologetically. "That's the way I learned to play the game. If you're not playing to win, then you're not helping the sport."

Restless Rod had reached the limit of his capacity to sit still. Abruptly he got up and excused himself, explaining that he had to go hit with Kenny. "It's the only way I'm ever going to get over this bug."

He gathered up his racquets and headed toward the locker room, moving with quick, purposeful little steps.

"That's Rod," said Mary Laver fondly, as her husband—still wheezing and snuffling—went out on the court a couple of hours later for his first-round match in Seattle. "That's his standard approach to any physical problem. Just keep taking your vitamin C and play through it. He thinks tennis is a cure for anything that ails him."

The stands at Pac West were cozy, with a capacity about the same as the high school gym of my small-town boyhood—not much more than a thousand seats. I suspected the club would have trouble filling even those modest numbers, however, be-

cause of the distraction of a competing sport. Seattle was in the
throes of basketball fever. The National Collegiate Athletic Association tournament, the U.S. college championship, was to be
on television that weekend, and the local University of Washington Huskies, a distant longshot, had somehow managed to
stay in the running.

If you were paying attention to the network news that week,
then you were aware that the Reverend Jesse Jackson was making a remarkably strong showing in the Democratic primary
campaign, and that the Reagan administration was making little
headway in its efforts to cope with the budget deficit. But what
I saw in the local papers was: basketball. And basketball was
what I heard people talking about in the motel coffee shop and
in the malls of Federal Way. (I also knew that my old colleague
Dan Rather, even while reporting the political news and the
economic issues with his usual conscientiousness, would have
been able to tell you which teams were favored in the next
round of the NCAA.)

Neale Fraser, whose antennae were tuned in with particular
sensitivity to sports news in every known field of competition
in practically every part of the world, came in with the morning
line on basketball. The Huskies, he reported, had a couple of
giants, both West Germans, who could put a ball through the
hoop from any spot on the court.

Considering the suffocating impact of "Final Four Frenzy"
—the Seattle media term for the local excitement over the prospect that the Washington Huskies might reach the last stage of
the national playoffs—it was surprising that the papers found
any room at all for mere tennis news. And it was all the more
surprising that the stands at Pac West were filled for a tennis
match, even Rod Laver's local debut in the Grand Masters.

His opponent happened to be the same player who had
recently beaten him—granted, in his flu-weakened condition.
"First-round singles," Al Bunis announced from courtside.
"The great Rod Laver, from Rockhampton, Australia, and Roy
Emerson, originally out of Black Butt, Australia." Bunis always
emphasized the name of Emmo's home town, and he always
drew titters from the crowd.

The background of this matchup extended a lot further back into history than their meeting a week earlier in Connecticut.

There was a Laver-Emerson rivalry before there was a Laver-Rosewall rivalry. For two or three years at the end of the 1950s, when the big names in Australian tennis were Fraser, Anderson and Ashley Cooper, Rod and Emmo—barely out of their teens—were jockeying for attention as the most promising of the next generation. In the early 1960s they were Number 1 and Number 2 in the world rankings. And the year Laver won the first of his Grand Slams, 1972, his opponent in three of the four big finals was Roy Emerson. Now it was Laver, at age forty-five, against Emerson, forty-seven.

If tennis was not a remedy for flu, then flu appeared to be an effective prescription for good tennis, the way Rod started out. He hardly missed a shot in running out the first set, 6–1.

Then Emerson got going. He scored two early breaks, and had a 5–2 lead before Laver steadied himself and then simply exploded in an outburst of brilliant shotmaking. Facing set point, Rod chased what appeared to be a winning crosscourt volley that was sharply angled across his forehand—chased it, reached it, and on the run fired back a spectacular passing shot. On the next point he nearly duplicated that shot for another winner, then followed it with two perfectly chipped backhand returns of service that Emmo couldn't handle. Suddenly Rod had break point, and it looked like another one of those Laver psychological coups.

But you could see Emmo fire himself up—you knew he had to be reminding himself that he had recently beaten this guy. He summoned up the service that used to be his bread and butter—that explosive curlicue. He staved off the break, served out the game and the set.

That took what starch was left out of Laver's flu-ridden body. In the third set he was hanging on to Emmo's heels like a weary terrier driven by nothing but instinct. When he crouched to face Emerson's service with the score 5–4 against him, Mal Anderson nudged me and said, "This is where Laver's really dangerous, when you're serving for the match. It's the hardest game to win against him."

But this time it was Emerson who pulled out the big shots at the right moment. The match ended with Emmo on top, as he had finished in Connecticut. The scores were 1–6, 6–2, 6–4. Roy had racked up another win against his old Grand Slam tournament opponent. And this one counted for prize money and bonus points.

Laver's loss suddenly added a little extra zest to the Grand Masters competition. If Rod, the overall choice to win the 1984 tour, could be upset—even though it might take an act of God to bring it off—and if Rosewall, who would reach the critical age of fifty before this tour ended, should happen to suffer a couple of his "down" days, as Torben Ulrich had called those rare, peculiar lapses . . . if this sort of thing should occur every so often in the course of the tour, then there was a chance for a long shot to pick up some points and some bucks. Possibly— though it was hard to imagine—he might even sneak in ahead of the two favorites.

Who was the dark horse?

Emerson, in spite of his sudden reemergence, didn't appear to be in good enough shape to sustain a serious run for the top prize. The post-match beers, which slid right off Mal Anderson's lean frame, stuck to Emmo. I was sure he hadn't lost an ounce of the ten pounds he wanted to shed. Besides, after two poor tournaments, he might have too much ground to make up.

Scott? Gene was in good shape and at forty-six had "youth" on his side. But he had ruled himself out of contention. By his own statement he was shooting for the middle of the pack.

Stolle? The obvious contender. Another of the youngsters— still just forty-five. And he had those two big wins over Rosewall last year.

But my choice was none of the above. It was Mal Anderson, the Good Guy with the Sweet Swing.

Anderson looked capable of beating anybody on a given day, and he was in shape not just for the one match but for the long tournament weekend—and beyond that for the season's grind. Like Rosewall, he was serious. He trained even during tournaments; hadn't I caught him at his secret morning road-work?

Besides, there were sentimental considerations in his favor. At forty-nine, Mal was beyond the "youth" class; he was in fact right on the cusp of Bunis's Law of Inevitable Decline. Certainly he still had all the tools: the strokes, the strength, the speed. All he needed, I felt, was a little more self-assurance, the confidence to face down Laver or Rosewall in some future crunch.

Yes, if there had been a pari-mutuel for the 1984 Grand Masters and I wanted to bet a long shot, I'd have stepped up to the window and bought a ticket on Malcolm J. Anderson.

Kibitzers

MY HORSE got off to a shaky start at Pac West, barely nosing out Gene Scott, 6–4, 7–5, and looking unhappy as he did it.

The other first-round matches were unremarkable. I did most of my watching from the balcony overlooking the court, where coffee and sandwiches (and beer of course) were available to the players, and where they usually hung out when they weren't on active duty. From the tables at the balcony rail they would keep a leisurely eye on the action below, occasionally commenting like kibitzers at a pinochle game.

Somebody noted the remarkable recent behavior of Krishnan, who at that moment was on the court struggling against Stolle. It seems that in Florida one day a group of the players got lost driving back to their hotel from the tournament site in Boca Raton. There was a dispute about which way to turn, and it was Krishnan, usually so mild and docile, who had seized command. "You've got to go *that* way," he told the driver peremptorily. About a half hour later it became evident that he'd headed them in the wrong direction.

"Do you realize," one of the passengers upbraided him, "that you were navigating us straight into the Gulf of Mexico?"

Krish didn't concede a thing. "It's my theory," he said, "that the earth is round."

The score on the court below was 5–1, Stolle.

"Do you know what Krish told me the other day?" one of the balcony loungers reported with an air of wonder. "He said that in 1959 he had the best overhead in the game!"

Krish? Violating his oath of modesty?

Among old tennis players no claim to supremacy ever goes unchallenged, so the balcony gang immediately compiled a list of rival overheads. It started with Fraser, Laver, Barry McKay and Jaroslav Drobny—though the Czech expatriate would have been almost forty in the year Krish had staked out as his own. It ended with Dick Stockton, who would then have been about six.

While the list was lengthening, Krish camped under an easy smash and hit it out by six feet. "In 1959," somebody observed, "that ball would have been good."

The gag reminded somebody else of Bill Talbert's story about taking Dick Savitt, the 1950s star, to play an exhibition with him at Choate, the Connecticut prep school Talbert's son attended. The two contestants were introduced with rather elaborate credentials—Talbert as "formerly United States doubles champion and Number two ranked singles player, former captain of the American Davis Cup team," and Savitt as "formerly the Number one American singles player and Wimbledon champion."

"Formerly," said some smart-ass kid in a stage whisper, "this would have been a hell of a match."

The mention of various old tennis players started Al Bunis on his own reminiscent quest of superlatives. The best match ever played in the Grand Masters, he volunteered, was a 1978 tournament final between Ulrich and Sedgman. It was witnessed by one of the biggest of all Grand Masters crowds, five thousand fans, at Pauley Pavilion, the Los Angeles basketball arena on the UCLA campus.

Playing quality tennis almost without let-up, as Bunis described it, Torben and Sedg battled even through two sets and then went to 6–6 in the third. In those days, the issue was settled by a nine-point, sudden-death tiebreaker. This match went to the absolute limit—the ninth and last point. Sedgman was serving.

In his usual attacking style, Frank came speeding in behind a good, solid serve. Ulrich, with his own "forward" strategy, charged in behind his return. Sedgman was already in position; he volleyed Ulrich's return. Ulrich cut off the volley, volleyed

back. The two aging warriors—Sedgman already past fifty, Ulrich a year younger—were standing each other off, face-to-face,
at the net. The exchange of volleys went on—too many to
count, almost too fast to follow. Finally, Sedgman slashed one
at a downward angle, a sure winner. But Torben somehow
reached it, returned it, and it went right past Sedgman for the
match.

"The crowd had been holding its breath right through the
final point," Bunis recalled. "When it was over, you could hear
everybody exhale, the whole stadium, all together. Then they
all stood up and cheered."

I asked Al if he had any favorite matches from his own playing days on the amateur circuit.

"I reached my peak," he said, "in my first-round match
against Sedgman in the 1951 U.S. Singles at Forest Hills. I battled him even for two games. Then he got lucky and ran off
seventeen in a row."

Krishnan joined the balcony group, freshly showered and
dressed after his match, his gleaming black hair plastered down
damp on his skull. I looked for signs of the new assertiveness
that I had been hearing about, but I couldn't see any change. It
was the same solemn, squarish gent I sometimes saw during
the off-court hours at one tour stop or another, striding solo
toward some shopping mall or, later, toward a post office with a
package to mail home to his family in Madras. Except for the
curious Asian gait and his deep exotic color, he could have
melted into any crowd.

If, as the new round of Krish stories suggested, the familiar
waddle was being replaced by a swagger, then maybe it was
his way of trying to psych himself up after his early defeats. But
if that was the case, then it wasn't working. He'd just lost to
Stolle 6–1, 6–1.

He drew up a chair at the outer fringe of the group and sat
nursing a consolatory soft drink with a serious, meditative
expression. I thought he might be further comforted by a reminder of better times, so I asked about *his* favorite tennis
match, Grand Masters or otherwise.

The loser's face brightened. True to the self-effacing Krishnan I could recognize, his favorite match involved two other players.

"Surprisingly," he said, "the match I liked best wasn't a close match at all. It was a runaway—1957 Wimbledon final. Lew Hoad beat Ashley Cooper, 6–2, 6–1, 6–2—something like that. The shots simply flowed from his racquet. He played tennis out of this world. I still have the picture in my mind of one particular shot. Hoad chased a smash to the Royal Box in the deep forehand corner, and just managed to retrieve it. He just got it back into the court, and it landed with a high bounce. A setup for Cooper. He had the whole court open, there was no way Hoad could get into the point. So Cooper just bounced the ball short into the backhand court.

"Well, Hoad sprinted the whole distance—diagonally, you understand—and he managed to reach the ball. Not only that, but he hit such a topspin backhand that it went right through Cooper for a winning point.

"Twenty years later," Krish went on, "I had occasion to write Hoad a letter. I told him I could remember that match, point after point. I could. I still can. I can still see Hoad hitting everything—topspin passing shots, half-volley winners. Everything!"

There was a match involving Krishnan himself, a much more recent one, that he remembers almost as clearly. Remembers it with a mixture of pain and pride.

It was the finals of the 1976 national singles championship of India, and Krishnan's opponent was his son, Ramesh—the only recorded instance of father versus son for a national tennis title. Ramesh was then the boy prodigy of Indian tennis, a fifteen-year-old contender, just as his father had been a generation before. Krish himself was on the verge of forty.

"I played a bad match," Krishnan senior recalls, wincing. "I wanted to make it a real match—it would be a good experience for my son, I thought. But I couldn't do it. Every time I had the open court, my mind would tell me to hit a winner, but something wouldn't let me do it. The pressure was terrible." He concluded with a smile. "He beat me in straight sets."

Altogether, Krish and his son met five times in official tournaments. Ramesh beat him every time.

Ramesh went on to what has all the look of an outstanding tennis career. He is the only really outstanding tennis player among the offspring of the Grand Masters, at least so far. Even as we spoke in Seattle, he was well on his way to a marvelous season, reaching the late rounds of a number of Grand Prix tournaments, winning one of them, and, at the age of twenty-three, battling his way into the upper levels of the rankings— among the top twenty-five players in the world.

Krishnan *père* has given his son's tennis-playing career the same sort of encouragement he got from his own father. He follows that career with a great deal of pride, but he does it mostly by reading about Ramesh in the sports pages, the life of a Grand Prix touring pro being as peripatetic as it is. The part-time life of a Grand Masters touring pro doesn't make it any easier for the two Krishnans to get together.

One place they make sure to coincide is Wimbledon, where Ramesh has been among the seeded players and his father has been a regular spectator ever since he stopped being a contestant himself. The Krishnan family takes a house in London for a month every Wimbledon season.

Krish says he wouldn't trade his own memories of the tennis circuit for his son's experiences on the Grand Prix tour. Like the Australians reminiscing about their own circuit days, he thinks today's kids are missing something.

"I told my son that traveling and playing tennis is the greatest education you can have. That's something you realize later. But there was not so much pressure on us as there is now on the young Grand Prix players who are making a career of tennis. We were thinking of tennis as something to do *before* making a career.

"We competed hard but we enjoyed it more. We used to meet people. We would go to their homes. Now the players don't seem to have much social contact with the world. You practice, you play your match, go back to the hotel.

"I have friends in the Indian community all over the United

States from my tennis years," he went on. "I have played tennis thirty-five years, so they know me or they know about me. When they see the Grand Masters are playing in their community, they come and look me up and invite me to their homes. Sometimes I have three invitations during one tournament. I have to tell them to get together, pick one home and have one dinner. Invite each other. It is almost always a very nice occasion."

Mal Anderson, who sometimes appears to be challenging Krishnan for the world's modesty championship, joined the balcony sitters, and contributed as his favorite tennis match a Laver-Rosewall encounter. It was the finals of the 1969 Australian Championships, the first held as an open tournament. "It went five sets," Mal said, "and for sustained high quality of play I don't think I've ever seen a finer exhibition of tennis. Laver won, but it could have gone the other way and I'd still think it was the best."

He considered some other possible choices. "There were a couple of Hoad-Gonzalez matches on the old pro tour that came pretty close. My own matches? Well, in the World Professional Championships at Wembley in 1959 I beat Rosewall in the semis, 6–4 in the fifth set, and then I beat Segura 8–6 in the fifth to win the finals. I'd have to say I played well. Possibly that was my best tennis ever. But this was the pro tour, remember. It was before open tennis, so it didn't have the prestige."

I mentioned to Mal that I'd seen him coming back from his early morning run the previous day, and complimented him on his self-discipline.

He looked puzzled. "I haven't been running," he said. "I had trouble sleeping so I went out for an early breakfast. There's a little place just down the road where they serve you a couple of nice eggs, potatoes, sausage—everything you'd want—for a dollar seventy-nine or so. It's not a bad walk, and I've been going down there instead of paying the prices at the hotel dining room."

As a matter of fact, Anderson went on to say, he didn't feel much like running any more than he had to. His leg was hurting

—that's what was ruining his sleep—and he preferred to rest it for the matches.

Anderson's frugality about restaurant prices was not remarkable. The Aussies, I'd already noticed, were canny about their travel expenses. At every stop on the tour they invariably searched out some low-priced fast-food joint while the rest of us were indulging ourselves in six-dollar eggs or double-digit lunches at the hotel. It was in keeping with the well-established reputation of Australian tennis players on the pro tour—a reputation which the Aussies themselves acknowledged in a phrase they used to describe themselves: short arms and deep pockets.

The tradition carried over into their senior careers. Pancho Segura, when asked about his greatest thrill in the Grand Masters, said it was "the time Frank Sedgman picked up the dinner check."

Ken Rosewall, who is widely believed to be one of the richest tennis players of his generation, is also the most notoriously deep-pocketed. In his own defense he once pointed out to an interviewer that "I come from an ordinary, hardworking middle-class family, and I was taught to be thrifty." Now he no longer bothers to defend himself. Asked how much he had changed physically since his early years on the circuit, he told a reporter, "I'm a little heavier now. In the wallet."

Casualties

When Anderson got up on Saturday morning the pain in his leg had taken on serious and recognizable proportions. It was sciatica, an affliction associated with the lower-back problem that is often identified as a "slipped disc" or "herniated disc." The pain travels from the spinal column along the sciatic nerve, which runs down the back of the leg. Almost any movement can be excruciating.

Anderson had made a commitment to play an exhibition doubles match that morning with Krishnan against Jody Rush and another local pro, as part of a clinic for kids. Mal thought about trying to find a substitute but "there didn't seem to be anybody available." He decided he might as well play as a way of testing the leg to see if it was in good enough shape for his semifinal match against Rosewall that evening. The answer was: No way! He called Bunis and reluctantly defaulted.

I was left with a worthless mutuel ticket in my pocket. Barely out of the gate, my horse had pulled up lame.

For all the vulnerability of aging athletes to illness and injury, a default in the Grand Masters is a rare event. When it does happen in a field this small, it leaves a gaping hole in the program of matches. A decision was quickly made to fill out the evening's card with an exhibition match in which Rosewall would be one of the contestants. But the question remained: against whom?

Stolle and Emerson would be playing the other semifinal. Ulrich, the designated substitute in any emergency, was playing only doubles in this tournament. Having bombed out, he had taken off to make a few bucks by doing another clinic some-where else in the area. Gene Scott had left Seattle after his loss. Neale Fraser's arm was as gimpy as his partner's leg. He had struggled through a losing doubles match wearing an elbow brace like a supersenior. Rod Laver's status was no better than "walking wounded." Finding an opponent for Rosewall was like canvassing the ward in a Civil War hospital for volunteers to fight at Gettysburg.

The choice was about to fall to Krishnan—by default, so to speak—when Laver stepped into the breach.

"Somebody filled in for me in Connecticut when I couldn't get out of bed," he said, his voice still foggy with flu. "It's my turn. Anyway, I need to play my way back into shape." He had told his wife that day, "I've got to find my game again!" He sounded a little desperate, Mary said, as if he'd been in a season-long slump instead of a couple of weeks' recuperation.

The Seattle fans were going to get the obligatory Laver-Rosewall match after all, in spite of Rod's early loss. They'd just get it one day early, and it wouldn't count for points or money. Which didn't seem to bother the contestants in the least. It was a chance to play tennis, after all, wasn't it? A whole lot better than a kick in the ass.

On Saturday night the stands were full of attentive fans. The tide of Final Four Frenzy, after lapping at the gate of Pac West, had abruptly receded. In the previous night's televised basket-ball game, the Washington Huskies had lapsed into a state var-iously described in the local press as "coma" and "nightmare," and wound up being eliminated by the University of Dayton. The Huskies would not be playing for a national championship before a hometown crowd. It was up to the Grand Masters to provide local sports enthusiasts with some compensatory ac-tion. I thought they did a pretty good job of it, even though it was only tennis and the scores weren't close.

In the one semifinal that was played for real, forty-five-year-old Fred Stolle gave an impressive display of his youthful at-tacking game and blew Emerson away. Fred's mere two-year age advantage looked more like a decade in the first set.

At the beginning of the second set, Emmo made a dramatic stand, carrying one game to the extraordinary length of twenty-six points. It was deuced no less than ten times. But ultimately Fred wore him down, and took the match by the unlikely score of 6–1, 6–0.

Now came the match the crowd really wanted to see: the Laver-Rosewall exhibition. They were playing one ten-game pro set, and Rosewall quickly ran up a lead while Rod tested his recently bedridden strokes, like a patient trying his legs in the hospital corridor.

Kenny was handling Rod's service. Mal Anderson, watching his semifinal being played by proxy, commented as if counseling himself for some future match, "Rosewall pins you back with that first return. If you hang back and let him get you into exchanges, then he runs you all over the court. You've just got to gamble against him."

Laver took some chances against Kenny's service, hitting a couple of big returns for a break. Suddenly they were back on service at 4–5.

Neale Fraser, making conversation during the changeover, asked me sympathetically, "Did you ever find anybody to hit with today?"

"Yes," I said, "I had a nice game against an eighty-three-year-old lady." It was a deliberate exaggeration. The agreeable, solid-stroking lineswoman whom I had been matched with by Jody Rush, the local head pro, couldn't have been half that age. But Roy Emerson had just joined us in the players' box, and I thought I'd give him something to work on. Emmo picked up his cue faultlessly.

"Eighty-three?" said Emmo. "Did you draw her in and then lob her?"

Another one of those lessons in tactics from a master.

On the court, Laver was back in trouble, not so much on tactics as mechanics. Double faults on service, errors on his ground strokes. Rosewall pulled away to a 9–4 lead.

Serving with match point against him, Laver blasted two big serves—one into the corner, the next down the middle. Then he came in behind a serve and volleyed away Kenny's return for the game. The crowd stood and applauded. Mal nodded approvingly and said, "When you're down, hit out."

In the next game, three Laver passing shots, all risky, caught the lines. Rosewall braced. They settled into a series of beautiful exchanges, chasing each other the length and width of the court. But the odds, which favored Rosewall in that sort of pattern, did indeed prevail. The one-set match went to Kenny, 10–5, and the crowd went home looking as if they felt they'd gotten their money's worth.

22

Relationships

TENNIS LORE is filled with examples of what baseball fans would call a "jinx." In tennis, a more sophisticated sport, it is described as a "psychological edge"—one player dominating another of comparable ability to an unreasonable degree. Bobby Riggs had that uncanny knack. Once he stamped his brand on an opponent, he seemed to own the guy for life. Over a stretch of a couple of years Bobby met Joe Hunt (then regarded as the most promising young player in America; soon afterwards a casualty of World War II) in the finals of fourteen tournaments. Riggs won every match. He beat Billy Talbert no less than thirty-two times on the circuit before Talbert finally caught up with him in a tournament final. Talbert, after staying up all night partying, managed to beat Riggs that one time by gambling on service aces and difficult placements on every crucial point. As for that other old crony from the circuit days, Gardnar Mulloy, he refers to Riggs as "the only guy I ever played more than twice without winning." Mulloy never won a single match in all the tournaments they played as amateurs.

Mulloy did manage to beat Riggs in an exhibition match in Woodstock, New York, in 1939. He didn't beat Bobby again until the finals of the national sixty-five-year-olds' championship on grass forty-five years later! That was at Cedarhurst, Long Island, where Gar beat Bobby 7–5 in the third, after being down 4–5.

Ken Rosewall had a hex on Fred Stolle, dating back to their years on the WCT tour, and Rosewall had beaten Stolle with surprising dispatch in the semifinals of the most recent Grand

Masters tournament, the one at Boca Raton. But there was a feeling in the ranks that this was only a pause in the turning of the worm. Or, as Neale Fraser put it, switching metaphors, "Fred's been Kenny's pigeon far too long." The finals at Seattle looked like the spot for Stolle to assert himself as a force on the 1984 tour, to start shouldering Rosewall aside, perhaps taking over the older man's place as the head of the tribe. That ominous watershed age of fifty was only months away for Kenny. Stolle's four-year edge could be critical.

The feeling was based on one particular performance by the younger man in the finals of a tournament at Naples, Florida, near the end of the previous season. I thought there might be something instructive in that achievement, so I asked Stolle to analyze it in terms of the psychology of the game. He thought about that for a moment.

"Muscles is so special," he said. "He doesn't hit the ball as hard as some other players, but he's so good and so consistent that I always used to be conscious of who I was playing when I should have been concentrating on the game. I always had the feeling that in order to beat Rosewall I had to get to the net. I *had* to. So I'd start to rush my shots. I was always playing Kenny instead of the ball.

"But that time at Naples, when I was down 0–6, 3–5, with Kenny serving for the match, I finally began to play the ball. Hell of a time to start, right?

"I began to charge the net, the way I always felt I had to, but"—he paused for emphasis—"I began to pick my spots a little better. What I mean by that is, I attacked when I was in control of the situation. Instead of getting passed I began to make the volleys. Kenny began to get a little nervous. And . . . well, you know how it ended."

Al Bunis later picked up the story for me, adding a little instructive analysis of his own.

"When Fred started charging the net," Bunis said, "he was forcing Rosewall to pass him. And passing requires more precision than volleying. Late in the match, when you're getting a little tired, it gets harder and harder to thread that needle. You miss a few shots, your confidence starts to slip. When Rosewall goes off, it's a breakdown of confidence, just like everyone else."

The match ended in a tiebreaker, 0–6, 5–7, 7–6, with Stolle in the rare position of winner over his nemesis, Rosewall.

It was just a week later that Stolle beat Rosewall again, in the championship tournament of the 1983 series.

When Rosewall and Stolle met in the finals at Pac West, it looked as if they'd gone back to their original script. In the very first game, Kenny moved right in and took charge, breaking Stolle's big serve. When Stolle broke him back, Kenny merely shook it off, and broke Fred a second time. Now, when Rosewall stepped up for another service turn you could almost see him tighten his concentration. He damn well wasn't going to blow his lead again.

Service is hardly Rosewall's strong point. As he says, it's not intended to be an outright scoring shot. His motion looks harmless; the ball comes in relatively flat and without much velocity. But there are some useful things to be learned by paying close attention to that particular part of his game. For out of that unprepossessing stroke he gets reasonable depth, unexpected angles, and, above all, a better start on the next shot than just about any other player in the game. He may be the perfect model for Neale Fraser's advice about stepping into the court —moving onto the attack—as you complete your service. But Rosewall does it in a way that's all his own.

For Kenny's service, like every other stroke in his game, is beautifully patterned, rhythmic, consistent. His follow-through takes him one modest step across the baseline; he lands in perfect balance; there is just the slightest pause, and then he either continues forward toward the net or, with a stylish little step, he skips back across the baseline to play the return.

It is all done with graceful little movements, almost as quick as a tap dancer's. And it is done with such immutable consistency that if they played tennis on snow, you'd see only one set of footprints at Rosewall's end of the court.

So now, here's Rosewall with his little tackhammer service up against Stolle with his sledgehammer. Rosewall lays in one good service after another. He holds, leads 3–1, and has established his psychological edge. Stolle, after those two early breaks, begins serving tentatively. He is not getting in behind it, and the returns are catching him out of position for the volley.

With Rosewall leading 5–3, Stolle hits a perfect drop shot barely over the net. Rosewall's anticipation is so keen—he is so concentrated on the ball—that you can see him start for it almost before Stolle's racquet makes contact. He covers the shot for a winner. In the following game, Stolle, visibly troubled, lets a ball drop unchallenged in his forehand corner, then double-faults for the set.

In the second set Rosewall lifts his game from merely precise to brilliant, and Stolle, conversely, is on a downhill trend. But being Stolle, he takes it all in good humor, with his solemn, deadpan style. When Rosewall, after holding service, sends the balls down to Stolle's end of the court by hitting a couple of practice serves, Fred calls back, in mock anger, "You won that game! You don't have to serve again!" A lovely offensive lob floats unreachably over his racquet, and Fred, without even looking up, gives his patented "Yours!" call.

At 4–2, Rosewall, who has been serving consistently down the middle to Stolle's backhand in the deuce court, suddenly hooks a beautiful first serve deep into the forehand corner, catching Fred off balance. He wins that game. In the next, Stolle, hardly looking like a challenger any more, double-faults twice, then nets a backhand for the match. It's the old script, all right: Rosewall the winner, 6–3, 6–2—just about the way it ended a couple of weeks before, in the semis at Boca Raton.

Stolle summed up the match afterwards as "a short day at the office."

I left the Pac West arena with the deflated image of Stolle in my mind. A few days earlier I had been talking with some of the members of the troupe about that whole mysterious psychological side of the game that is involved in winning streaks and losing streaks, in slumps and rolls, and what Torben Ulrich called "the winning and losing relationships that develop between tennis players." Stolle, after last year's mini-string of

successes, seemed to be falling back into his old "losing relationship" with Rosewall. Emerson customarily fell apart
against Stolle. Krishnan—poor Krish, as I was beginning to
think of him—had a losing relationship with everybody. I wondered how he was going to win a match on this tour; if there
was any possible way to break out of a slump like his.

"It's especially difficult," Torben said, "to get into a tournament rhythm when you never get to play more than one
match. I remember something Krishnan said in his first season,
when he had been losing in the first round every time. And it
was so sad, you see, the way he said it. He said, 'I don't know
how to win any more. I have no practice at it.'"

"The trouble with Krish," said Al Bunis, "is that he never
won Wimbledon. The others did, most of them. So he starts
with a mental handicap against these guys. They're not his opposition, they're his heroes. But you know, if you keep practicing against somebody every day, sooner or later you discover
he's only an ordinary human being, who sweats and makes
errors. You realize he's got a problem on the forehand that
you'd never noticed before. You get lucky and win a set. That's
all you need to break the chain.

"Last year Krish started out the same way. But he began
practicing with Alex Olmedo. Olmedo won Wimbledon. Olmedo was still fast, still had some big shots. But you know who
Krish got his maiden win against? It was Olmedo. Nice match.
Well-played match."

Ulrich recalled that when Sven Davidson first joined the
Grand Masters, early in its history, he had as hard a time as
Krishnan in establishing a winning form. "He was losing every
match one and two," Torben recalled. "He was just coming
from the computer business—that's his special field, you know
—and he hadn't been playing competitively for some years. But
while he was losing all these matches he was training. He was
running a few miles a day, and he was playing a few hard sets
of practice every day after he got knocked out of the tournament. He didn't just sit around and wait for the next stop on the
tour, he was everybody's practice partner. He kept playing

every day. Pretty soon he was still losing, but it was two and three. Then it was four and five."

We were standing in line together at a buffet luncheon, one of the purely social events on the Seattle calendar, and Torben paused to select a few items for his paper plate before returning to the Davidson saga. "I remember," he said, "how happy I was for Sven when he finally broke through and won his first Grand Masters match."

I asked if he happened to remember who it was that Davidson had finally managed to beat. I should have known.

"It was me," Torben said contentedly. He sopped up a bit of chili with a small piece of croissant and dabbed at his beard with a paper napkin. Torben's plate, I noticed, contained exactly what he had once described to an inquiring reporter as his diet—"some croissant, some frankfurter, whatever is there." He didn't exclude any kind of food, just as he didn't exclude any reasonable experience—playing the clarinet, painting pictures, submitting to the discipline of a Zen retreat. He had a tolerance of cholesterol and carbohydrates like his tolerance of human behavior. It was Torben who, when the subject of tennis manners came up, refused to condemn McEnroe or Nastase, even though you knew he would never emulate them. What Torben demanded of himself was restraint. Moderation.

At least that was true where food was concerned. Although he was sampling everything, I noticed he took only a tiny portion of anything.

I also noticed, for the first time, how deeply seamed his face was under the camouflage of beard. Hell, he was fifty-six years old, and that "curve of declining potential" was dipping fast.

I asked him, in a slightly different way, a question I had raised a month earlier, at the start of the tour: What did he intend to do after his Grand Masters playing days were over?

Again, that benign but enigmatic smile.

"I don't think about it," he said.

23

Trivia

THE PSYCHOLOGICAL SIDE of tennis came in for a few last licks at a farewell social event before the Grand Masters checked out of Seattle. It was an impromptu wharfside dinner organized by the Pac West management for whatever members of the troupe they could round up after the finals.

"The mental part of the game," Mal Anderson said, shaking his head as if the subject defied understanding. A waitress mistook the gesture as a refusal of another beer. Mal quickly disabused her of that notion and lifted a fresh bottle from her tray.

"It's so important," Mal went on, "to believe you are going to win, to know you can beat the other guy. But who knows why some people have other people's number? Ashley Cooper could beat Fraser just by walking onto the court. Fraser would have him two sets to love, five-love, and you'd think, 'Oh-oh, Fraser's in trouble!'"

At the other end of the table, Neale winced reminiscently at his thirteen consecutive losses to Cooper, his chum and sometimes doubles partner.

Rosewall, seated across from his wife, was engaged in a conversation about resort development with a Pac West associate recently returned from a business trip to Australia. He found real estate development interesting, Kenny said, but only as a bystander. He had no head for business himself, Kenny insisted. Although he has made a lot of money in real estate, it has always been as an investor, following somebody else's lead.

Somebody asked Rosewall what he would have done for a living if he hadn't been a professional tennis player. The idea seemed so remote that Kenny had trouble coming up with a possible answer. But finally he recalled that before he left school to concentrate on tennis, at the age of fifteen, he was taking courses that would have led him into bookkeeping or accounting. "I suppose it would have been something like that," he said dubiously.

A huge platter of miscellaneous shellfish was brought to the table, provoking a discussion that led to snails, or escargots (the French term preferred by the Australians). Escargots seemed to be just about the only form of shell-dwelling edible not represented on the platter. The very mention of the little crawly beasts sent a young woman from the Pac West staff into squeamish giggles.

"I like escargots," Rosewall announced firmly. "But I like them fresh out of the field. It's hard to get them fresh, you know, because it's so tricky chasing them."

"It is?" the young woman said.

"Yes," said Rosewall, deadpan. "I did a bit of that back home to get ready for the Grand Masters."

I recognized it as one of Rosewall's rare flights of levity, but the girl merely nodded amiably. Anderson joined in. "That's how Kenny keeps fit, you know. It's how he developed his famous speed of foot—chasing escargots.

The party wound up, as Grand Masters gatherings often did, with an exchange of Torben Ulrich stories. "Torben," said Al Bunis, by way of preface, "has a background of experience that is absolutely unparalleled in the history of the game. He has been a touring player, amateur and pro, for thirty-odd years. And believe me, they have been *odd* years."

The other day, Bunis reported, one of the Seattle reporters had asked Torben what advice he would have for youngsters who were thinking about a career as professional tennis players.

Torben stroked his beard thoughtfully. "I would tell them, 'Watch the ball. And remember there is suffering in the world.' "

It sounded like Torben, all right, though he wasn't present to confirm or deny it.

Somebody recalled the time, back in the amateur-circuit days, when Torben and another player were practicing for a tournament at some club in England. A couple of club members were hanging around, waiting to get on the court. One of them finally asked, in the oblique British style, "Have you been playing long?"

"All my life," Torben answered.

A few minutes later the member tried a more direct tack: "How much longer are you planning to play?"

"I intend to go on for many years," Torben assured him.

It would have been nice to believe it was still true. But I wasn't so sure.

Back at the motel the dinner group joined up with the Lavers, who were entertaining family: Mary's daughter, Ann, and her husband, Kipp Bennett. They lived in Spokane, Washington, across the state, and had been spending the weekend in Seattle watching the tournament and visiting with the in-laws.

The Lavers and the Bennetts had just settled into one of those trendy trivia games at a table in the bar. The questions were heavily weighted toward obscure Americana, but Rod was doing better than you'd have expected of an Australian bloke on minor events in the Truman and Eisenhower administrations. Mary and Ann were taking care of old movies and show tunes. Everybody began to stumble on literary miscellany like the names of William Faulkner's mythical Mississippi county (Yoknopatawpha) and Dr. Doolittle's imaginary two-way animal (the pushme-pullyu), so some helpful kibitzers started making up more relevant questions, including, inevitably, some dealing with tennis trivia.

It was a moment I had been ready for ever since my educational encounter with Bobby Riggs at Boca Raton. In the course of checking out one of Bobby's "oddities," I had come across a tiny gem of tennis history, and I served it up to Laver now like a twist into his backhand corner.

"A famous Australian tennis player, Frank Sedgman," I began in TV-quizmaster style, "was the last man to sweep all three Wimbledon titles—singles, doubles and mixed—in a single year. Now, for the trivia championship of this bar, name the Australian player who made a sweep in reverse—got *beaten* in all three finals."

"I know," said Laver immediately, crashing the return as if he'd just been waiting for that serve into the corner. "It was 1959, and the player was me."

"Wrong," I said.

"Had to be," Laver insisted.

I volleyed the return. "It was 1946, and the player was Geoff Brown. Lost the singles to Yvon Petra, lost the doubles with Dinny Pails, lost the mixed with . . ." I couldn't remember, but I was sure of it.

Laver wrinkled his freckled forehead and flipped back through a couple of decades of tennis matches. "I *know* I lost the singles—that was Olmedo's year. Bob Mark and I got beaten in the doubles by Emmo and Fraser."

He stopped. "Maybe you're right. I might have won the mixed. That could have been one of the years I played with Darlene Hard, and she was tough. When we walked out on the court, she told me, 'Okay, I'll serve first and take the over-heads.' We could have won it that year."

A waitress interrupted to take the last orders before the bar closed. She began clearing the tables of a platoon or so of dead soldiers.

Rod was still thinking. "Nineteen fifty-nine," mused the only man who ever won two Grand Slams. "I had a chance to be famous, and I blew it!"

PART V

Freeze-Out in the Hotbed

The Generation Gap

"Who's the best player you ever faced? The best you ever saw? How would you rate the players of today against your own generation? You in your prime versus McEnroe now—how would you have done against him? You against Connors . . . or Lendl . . . or Borg . . ."

I heard those questions asked of Laver, Rosewall and the other Grand Masters at every stop on the tour. By reporters in their locker room interviews, by fans trying to make verbal contact with their heroes while waiting for an autograph to be signed.

The issue of yesterday versus today had been ruled on by Gardnar Mulloy at Boca Raton ("Our first ten would beat their first ten . . ."). But that didn't settle anything, of course. The same questions came up so relentlessly that the players could have saved themselves some trouble by having their answers printed in the tournament programs, along with country of origin and record of past championships.

The effort to span history, compare generations, rank players across the decades—all this is standard exercise for fans of any sport. Tennis is no exception. There is a continuous search for the All-Time Champion, the hero of heroes.

Then who is the *champions'* champion, the best according to those who should know best?

If you took a poll of Grand Masters past and present, you would have a jury of about seventy players whose credentials cover the whole post–World War II period from the mid-Forties to the mid-Seventies. Ask them to name the best of that era, and you'd get no unanimous choice. But I'm convinced, from my own substantial sampling, you'd get a pretty solid consensus, with six names leading the pack. In probable order of rank:

1. Jack Kramer   4. Frank Sedgman
2. Pancho Gonzalez   5. Lew Hoad
3. Rod Laver   6. Ken Rosewall

After that, you'd get a scattering of votes for the likes of Pancho Segura, Tony Trabert, Roy Emerson, John Newcombe, Arthur Ashe, Stan Smith; a mention of Ilie Nastase, Manuel Santana, Ted Schroeder; a sentimental nod at Vic Seixas, Jaroslav Drobny, Budge Patty.

But that first half-dozen would stand pretty much unchallenged as the class of the postwar era. And Jack Kramer's name would lead the rest.

What was so special about Kramer?

Players who faced him at his toughest, on the pro tour where big bucks were on the line—players like Frank Sedgman—draw you a picture of Big Jake that amounts to an extraordinary combination of generalship and weapons.

Kramer's one-two punch of big serve, big volley is legendary. His forehand approach shot, with a vicious sidespin that made it kick away from a right-hander's backhand, was one of the game's model strokes. But it was the relentlessly aggressive way he used those weapons and his strategic command of the tennis battlefield that were really unique. He understood the percentages of every shot to and from any spot on the court, and he had the self-discipline to play them. As one of his lesser contemporaries, Julius Heldman, once observed, he had "good match temperament almost from the beginning . . . [and] a champion's determination to win."

Like Kramer, each of the other players in the Dominant Half-Dozen was distinguished not by a single outstanding feature but by some combination of qualities. No player makes it to the upper levels without a winning shot—some stroke that he can count on to hurt you, and that he hits better than almost anybody else around. But with that, they all had some special athletic skill or some sheer strength of temperament that carried them above the crowd. *Gonzalez* with his monster serve *and* his extraordinary predatory style—his special taste for the kill. *Laver* with his demoralizing topspin bullets and his creative imagination. *Sedgman's* rock-firm volley and his dazzling speed at getting to the net. *Hoad's* brute strength of shot and his utter disdain of risks. *Rosewall's* precise, forcing backhand and his impeccable footwork.

They were the best of the postwar era.

If you wanted to push the chronological limits back further into the past, you could call on the credentials of the *Old* Old Guard—those Grand Masters who had experience on the circuit during the 1930s, who played against some of the legendary stars of the *prewar* era and had a closeup look at others. Their consensus would give you another half-dozen players as the Best of *Their* Time:

1. Don Budge
2. Bill Tilden
3. Ellsworth Vines

4. Fred Perry
5. Gottfried von Cramm
6. Bobby Riggs

What was special about *Budge* was practically everything— the all-around force of his game; his return of service, which probably outdid Jimmy Connors's vicious returns in depth and velocity; the punishing "heavy" quality of his ground strokes, particularly his brilliant backhand, which kept opponents back on their heels. *Tilden* was distinguished by a service that combined cannonball impact with rifle marksmanship; total command of spins of all sorts; and a sense of drama that enabled him to control the flow of a match. *Vines* hit the ball as hard as anybody before or since, and, according to Kramer, "could do more with it on a given day than anybody." *Perry,* England's last Wimbledon winner (1934–'35–'36) earned his place with a spectacular running forehand and general athletic ability— strength, speed, quickness of reflex. *Von Cramm,* who was once described as "the greatest player who never won Wimbledon [he was a finalist three times] or Forest Hills [a finalist once]," had a complete arsenal of elegant strokes and a feeling for the game that was both scientific and passionate. *Riggs* makes the list with his remarkable agility at the net, his array of touch shots—especially his lob—and his almost fiendish tenacity.

Some members of the jury would scratch Von Cramm or Riggs in favor of Jack Crawford, Australia's first Wimbledon champ (1933). Or they'd cast an admittedly hearsay vote for René Lacoste or Henri Cochet, the artistic French players who put a crimp in Tilden's long string of successes in the late 1920s.

Otherwise, you can put those two lists—the six Prewar Best and the six Postwar Best—together, shuffle them a bit to get Budge and Tilden up at the top (most voters would put one or both ahead of Kramer), and you'll have about as good a selection as anybody's of the Best of All Time.

Among current players, who might qualify for the Grand Masters' list of all-time greats?

"You'd have to find room for Connors and McEnroe," says Bill Talbert, who has seen them all and played most of them. "Maybe you'd have to give Johnny a little more time to prove himself, but off his performance so far, you'd have to rate him up there with the very best."

That vote is widely seconded among other senior players— more enthusiastically about McEnroe than about Connors. The name that is strikingly absent from this short list of new candidates is Bjorn Borg, who won an astonishing five consecutive championships at Wimbledon (1976–1980) even though its fast grass favors net rushers and historically has discouraged baseline players like him.

Borg has his advocates among the Grand Masters, like Gene Scott ("Borg proved that you could rally on grass") and Sven Davidson, Bjorn's predecessor as Sweden's greatest ("Borg would produce winners where most players would have been dead—from way out on the flanks; he was the greatest counterpuncher of all time"). But most of the Grand Masters, brought up in the attacking style of the serve-and-volley game, find Borg's *counter*attacking style alien. They feel the same way about other recent winning baseliners like Guillermo Vilas and Ivan Lendl. The old boys seem to regard their success as a mere blip in the natural trend of the game, a kind of historic aberration that inevitably gets corrected, like fascism or the early seventeenth-century craze for tulip bulbs.

Frank Sedgman says flatly that Borg was overrated, that he rose in a kind of vacuum. There happened to be nobody around with the necessary combination of tools and smarts to stop him —until McEnroe arrived to save the day for the serve-and-volleyers.

Gardnar Mulloy insists that Borg's success would have been restricted to the slow clay courts if his opponents had only kept their wits about them and remembered that tennis is a game most often dominated by the offense on a fast court, but that you need a little finesse to mix in with your aggression.

I asked him to explain.

"I watched Borg play," Gardnar began in his characteristic lazy style, "and then I talked to Laver, I talked to Vines, to Perry, Gonzalez and Kramer and Hoad and Budge." He was approaching the issue gradually, like a man working his way up to the net from behind the baseline. "Every one of them with the exception of Hoad had the same observation: Borg is a looper—he hits that topspin hard, with his exaggerated grip that makes the ball travel over the net in a high arc. Well, with a looper, every once in a while he's going to hit the ball short. And when he does, we're going to come in under it and put it away.

"And in between, every once in a while, we're going to drop-shot him. Bring him in to the net. Borg was very uncomfortable at the net. Hoad was the only one who'd play it a little differently. Hoad said, 'I'd come in for the short shot and take it on the rise.' "

While the majority of the old-timers, in other words, would have taken Borg's high looping drives in the air and volleyed them for winners, Hoad would have waited and taken the ball on the bounce—*early* on the bounce. He would have hit an approach shot to set up a *surer* volley. Or he would have tried for an outright placement.

Either way, goodbye Borg. According to Mulloy.

Personally, I'm not so sure. *Ranking* players from different eras is tricky enough. *Mind matches* against players of another era—now that strikes me as flimsy stuff indeed. Yet it's an exercise that players indulge in at the slightest provocation.

Jack Kramer once ventured that Gonzalez at his prime would beat Laver at the top of *his* game, "regularly," that Riggs would take Rosewall, and Budge would handle Connors at his best.

Gene Scott once conceived an entire "fantasy tournament" bringing together thirty-two of the greatest tennis players in history—each at his prime. Bringing them together in Scott's imagination, that is. The field ranged from the Doherty brothers, turn-of-the-century Wimbledon champions, to stars of the 1970s like Laver, Rosewall, Smith and Ashe. Bill Tilden was seeded first.

Assuming an "ideal" surface (moderately fast, true bounce) and taking into account all sorts of individual strengths and weaknesses, even psychological factors, Scott constructed a draw and calculated the winners of all thirty-one matches. He even decreed the scores. It was like playing God, with a tennis court for the cosmos.

Gene's universal all-star tournament came down to a semifinal round in which Pancho Gonzalez eliminated Tilden in four sets while Laver did the same to Budge. (The luck of the draw had matched Kramer against Budge in the quarters, and Don was the survivor in a fifth-set tiebreaker.) Then in the finals, Gonzalez put Laver away 6–3, 7–5, 7–6. Pancho's service proved just too much for Rod to handle. In Gene Scott's imagination.

You'll notice that the finalists were both players from Scott's own era. (Although a decade older than Rod and Gene, Pancho was still very much a factor in tournaments of the late 1960s.) You'll also notice that the winners in Jack Kramer's mind matchups—Budge, Riggs, Gonzalez—were all players *he'd* faced. Which exposes a great fallacy in these all-time rankings and interera matchups, even the ones devised by the ultimate experts, the champions themselves.

For there is something special in the makeup of a tennis

champion, and part of it is the inner belief that nobody could've played the game any better than the guys you couldn't beat.

The players may tip their hats to their ancestors, as Gene Scott did in seeding Tilden first. And they may be willing to keep the door open for deserving newcomers like McEnroe and Connors. But each generation really wants to believe that it was the best, its stars the brightest. Our guys could take their guys . . . .

It's the tennis version of the generation gap.

The generation gap also works in reverse. Youngsters think nobody really played the game until *their* group came along.

If I needed any evidence of that, then I certainly found it when the Grand Masters took their venerable act to Southern California, that hotbed of young tennis talent.

The tournament site was the West End Tennis Club, an oasis deep in the oil refinery landscape along the freeways south of Los Angeles. West End is what is sometimes known as a "players' club," meaning that its membership includes a number of men and women with sectional rankings and kids with serious tennis ambitions.

Turn off the San Diego Freeway at Torrance, almost any afternoon, make your way through the side roads to West End, and you'll find its landscaped acres of cement tennis courts populated with scurrying teenagers being put through their paces by a corps of businesslike pros. The place exudes the nervous energy of a hotel kitchen at the peak of the dinner hour. West End is one of those pressure cookers in which junior tennis players are brought to a state of readiness for national competition.

The chef, a burly Swiss-born teaching pro named Robert Lansdorp, is credited with developing a number of California players, among whom Tracy Austin and Eliot Teltscher are the most prominent. Lansdorp introduced me to his current phenom, a tall, beautiful child named Stephanie Rehe. In repose, she had the delicate lines of a Tenniel drawing of Alice in Wonderland—if you made allowances for the electric-blue warm-ups in place of the little white pinafore. When I saw her hit some tennis balls, she reminded me less of Tenniel than of that LeRoy Nieman painting of Laver and Rosewall—an explosion of color, all blur and force. She was running through a ground-stroke drill, hitting forehands alternately crosscourt and down the line. The shots flew off her racquet with the satisfactory thud of a tennis ball hit exactly in the middle of the sweet spot. Hit very hard.

She was only fourteen, Lansdorp informed me proudly, though she could have passed for a couple of years older, and indeed had been cleaning up in the 18s bracket. She could be ready to try her wings in grown-up competition this year—a tournament or two on the women's professional circuit in the summer, after her junior high school term ended.

I asked Lansdorp what Stephanie and his other young charges thought about the Grand Masters, who had been playing on their premises for the last couple of days.

"Not much," he said. "I encouraged the kids to come out and watch them. I handed out free tickets. But they're not impressed. Now, you know, it's all wristy topspin—hitting the hell out of the ball. And speed! Lendl and Jimmy Arias—those are the models for young players today. When they watch the Grand Masters, all they see is two old men stroking the ball. And they think: Those guys are so *slow!*"

What if they could have seen the old guys a couple of decades earlier, I wondered, when they were streaking around the court like Arias and hitting the hell out of the ball themselves?

Lansdorp shrugged. "It's a different style."

I consulted Fred Stolle, the Grand Master with the most recent Grand Prix experience. Was there really that much of a change in tennis? Or was it just the difference in ages?

"The main difference between the tennis of our generation," he said, "and the way the game is played today is topspin. *Everybody* nowadays hits with topspin, and they hit the ball consistently harder than we did. It's the result of the improvement in the racquets. If you tried to play with one of our old wooden racquets nowadays, you'd break your arm. Doubles

—the difference there is you won't see them chip and dink the way we do. Well, McEnroe does. But otherwise, you've just got to put your body armor on before you go out there."

It was the same thing Bill Talbert once said, much less amiably, when somebody asked him his impression of present-day tennis.

"Violence!" Talbert said simply, and started to turn away.

The reporter didn't get it.

"Violence!" Talbert repeated. "That's what comes to my mind when I think about contemporary tennis. Two guys flailing away at each other, with nothing but topspin to keep the ball in the court. The game has been reduced to one simple idea: Get out there and hit the ball as hard as you possibly can. Young players nowadays seem to have no idea of tempering their shots or varying them or applying finesse or any other quality except brute force!"

It was a remarkably passionate statement from a man who usually expresses disapproval by mere hauteur.

Force and topspin, of course, are the hallmarks of the baseline style practiced with considerable success by a whole parade of recent young players following in the footsteps of Borg and Vilas. Among the ones who have crashed the upper brackets of the computer rankings are not just Lendl, the hollow-cheeked Czech, and Arias, the bouncy American, but also Jimmy's young compatriot, Aaron Krickstein, and the brawny South American Andres Gomez. They are players who prefer to slug it out from the backcourt instead of maneuvering into an attacking position up forward. They range along the baseline, most of them very speedily, sending back everything that's thrown at them. Their way of establishing an advantage is by sending it back faster and harder than it came. Their preferred way of scoring is not by the volley but by the outright placement or the forced error.

No wonder their young admirers at West End got no thrill out of a Grand Masters match between Gene Scott and Ken Rosewall. "They didn't see the way Rosewall did it," their mentor, Robert Lansdorp, lamented in a tone of frustration. "They didn't see the way he just picked Scott apart, the way he played the whole court, used every foot of it, the way he drew him from side to side. All those beautiful shots . . .''

Lansdorp went into the clubhouse shaking his head, followed by a couple of his teenage pupils, who exchanged mystified shrugs.

The Scott-Rosewall match had been played in an unnaturally cold wind, like the mistral that blows through the south of France. It stiffened the bear on the California state flag that flew from the clubhouse staff. It had a similar effect on the spectators, mainly oldsters like me. But Rosewall's amazing accuracy seemed unaffected by it. He was expertly taking advantage of shots held back by the wind—taking the short ball and using it in the way that was foreign to the baseliners. He would hit a deep underspin approach shot into the corner and follow it in to volley away the return.

Scott, to give him credit, kept hanging in there, kept hitting out, trying to find a groove. But any time he seemed about to put a game up on the scoreboard, Rosewall would play a point that turned it around. He was relentless. At 4–1 in the second set, Scott—with beautiful anticipation—managed to cover a perfect Rosewall drop shot and returned it at an extraordinary angle past Kenny's outstretched forehand. Instead of conceding the point, Rosewall chased the ball the entire diagonal length of the court, calculating that the wind would bring it back to him. That's exactly the way it happened. Kenny caught up with the ball just as it was about to disappear into the courtside shrubbery. Then he hit it past Scott into the open court for a winner.

On the last point of the match, Rosewall hit five or six consecutive crosscourt forehands, all quite flat, none of them terribly severe. But each one cut a slice out of the court, reducing Scott's playing area, until the last one drove Gene right off the court. Now Kenny switched his aim and hit away from Scott, straight down the line. The match ended 6–1, 6–1, with a smattering of applause from us old-timers in the stands.

It remained for Mal Anderson to make an impression of sorts on the younger generation. His first-round match against Roy Emerson was going along uneventfully—Mal comfortably in the lead—when I left the stands and went out to my car for an extra sweater. Normal tennis-watching getup was proving insufficient for the rigors of California weather. When I came back I had to wait for a changeover, so I stood and watched the game from a kind of terrace overlooking the sunken concrete pavilion.

A couple of (I guessed) sixteen-year-old boys from the Lansdorp kitchen were standing next to me. They weren't going in, just pausing for a moment on their way to the locker room after their own game. I held my tongue while they exchanged disparaging remarks about the slow pace of play. Then Emmo came charging in to the net behind a textbook approach shot, only to be met by an even prettier backhand pass down the line from Mal. One of the kids nudged the other and said with grudging admiration, "That old guy hits the ball so far out front, it's unreal!" Score one—finally—for the older generation.

A few moments later, Anderson, having won the first set, 6–3, pounced on a second serve from Emmo and hit a crosscourt winner, taking the first game of the second set. Then he went up to the umpire's chair and withdrew from the match. Mal's bad back, the sciatic nerve problem that had overtaken him in Seattle, was acting up again.

"I might have been able to finish the match," Mal told me in the locker room, "but then I'd have to default the semis again. You don't want to do that if you can possibly help it."

He hobbled toward the shower, an incredible specimen of an athlete on the verge of fifty but looking, I feared, every bit like the younger generation's idea of an old man.

25

Big Jake

THE WEST END KIDS have picked the wrong models. The sun is already setting on the heyday of the slugging baseliners. They *are* only a momentary blip in the great story of tennis.

That was the word I got when I drove north on the freeway one afternoon to the busy, pretty community of Westwood. I got it straight from the horse's mouth. I got it from Jack Kramer.

Big Jake, now in his midsixties, is a kind of living landmark of the game, occupying a place in the modern history of tennis as significant as, say, the old grass courts at the Newport Casino. He describes his career in the following sequence of occupations: amateur tennis champion, professional tennis champion, tennis promoter, tennis TV commentator, tennis players' union director and international tennis executive. These experiences have given him a vantage point on just about everything that has transpired in the sport in the whole post–World War II era —and not just as a bystander. He helped make them happen. Big Jake is a nearly lifelong resident of Southern California, and an assiduous student of the game would no more think of passing through Los Angeles without checking to see what was on Jack Kramer's mind than a country music fan would think of leaving Nashville without checking out the Grand Ole Opry.

In a no-nonsense office at the base of a Westwood high-rise, I looked in on Big Jake—a tall, jaunty man with slicked-down sandy hair, an irrepressibly friendly manner and an outdoorsy look. It seemed out of place behind a desk with a busy telephone. Besides his continuing tennis activities, Kramer owns a

busy thirty-six-hole golf club, and in connection with that, op-
erates a banquet and business-conference service.

In a brief history lesson he explained the rise of the baseline
players during the last decade or two. When open tennis arrived in 1968—with a lot of help from Kramer—it gave a shot in
the arm to the game in countries where clay happened to be
the standard surface and the baseline style the standard pattern
of play. "We encouraged tennis in Spain," he said. "We encouraged it in Italy, to some extent in South America. We talked
Forest Hills into getting rid of grass. Clay courts would help
televise the sport better. It's more interesting to watch a match
on a slower surface because the ball's in play longer, you get
different kinds of rallies, et cetera.

"But it was a two-step process, and clay was only a transi-
tional phase. The idea was to get to concrete. Because a concrete court of a certain moderate speed will give the defensive
player a shot, but the advantage still lies with the big serve and
volley. The kind of topspin used by Borg-style clay-court players is not effective on a hard surface. They use so much topspin
that the ball falls short. On clay those guys *want* you to come
in under their short shots because you won't have secure footing. But on a hard surface, with secure footing, you can plant
yourself and volley the ball away. They can't get away with that
topspin on concrete."

Kramer uses the term "concrete" to include not just the
traditional California cement surface but any kind of paved
court in which some form of asphalt vinyl composition is trow-
eled over a base of poured concrete. Perhaps the most prevalent example is Decoturf II, the surface used at New York's
National Tennis Center and many other tournament sites.

The transition from clay to paved surface lasted less than a
decade, but that was long enough to make the old American
grass-court circuit fade away. Those festive "tennis weeks" at
places like Newport and Southampton, so fondly remembered
by Bill Talbert and the Aussies, were replaced on the tournament schedules by businesslike clay-court events in the popu-
lous urban environments of places like Washington and
Louisville. But their day was brief.

"Now," Kramer pointed out, "you've got the Canadian Open that went from clay to concrete, you've got some of the big indoor events around the world on the hard surface, you've got Cincinnati and our new stadium in Los Angeles, and you've got the U.S. Open. You've got eighty percent of the big-money, prestige events being played on concrete surface, and that's gonna appeal to the serve-and-volley player. The players in the colleges and high schools are gonna see this, and they're gonna go back and try to be more aggressive and develop bigger serves and stronger volleys, and the baseline game is not gonna be as popular as it was for a while there.

"Because you're not gonna beat McEnroe from the back-court. That was one of Borg's problems. He retired to get away from McEnroe. McEnroe's game is gonna beat Borg's game, it's gonna beat Lendl's—though Lendl is still so young and such a great athlete that he can still make slight adjustments to his game. He has to learn what to do with a short ball. What Lendl tries to do with a short ball is to hit a placement, which is how you make errors."

Kramer's prescription for dealing with a ball that your opponent fails to drive deep in your backcourt follows the same rule that Kramer applied to every situation in tennis: Play the percentages! Don't go for an outright placement winner, just slice the ball down the line and come in to the net, where you've got a better chance of putting the ball away.

Big Jake hunched forward with a slight movement of his shoulders, like a man preparing to hit that scoring volley. "So," he summarized, "with these fast surfaces, we're gonna see more McEnroes than Borgs in the years to come. The game is gonna be played more like it was in the Thirties, the Forties and the Fifties than it was in the Seventies."

I think it's worth noting, in the light of Kramer's analysis, that when McEnroe trounced Lendl on the "concrete" in the finals of the 1984 U.S. Open, Lendl played inflexibly from the backcourt. And when Ivan reversed that outcome in his stunning 1985 victory, it was by making some marked adjustments in his game—playing aggressively and hitting admirable volleys.

Jack Kramer speaks, of course, as the very model of the fast-surface game. He was perhaps the outstanding practitioner of the aggressive California cement-court style, and perhaps the outstanding product of the protégé system that turned out several generations of champions for the United States Lawn Tennis Association. Taken under the wing of the USLTA's Southern California section as a promising Los Angeles junior, he was subsidized with a club membership, something his father, a railroad engineer with a passion for sports, couldn't have afforded. Young Kramer's high school schedule was arranged for him by his sponsors. All his classes were in the morning, leaving afternoons free for practice and for lessons from high-priced pros. The bill for the lessons, like the dues bill at the club, went straight to his sponsors. He was put on the sporting good companies' "free list" for racquets and other equipment. He was transported to tournaments for the essential toughening experience of match play. And for further tempering, he was matched against big-time players when they happened to be in the area.

In other words, it was the California version of Australia's junior development program. The big difference: Instead of being given jobs, the California kids were kept in school.

One of the grown-ups young Kramer was matched against was Bill Tilden. They played a couple of practice sets when Kramer was fifteen. Tilden was then in his midforties.

"We played about even," Jake recalls, pointing out that Tilden was playing under the most serious handicap of age—not a loss of physical skills but a lack of competition. There simply weren't enough people for Tilden to play, because it was routine in those days for tennis players to quit playing seriously by the time they reached their midthirties. It would remain true until the older ones were encouraged to stay in the game by two developments. One was open tennis. The other: the Grand Masters.

"That's why Rosewall and Stolle and some of the new bunch in the Grand Masters have such a break over the Sedgmans and the Gonzalezes and some of the others at a comparable age. It's because they never stopped competing on a tennis court. That's why Rosewall has had an easier time than most players holding his form, because he never stopped playing in the toughest competition he could find. He's naturally disciplined, stays in shape. Hasn't changed physically since I saw him as a kid.

"First time I saw Rosewall play was an exhibition against Hoad—can you believe it, January 1, 1947. The exact date. It was an exhibition in Australia, and Ted Schroeder and I were going to play the feature match. We'd just won the Davis Cup down there. We were at Kenny's home club—Rockdale or something like that, just outside of Sydney. I'm in the locker room getting dressed, and I'm watching these two twelve-year-old marvels out the window. Little Kenny and Lew.

"Kenny beat Hoad six-love in the first set, but all the points were good ones. I said, 'Let them play another set.' And Muscles beat him another six-love set. Hoady got better as a junior, and then they had a seesaw, back-and-forth, win-and-lose competition. Went on for some years."

At the time of that prophetic exhibition at Sydney, Kramer himself was an overage prodigy of twenty-five, his maturation delayed by service in World War II.

Like Bobby Riggs, but for different reasons, Kramer had grown up with a taste for betting and a keen sense of the odds governing all kinds of situations, chance or skill. His knowledge came out of boyhood poker lessons learned from an unimpeachable source. He had been taught the game by Las Vegas poker dealers, boarders in Jack's family home at a time when the Kramers lived in the gambling capital, which was then also a railroad town.

Later, in Los Angeles, the laws of percentages were translated into tennis terms for him by one of his sponsors, Cliff Roche, an automotive engineer with some well-calculated theories about the game. Young Jake refined those ideas into winning maxims like these:

· On a fast surface, where the server holds an automatic advantage, don't waste your energy trying for a break in the early games of a set—not unless you find yourself at 0–30 in your favor. At 4–all in the set, go for it, but not if the server gets you 30–0.

· The lowest-percentage shot—the one you've got the least chance of pulling off—is the backhand crosscourt winner. When faced with the temptation of a short ball to your backhand, the odds favor slicing it down the line and coming in for a volley.

· The percentages in general lie with the aggressor. Other players, almost throughout the history of the game, had made a practice of attacking behind a strong serve. And some played matches in which they attacked on practically every shot. It remained for Kramer to make continuous, power-hitting attack the constant pattern of his game, leaving the opponent with no sanctuary and no chance to mount an attack of his own.

The single sentence in Jack Kramer's autobiography that leaps out most starkly at the average club player, with his average, tentative second serve, is this one:

"If you don't come in on your second serve, your opponent will."

It's the tennis equivalent of that famous motto of the French armies in World War I: *"L'attaque! Toujours l'attaque!"*

With his deadly combination of power and percentages, Kramer at twenty-six stood as unarguably the Number 1 player in the world of amateur tennis. The year was 1947. He had won the Wimbledon Singles and Doubles, the U.S. Singles (for the second year) and doubles (his fourth title), and had led his country's Davis Cup team to two successive victories. There were no worlds left to conquer.

Having quit college after one year, Kramer found himself in somewhat the same position as his Aussie counterparts who had committed themselves to tennis as teenagers: no degree and no marketable skills. He also had a wife, and they'd started a family.

When an offer came from Bobby Riggs, the professional

champion, to challenge him in a nationwide head-to-head barnstorming tour, Kramer leaped at it without much hesitation,
even though it looked like a dead end, the life span of a professional tennis player being as limited as it then was.

The tour opened at the old Madison Square Garden in New
York (a dozen blocks or so uptown from the present site) the
day after Christmas, 1947. For public interest and dramatic circumstances the match stands as one of the most memorable
events in tennis history. One of the worst blizzards in the city's
records filled the streets with more than two feet of snow. Drifts
piled up as high as four or five feet. But sixteen thousand seats
were sold, only about a thousand less than the Garden record
set just ten years earlier at a Vines-Perry match. More remarkably, when play started that wintry evening, fifteen thousand of
those seats were filled. Riggs remembers that when the warm-
up rally ended and the umpire called "Play!" he was taking
bets from some spectators in the courtside boxes. Kramer recalls that once the match started, Bobby was all over the net.

With his moderately paced swarming offense, Riggs won
that opening match 6–2, 10–8, 4–6, 6–4. But by the end of the
1947–48 tour, Jack Kramer, escalating his power attack, had
added the professional championship to his amateur laurels
and stood, uncontestably, as the Number 1 tennis player in the
world.

Two years later it was Kramer's turn to be challenged by
still another California hotshot graduating from the amateur
ranks. The new kid was Pancho Gonzalez, a remarkable twenty-
one-year-old combination of talent, strength and competitive
temperament. Kramer gave him an astonishing drubbing, winning three out of every four matches in a grueling itinerary of
123 stops promoted by Riggs.

For a few more years Big Jake took on all comers—Segura,
Sedgman . . . then, in limited competition, Hoad and Rosewall
and Trabert. Mighty Don Budge took a shot, in a comeback
effort. Kramer knocked them all off, and then, overtaken neither
by age nor the opposition but by his physical problems, retired
while still in his early thirties. Except for occasional reappear-
ances, he confined himself to the sidelines as promoter of the

tour, picking up the entrepreneurial reins from Riggs. He demonstrated a business knack and promotional flair to match his performing skills, and brought a degree of stability to an enterprise that had historically been flimsy and chaotic. Pro tennis gained a measure of respectability under Jack Kramer.

But it was still not quite respectable enough for the tennis establishment. Although Kramer was the most vocal lobbyist for open tennis, the idea of mixing the breeds, amateur and pro, in a tournament draw remained anathema. The ruling principle of the sport was a form of apartheid almost as rigid as South Africa's. When, for instance, the pros organized a benefit tournament for a former amateur champion, Art Larsen, who was disabled in a motor scooter accident, the USLTA wouldn't let any amateurs participate.

What changed things in the late 1960s was a simple fact of life: Professional tennis now had all the clout—meaning all the players. First one by one, then in pairs, finally in groups, the best had been turning pro. Amateur tennis was being reduced to a second-rate sport.

When the British LTA in 1967 decided to face facts and try a professional tournament at sacrosanct Wimbledon, it was Jack Kramer they called in to help them run it and to mobilize the talent. He delivered a lineup that made you wonder what had taken the tennis moguls so long to come around: Gonzalez, Sedgman, Hoad, Andres Gimeno, Butch Buchholz, Fred Stolle, Dennis Ralston . . . and the finalists in that historic event—who else but Laver and Rosewall. In one of those historic matchups we noted earlier, Laver took that one in three sets, the last set going 12–10.

The next year Wimbledon and Forest Hills went open. The shape of the sport was changed for all time.

At his office in Westwood, sixty-three-year-old Jack Kramer reviewed those events of the years when "we opened up the game." He spoke in his habitual tone of sunny geniality, with an air of generosity about past conflicts. But a pained expression came over his face when I asked him about the current state of tennis.

He ticked off a number of problems which he considered threatening to the well-being of the sport. Ultimately, he said, tennis cannot hope to survive unless it submits to self-regulation as other sports have done.

"You look at golf," he said, gesturing toward some bright fairway off on the horizon. "You look at the franchise sports like baseball and football. They've got responsibility, and there's someone callin' the shots.

"But in tennis, we've got a situation where the top players want to play five or six months, and the rest of the time play exhibitions where they don't have to win to collect the big dough. Where does that leave the kids down at the lower level of the computer rankings?

"The way this game works, players don't start showing a profit until they get into the top one hundred. Until then, they've got all the expenses of travel and training and coaching to make back. If they've got real ability, they get up into the top fifty, and now they're paying taxes and putting something aside for an investment, and they're signing five-year endorsement contracts.

"But," he went on, "it's the top seven or eight that get all the television exposure, all the publicity. And they start makin' two or three million a year in contracts *off* the courts. Because they are in the feature matches, the ones on TV, and the cameras are showing the patches on their shirts and headbands, and the trademarks on their shoes. That's what they're collecting all that off-court money for.

"But if the top seven or eight don't cooperate with the system—if they don't enter enough of the lesser tournaments, the ones with the small prize money—then we're going to lose the bottom end. A lot of the tournaments are gonna say, 'We can't compete any more—which they're already saying. There'll be no place left for the lower-ranking kids to play and learn the game and make a buck.'"

In theory, the men's side of tennis *is* regulated by a worldwide governing body, the Men's International Professional Tennis Council. Usually identified simply as the Pro Council, it includes representatives of three major forces in the tennis world: the players, the tournament directors and the International Tennis Federation (which is basically the old amateur tennis establishment updated and brought into the modern world of open tennis).

But in fact, the Pro Council has no authority over a number of crucial areas of tennis activity, including those big-money exhibitions and other special events. Furthermore, the Pro Council is often caught in a crossfire of conflicting interests involving its own membership plus two other major forces in the sport. One is the sponsors, the other is the management groups like IMG and ProServ, which represent the players as agents but also stage some tournaments and special events. They also produce broadcasts of tournaments and sell them to sponsors and/or television stations or networks. All of which means that somebody with a financial stake in a tournament can decide whether or not a player will enter that tournament rather than another one. That somebody representing a player is in a position at least theoretically to influence how he will be seeded, what kind of television exposure he gets and therefore what kind of position he is in to show off a product he endorses.

"Tennis is a game of superstars," a USTA spokesman once told me. "In the last analysis, it's the players who run the game."

"The stars are creatures of their agents," another insider observed on another occasion. "In the last analysis, the big decisions in tennis are made by the management groups." He went on to point out that often this power has been wielded to the advantage of the sport, since the management groups have been instrumental in bringing sponsor money into the game and in putting some shaky tournaments on a firm footing.

Nevertheless, the number of professional tennis tournaments in the world keeps declining every year, while the superstars thrive. But the market for the also-rans is shrinking. And the Pro Council remains battered and sometimes immobilized by the internal conflicts of the game, which have even been taken into those other courts, the courts of law.

"All it takes," insisted Jack Kramer, "is someone with the right to say to a player, 'You're gonna play twenty tournaments a year, and you're gonna play three to five of them in places that need your help to keep them going.' But," he lamented, "everybody is abrogatin' their responsibility, and I can't stand it! I helped form all these things!"

He was voicing the frustration that had recently prompted him to resign from the Pro Council, of which he was a charter member. He served as a representative of the players' union, the ATP (Association of Tennis Professionals), another one of the things he helped form.

The pragmatic answer for tournament directors confronted with the problem of luring reluctant tennis stars into lesser events has been to offer them appearance money or guarantees. Under the table, since that kind of payment is prohibited in events under the Pro Council's jurisdiction. It's a rule that Guillermo Vilas, then the world's fourth-ranking player, had lately been suspended for violating. The suspension was subsequently lifted, and Vilas was fined $20,000—a mild one-third of the $60,000 he was charged with collecting for entering a tournament in the Netherlands. Jack Kramer had supported the sanctions against Vilas. Appearance money is, in effect, a professional equivalent of the old deceptions Kramer knew as "shamateurism," and he regards it as both unfair and unnecessary.

"A player deserves more money than Vilas, more than McEnroe or Connors, if he plays better that week," Jack told me. "Those top players are already getting the perks of their high ranking and drawing power. They are seeded in the tournament, so they have a kind of guarantee of getting through the early rounds and into the bigger money. They get to play on the best courts, where there's less risk of losing points through bad bounces, et cetera. You never saw Borg playing out on Court 16, where the ball won't bounce. That's why Borg, when he had that comeback for a little while, wouldn't play the qualifying rounds—because he'd have to play on the outside courts with their bad bounces.

"On top of all this," Kramer continued, really getting into the subject like a player working his way into a match, "on top of all this, the high-ranking players are getting the financial advantages of television, showing their endorsement products like I was saying.

"So I say to Vilas and the rest of them: 'You're gettin' the breaks to play the game. The game was there when you started, and I can remember when you were lucky to get into a tournament. Now you're up here because of a system that's designed to be fair to you at eighteen and fair to you at thirty-eight. So keep it going! Adhere to the rules or you'll kill the tournaments! You'll kill the system, you'll kill the game!' "

Kramer interrupted his address to the unseen audience of current tennis players and took a phone call. When he hung up, he turned back to me and concluded, "In tennis, a player has the responsibility to leave the circuit at least as good as he found it."

That tennis version of a copybook maxim was one I'd heard from many players of the amateur era—Riggs and Talbert, Sedgman and Rosewall, Fraser and Anderson. I'd heard it in several variations: "Every player owes something to the game. . . ." "You've got to put back into tennis some of what you took out. . . ." "A player has to leave something for the players that come after him. . . ."

It hadn't occurred to me until now that this might no longer be accepted as an article of faith in today's professional game. It might be one of those pieces of traditional wisdom, like old saws about thrift and virtue, that fail to make it across the generation gap.

Torben Ulrich says the whole issue of guarantees makes him feel sad. The basic idea of open tennis, he observed, was to eliminate dishonesty and deceit. Open tennis was supposed to be "a democratizing process, which eliminated payoffs for the big stars at the expense of the journeymen. It made *everybody* a star. But now, it seems, there are stars and superstars. Or maybe superstars and not-so-super stars." It was, he said, like the commercialization that infects the arts in contemporary society. Some artists only want enough money to practice their art, but others sell out for the big dough.

Sven Davidson was less inclined to condemn the superstars,

but he was just as tough on the practice of guarantees. "If it was me on the Pro Council," he once told me, "I would have said, 'This is a matter for the Dutch tennis federation to police. [The offending tournament in the Vilas case, remember, took place in the Netherlands.] And until it is taken care of, everybody suffers with everybody else—no Grand Prix tournaments in Holland for the next three years! Period!' "

But not even the fraternity of senior players is unanimous with Kramer in opposing appearance money. Gene Scott, for example, as a tournament director and promoter himself, takes the position that the only thing wrong with guarantees is that they violate a rule—a rule that, he says, can no more be policed then Prohibition. If a guarantee could be offered openly and legally, then, he says, there could be no reasonable objection to it as a professional's way of cashing in on his personal skills and earned prestige.

Well, I have an objection. The essence of sport, after all, is competition. The idea of any game is, within certain limits of behavior, to excel over the other player. To win. Otherwise it's not sport at all, it's just theatre. Mere performance. A guarantee gives a player the rewards of excellence without the need to win. It's just contrary to the basic idea of sport.

Kramer had been amiably philosophizing and reminiscing for a couple of hours, and I figured it was time to get down to business: the subject of the aging process in tennis. I asked him what conclusions he may have reached about it from his own experience and from his observation of senior players in the Grand Masters.

"Well," he said with a thoughtful frown, "it's different for everybody. Sometimes it happens mentally, and it happens at an early age, especially for clay-court people. Look at Borg [who retired at twenty-six]. Look at what happened to Tracy. [Tracy Austin, Robert Lansdorp's prize pupil, won the 1979 U.S. Singles at the age of sixteen, was forced off the circuit by chronic injuries a few years later, but seemed unable to get back into competition even after the physical symptoms were relieved.] Clay courters have to grind it out. They get tired of running.

"My own time was very short because I had this arthritis of the hip. I had started feeling lower back problems in 1951. I was thirty. I had trouble sleeping. I had to take all these pills just to get out on the court. Cortisone and butazolydene.

"After I beat Pancho I played two more tours—against Segura and against Sedgman—and I didn't play as well as I had. And my wife and mother were concerned about all these drugs I was taking. I was a junkie on muscle relaxants. Eventually I had to have an operation for a hip replacement. Gene Scott—I admire him for the way he toughs it out, but sooner or later he'll have to have the same operation I did."

The telephone interrupted him again. He resumed a few minutes later as if he'd been mulling over a peroration while listening to his caller.

"Tennis," he said, "is a game in which you have to get your strokes down by the time you're seventeen or you may never get 'em. If you don't have a second serve by that time, you're probably not gonna make it. And it's very hard if you don't have a nice backhand with spin by that time—over and under. Now you got to learn how to play your strokes when the pressure's on. And then it's a question of how long you can maintain the discipline that's necessary in your life in all ways to keep you at that level you achieved at around twenty-one or twenty-two.

"In certain ways you'll keep improving. I played better professional tennis than I played amateur tennis, because, let's face it, there's a lot that comes from the experience of competition. Riggs improved me, and I improved Gonzalez."

He stopped himself with a kind of apologetic smile. "I guess I keep dodgin' around the question, but . . . well, I think you can probably, if you want to do it, play as well at thirty-five or thirty-six as you did when you were twenty-two or twenty-four. But, boy, you've got to pay a hell of a price in discipline!"

Kramer's prime example of the cost of playing serious competitive tennis in midlife is Pancho Gonzalez. Kramer had a chance to watch his old antagonist play in the Grand Masters when they held a tournament in conjunction with Jack's Pacific Southwest tournament in Los Angeles, and again when Jack served as television commentator at several Grand Masters tour finals.

"Watching Pancho play in some of those matches," Kramer now recalled, "I used to keep saying to myself, 'Why's he doing it?' Because the little moves he used to make automatically that he just couldn't make now would aggravate the hell out of him. Pancho always was a disagreeable guy on the tennis court— that's all there was to it. But it used to only be bad calls and maybe the ball kids that would really get to him, and now it was *everything!*

"I didn't know if the explanation might be money or what. So I told him, 'God, it can't be worth it to you, kid!' He told me, 'Jack, I liked the idea of these tournaments for the old players, and I thought I could be helpful to the guys. And I thought it was worth going through the pain'—he was having trouble with his shoulder all the time—'and I wanted to be a part of something I thought should happen.'

"So I admire him for doing it, but I don't know why he did it. I don't know why any of them do it. I don't know why they still want to go out there and fight and compete and go through the agony. Because there's not much fun in losing, and if you don't train, you're not gonna win, at any age."

He leaned back in his chair and stretched—an old pro taking a breather at the end of a tough match. "As far as the other Grand Masters, it appeared to me that Torben played damn near as well into his forties and fifties as he ever played. Of course, he was a physical fitness freak, as was Sven Davidson. Some of the other players, like Seixas, were having their physical problems.

"The most amazing thing about the game they play," he added with a chuckle, is that they do it without giving up their evenings. Because, no doubt about it, these fifty-year-old guys still like to socialize. Well, my hat's off to 'em!"

26

In the Trenches

JACK KRAMER said it for all the old champions: Amateur tennis was fun, but it was on the pro tour that you earned your spurs.

When tennis players reminisce about the amateur circuit, about Wimbledon or Forest Hills, Newport or Southampton, they tend to wax nostalgic. They remember big parties, pretty girls, locker-room high jinks and after-hours capers with their buddies.

When they recall the pro tour—if they were among the relative handful good enough to have played it—there is rarely any such sentimentality, only a kind of fierce pride. It's like the difference in old soldiers' war stories—the difference between being in uniform and being at the front.

The military analogy is very much to the point. Listening to accounts of the pro tour from old soldiers like Kramer and Sedgman and Rosewall, I got a clear, constant impression of something like trench warfare. Those who survived it are united by lasting bonds of mutual respect, if not always affection. The circuit produced champions; the pro tour produced heroes.

When Jack Kramer abdicated as king of the pros after the 1953 tour, he put his crown up for grabs among an expanding group of contenders, all under contract to him. There were the veterans: Gonzalez, Segura, Sedgman and, in his one-season comeback attempt at the age of thirty-eight, Don Budge. They were joined by a succession of younger stars whom Kramer picked off, one by one or sometimes two by two, as they rose to the top of the amateurs. They included Sedgman's old doubles partner, Ken McGregor, and another solid Australian player,

Dinny Pails; America's young power-hitter, Tony Trabert; the Peruvian-American, Alex Olmedo; and that pair of former child marvels, Rosewall and Hoad.

In that circle of champions, competitiveness was a matter of instinct, like sex or survival. Although the guarantees in Kramer's contracts meant that a player's take for any given match would be the same whether he won or lost, the ultimate stakes for winning were enormous. Whoever came out on top at the end of the tour could command top dollar, as much as $100,000 a year, while a loser might not even get into the act the next year. Gonzalez, for example, after his defeat by Kramer, had to sit out for two years while Sedgman and Segura took their shots at the champ. And then, to his unending outrage, when he came back for the 1954 tour, it was at less than half of his original market value—about $35,000. Even when he came out on top, his percentage the following year was less than Tony Trabert was getting as the star graduate of the amateur circuit.

The mood of the pro tour was one of unrelieved pressure. Kenny Rosewall says of his maiden voyage in the pros—a hundred-match tour against Gonzalez—that "it was like playing a hundred finals."

In these circumstances the clubby old rules of gentlemanly behavior sometimes went by the boards. This was both more and less than sport; it was a grim and gritty business. Kramer himself had set the standards in his first (1950) head-to-head tour with Gonzalez. Noting Pancho's voracious taste for soft drinks, and convinced they were nothing less than poison, Jack, as promoter, arranged to have a nice cold soda waiting for his young opponent at every changeover.

Gonzalez, on his part, tried to intimidate his opponents physically. Pancho in repose is a large and menacing figure. Rosewall—whom Pancho towered over by more than half a foot —recalls instances when Gonzalez grabbed hecklers and even officials by the lapels. Once he threw his racquet at the umpire's stand, rattling it ominously, during a change of courts.

So intense was the competition among all these gladiators that the feature match on any given night routinely went the full five sets, and the concluding doubles would then be played out after midnight before a handful of diehards in the stands.

Gonzalez and Hoad were especially tough against each other, neither willing to yield an inch. Their sets sometimes went 20–18 or 24–22 in those days before the tiebreaker.

Psychologically as well as physically, the tour was a punishing experience. Jack Kramer says that some players simply never recovered from the shock of their baptism in the pro game. He cites Alex Olmedo as an example of an authentic champion who, after a sudden, early rise to the top of the amateur heap, was simply stunned by the terrible beatings he took as soon as he stepped across the line into the pros. He wasn't used to losing, and he couldn't seem to adjust to it. Eventually, Olmedo got a few good wins on the tour, but his game was never quite the same, and he soon faded out of the competition. Kramer, incidentally, thinks the same phenomenon may explain the careers of some recent players who, obviously talented, turned professional perhaps a year or two prematurely, got clobbered and gradually sank from sight—players like John Alexander, Billy Martin and Billy Scanlon.

It was Pancho Gonzalez who emerged from the bloody free-for-all with Jack Kramer's abandoned crown clenched in his predatory jaws.

"Pancho" was a nickname he detested. It smacked of ethnic stereotype, reminding him of the indignities often experienced in California by people of Mexican antedecents like his family. Eventually he acquiesced to the nickname, but he prefers to sign himself "Richard Gonzalez." In private, some of his colleagues called him "Gorgo," for Gorgonzola. It was a kidding reference to a sportswriter's misguided comment, calling him a "cheese champ" because he got to the top only after Kramer's retirement cleared the way.

Gorgo's ferocious style made him a legend among his own peers. Kramer says Gonzalez appeared to like nobody except Lew Hoad, his fiercest rival, and his own father, who sometimes visited him on the tour. Rosewall says he exuded "a general air of violence" on the court. Gene Scott, who came up against Gonzalez only some years later, in early open tournaments, when he had presumably mellowed a little, once wrote a description of Pancho as playing "in a leopard-like crouch from beginning to end of a match . . . without straightening up between shots." His prevailing mood, Scott said, was one of "controlled rage."

On the tour his rage was directed as much against Kramer, who he felt was exploiting him, as against any given opponent. Eventually he and Kramer were reconciled. With his success on the tour, Gorgo was earning over $100,000 a year. He had also earned Kramer's lasting respect as the toughest competitor in the game. "At five-all in the fifth," Kramer says, "there's no man in the history of tennis I'd bet against him."

Kramer once tried to enlist Gonzalez in an attempt to fix a tour in the interests of building up the gate—an episode Jack later recalled with some embarrassment, but also with admiration for Pancho. It happened at a time when the competition was sagging. Jake offered Gonzalez a bonus if he would carry the newest challenger—inexperienced, undramatic Ken Rosewall. The idea was not to dump any matches, just to let Rosewall stay close enough to maintain interest.

Gonzalez reluctantly agreed, but after a few stops on the tour he came to Kramer in anguish, protesting that the effort to play contrary to his normal killer style was ruining his concentration. Kramer, abashed, told him to forget the deal, go out and play his game and, incidentally, keep the bonus.

"When Gonzalez was on," says Alex Olmedo, "he was unbeatable! He *destroyed* Trabert. He would never lose a match to Ashley Cooper or Mal Anderson. A *mean* player!" he adds in a tone of frank admiration. "He had no pity on the other player. He could be twenty matches ahead of you on the tour, and he would still beat you love and love."

Olmedo is one of those veterans of the pro tour who talks like a Gonzalez fan, the way later players talk like Laver fans. He still refers to Gorgo as "my idol."

While I was in Jack Kramer territory in Westwood, I drove

up the freeway a few more exits and checked in with Olmedo on *his* turf, the palm-fringed courts at the Beverly Hills Hotel, where he presides luxuriously as head pro.

Olmedo is a man with a reputation for mean temper himself, but you'd never guess that from his easygoing manner and the habitual smile on his Inca face, the handsomely chiseled features that inspired his nickname, "the Chief." At forty-eight he looked in peak playing condition; it was the result, he acknowledged, of conscientious exercise and getting on the courts frequently with good young players.

Crowded out of the Grand Masters after four years, the Chief said he had enjoyed that competition, enjoyed the company ("seeing Frank Sedgman is like seeing an old movie star"). But, he said, he didn't really miss the senior circuit. The tennis he preferred to remember was the tennis he and his old rivals played on the pro tour. Some of the matches that are most deeply etched into his mind are a couple that he happened to see from the audience before he joined the tour himself. The players: Gonzalez and Hoad.

"Both guys were such great players with big serves," he recalled. "Gonzalez would hit that serve, and Hoad would return it like a ping-pong ball. They would go corner to corner. Boom! *Boom!* BOOM! People would stand up and applaud, thinking the point was over, and it would keep going two or three more shots. Or two or three more *exchanges*. People would be *screaming*. I tell you, man, that was *tennis!*"

The player most people know as Pancho Gonzalez ruled the pro tour from 1954 to 1960—with the possible exception of one year, 1959, when he began easing his way toward retirement, and Lew Hoad seemed, at least to many observers, to gain the upperhand. A year or two later, Gonzalez had pretty much made the transition from playing pro to club pro. But he sprang back to life at the age of forty, with the arrival of open tennis. And he remained a major force in professional tennis for a few years after that, winning some tournaments and playing some spectacular matches in Grand Slam events, where the heat of competition burned at its most intense.

Gorgo's match against Charlie Passarell in the opening

round of the 1969 Wimbledon was the lengthiest and one of the
most brilliant in the century-plus history of the All-England
championships. It went 22–24, 1–6, 16–14, 6–3, 11–9—no less
than 112 games in all, a remarkable total even in that pretie-
breaker era. Gonzalez, then forty-one, outlasted his twenty-
five-year-old opponent, and you'll notice from the score that
Pancho was two sets down, barely hanging on, when he started
his comeback.

That year, forty-one-year-old Pancho Gonzalez was ranked
Number 8 in the world behind Laver, Tony Roche, Newcombe,
Okker, Rosewall, Ashe and Cliff Drysdale—pretty fast company for a man verging on senior status. The next year, 1970, he
had a win over Laver, the reigning Grand Slam champion; and
in 1971, at the age of forty-three, he won Jack Kramer's Pacific
Southwest tournament in a field that included Stan Smith and
nineteen-year-old Jimmy Connors.

Gonzalez in the Grand Masters, just three or four years later,
was a different story.

From the record, you would have expected Pancho to dominate the new competition for forty-five-year-olds. But a 7–6,
6–4 loss to Torben Ulrich in one of the early Grand Masters
events, in 1974, proved all too prophetic. It was the first match
Gonzalez had ever lost to Ulrich—but there were several more
after that.

Gorgo had his wins, the best a tough three-setter over the
Number 1 Grand Master, Frank Sedgman, before that biggest
of all Grand Masters crowds—the 7,000-plus in Johannesburg,
South Africa. But Gorgo struggled—and sometimes lost—
against players he would have eaten up in the old days. He had
several losses to Sven Davidson, a couple to Seixas. Rex Hartwig beat him. So did one of his old pro tour whipping boys,
Mal Anderson. There were those times when, as Jack Kramer
noticed from the sidelines, "everything seemed to get to him"
—when Gonzalez lost his temper and berated the officials or an
opponent, disrupting the normal gentlemanly atmosphere of
the Grand Masters.

Pancho afterwards was usually remorseful. He was once
asked to comment on the disruptive behavior of Ilie Nastase.

"I think it's terrible," Pancho replied, "but I'm the wrong one to say so." He quickly raised the Gardnar Mulloy defense, however, pointing out that neither in the Grand Masters nor in his earlier tennis incarnation did he use profanity, nor did he prolong the interruption beyond an explosive outburst.

As the old saying goes: "Different times, different manners."

Gonzalez's abrupt decline in the few brief years between his open tournaments and his Grand Masters tournaments is a complicated thing to explain. For one thing, he had pretty much withdrawn from competition and returned to the teaching pro routine—and inactivity had taken more of a toll than he probably realized. Never exactly a fiend for conditioning (as a kid on the tour he was a heavy smoker, addicted to junk food as well as those poisonous soft drinks), Gorgo in his late forties was not disposed to get back in shape to compete against players who could hardly be called his peers. As one observer saw it, he trapped himself in a vicious circle. Competitor that he was, he couldn't stand the idea of losing, so he pretended he didn't really care about winning; and the result of his lackadaisical play was that he lost even more.

The last time I saw Pancho Gonzalez play tennis was in 1975. It was not in the Grand Masters but at the time and place of the "heavyweight title" match between Jimmy Connors and John Newcombe, a television event in which I had a small role. The site was Pancho's home court at Caesar's Palace in Las Vegas, and the morning before the big fight I watched him play a couple of sets of doubles with some of the visiting tennis celebrities: Tony Trabert, Ham Richardson and, if I remember right, Connors's sparring partner, Vitas Gerulaitis.

Playing in that characteristic catlike crouch, Gonzalez commanded the court—less with his authoritative serve and his marvelous chip returns then with his sheer animal presence. Afterwards, as the group left the court, Pancho challenged one of them—I forget who—to a set of what he called "suicide singles."

"Suicide?" I asked from my vantage point behind the fence.

"Yeah," said Pancho. "If he beats me, I'll cut my throat."

The last time I talked to Pancho Gonzalez was while writing the preceding paragraphs about his experience in the Grand Masters. It occurred to me that he might have his own explanation for his relative lack of success in the senior group, so I phoned him at the pro shop at Caesar's Palace. He staunchly insisted that it was simply untrue that he ever gave anything but his best effort in the Grand Masters, no matter who the opponent was. But he just as firmly refused to discuss the issue beyond that flat statement.

The net result of Gonzalez's career after forty-five is an image far different from that of the ferocious giant of the pro tour. Some of his old comrades in the Grand Masters talk about him not in terms of his performance on the court but of the extracurricular activities.

"My strongest memories of Pancho," says Sven Davidson, "are those Sunday nights after the tournaments when we didn't have an early flight on Monday morning, when our local social obligations were over, and we would all have dinner together. And then we would assemble somewhere in the hotel for The Game. Pancho was always first there—after me. Or sometimes even before me."

Sven was seeing every detail in his mind's eye as he described it. He continued in a kind of nostalgic glow, the sort of mood you never saw when players talked about the barnstorming tours.

"I would arrange the decks of cards," Sven said. "Pancho always ordered the beer. And paid for the beer—he always wanted to treat the rest of us. And we would play poker till one, two, three A.M. And we were having a *ball!* You could win a hundred dollars or you could lose a hundred—it was no disaster.

"Those were some of the best times in the Grand Masters. And those are my best memories of Pancho."

27

Allowing the Wind

THE PLAYER who succeeded huge, menacing Pancho Gonzalez as ruler of the pros was slight, unprepossessing Kenny Rosewall, the overmatched challenger Pancho once had to carry.

It was 1961 when Rosewall shot out to the front of the pack —the pack then consisting of Mal Anderson, Ashley Cooper, Pancho Segura, Andres Gimeno, Barry MacKay and, off and on, Gonzalez and Hoad. Rosewall by then had served four years in the trenches. He had remade his game to suit the pros' special, brutal kind of warfare. The onetime counterpuncher had become an attacker—the same transformation Bobby Riggs had put himself through a decade earlier. It was a matter of self-preservation, Kenny told me, under the deplorable playing conditions of the pro tour.

"We played in a lot of little places, on dim, dark courts," he recalled. "Dance halls, amusement parks, hockey rinks. On some pretty strange surfaces, too. We played on boards laid over the hockey ice—it would get pretty slippery from the condensation. We played on canvas over ice and canvas over boards. Those were all good surfaces for the big serve-and-volley game. The ball would skid and take off. If you didn't serve and volley before you went on the tour, you learned soon enough."

He shook his head as if he couldn't quite believe his own memory of that bruising educational experience. Wilma Rosewall smiled sympathetically at her husband.

We were sitting at a table in the West End club's rustic snack bar on a Saturday afternoon. Normally Rosewall would undoubtedly have been out on the court warming up for his semifinal against Fred Stolle that evening. But "warming up" would only have been a figure of speech. Even conscientious Ken had been driven to cover by the cold wind of the California mistral.

You won't catch Ken Rosewall shedding any tears for the good old barnstorming days—no more than any of the old vets. The weeping sounds you sometimes hear when the subject comes up are about money: what piffling sums they played for back then and how rich they'd all be if only they'd been born twenty or thirty years later and were playing the Grand Prix now.

Jack Kramer points out that they did pretty damn well for their own time. At $75,000 each in their 1950 tour, he and Gonzalez were making as much as Joe DiMaggio. But there were constant reminders of insecurity. For Kramer also remembers driving all day with Budge, Gonzalez and Segura to a remote town in Scotland where he'd misguidedly booked his troupe during a tour in Britain, playing an exhausting evening of tennis in a dim music hall, and getting $400 to split among the four of them for their pains—out of which they had to pay for gas and their hotel rooms. And Rosewall and Laver, during that era when pro tournaments were held in obscurity, with uncertain financing, once played the finals of a four-day event at Forest Hills for which they collected not a dime between them.

By contrast, Rosewall told a recent interviewer, "there's so much money around these days that half of the new players shouldn't even be playing, compared to some of the older pros who played before the big money came in. Many of today's players couldn't make their Davis Cup teams or become national champions, but they can make a very good living with all the money available now, just by playing in the first round of forty-five or fifty tournaments."

Kenny says he has no complaint personally—pro tennis didn't do too badly by him, all things considered. The investments he began making with his earliest tour earnings have panned out well—especially the resort hotel he bought into, along with Sedgman and Hoad, and some resort acreage he acquired well before it began escalating in value. The Rose-walls still live in Sydney, but far removed from the blue-collar neighborhood of Kenny's origins. They have a substantial house with a pool in a suburb with the euphonious name of Turramurra. A visitor describes the setting as a cross between England and Beverly Hills.

"I did all right," Kenny acknowledged, with just the faintest hint of a grin crossing his usually impassive face.

A couple of Robert Lansdorp's teenage students came through the West End clubhouse with professional-looking racquet bags slung over their shoulders. They passed Rosewall without a sign of recognition.

I asked Kenny if he had any thoughts about the current crop of young players or the trend in playing styles.

"Well, the game is not so pretty nowadays, is it?" he said. "All that wild swinging. But that's the style now, and the kids imitate the players who are successful."

He glanced toward the two youngsters, who were horsing around in the corridor just outside the snack bar. His solemn face, with its long jaw and heavy eyebrows, gave nothing away, but I sensed that he was thinking: "I could still handle most of their wild-swinging role models. Most of them. On a good day."

The playing conditions on the barnstorming tours as Rose-wall described them could hardly have been much worse than the conditions he faced that evening in the Grand Masters semifinal. The cold wind, which had played havoc with the first-round matches, was now churning up a surf on the club's little outdoor pool. The few swimmers I saw braving its frigid currents must have been members of the Polar Bear Club, an institution I formerly associated with latitudes like New York's and locales like Coney Island at a time of year when your crawl stroke has to be strong enough to break ice.

By match time the wind had turned into something approaching gale force, and the temperature had dropped so low that the scant two hundred or so spectators who turned up were accoutred in various local versions of Arctic gear, hauled up from God-knows-what previous incarnations, lived in other climate zones. Ear muffs, mittens, knitted caps, lap robes, mukluks, even a couple of ski masks; surveying this extraordinary array of tennis-watching getup as he prepared to introduce the players, Al Bunis began by announcing: "We are giving a prize for funniest costume, of course." He waited for his words to penetrate the wind, paused expertly for the laugh, then added, "And looking around this stadium, I'd have to say that most of you are in the running."

The man next to me appeared to have a particularly good shot at the trophy. He was dressed like one of those 1920s cartoons of a football fan—bearskin coat down to his ankles.

Football, a brutish sport, pays no attention to nasty weather —in fact, thrives on it. But the only thing approaching the West End freeze-out in my tennis experience was the Bavarian Championships, a German clay-court event conducted in a woodsy park just a trolley ride from downtown Munich. This was back in the amateur days, and the Bavarian was a significant summer event for European players avoiding the American grass-court circuit.

When I innocently boarded the tram one sunny July morning in my New Yorker's seersucker jacket, I should have suspected trouble, seeing the rest of the crowd carrying blankets and dressed for a raw November day in the Yale Bowl or worse. By midafternoon, when the sun declined behind an Alp and the wind began bending the pine trees, the locals were all happily snuggled into their furs and woolens, nipping at flasks of schnapps and cheering the long rallies, while I—nose numb, teeth chattering and fingers too stiff to write scores on the draw sheet—was urging convinced baseliners like Boro Jovanovic and Fausto Gardini to come to the net, for the love of God, and get the point over with! The injunction of course was lost on players to whom the forecourt was foreign territory; into which, as the saying goes, they ventured only to shake hands at the end of a match.

The problem of the wind at West End was defined early in the Rosewall-Stolle match when Kenny hit a backhand lob straight down the line and it blew wide all the way across the court on his *forehand* side.

Otherwise, Rosewall was hitting with his usual uncanny accuracy against his good-humored sometime pigeon. After a few experimental misses Kenny seemed to develop an exact sense of where to aim the ball in order to make it land somewhere else. As Krishnan observed from his place on the sidelines, "He allowed the wind." He began hitting the lines as if the match were being played indoors. It wasn't until the fifth game that he committed a real unforced error. And in his first three turns to serve he laid his first service in with a frequency that exceeded seventy-five percent. He breezed, so to speak, through the first set, 6–3.

Stolle meanwhile was playing it for laughs, as if that was all he could hope to get out of the match. When a ball coming at him blew long over the baseline, he deliberately fanned at it— a parody of a bad swing. On the change of courts after the first set he bent into the wind and trudged to his position like an Arctic explorer tramping through snow drifts.

Midway through the second set, Stolle suddenly seemed to get hold of himself, and the character of the match changed drastically. Fred's own postmatch explanation: "At the beginning I couldn't figure out the wind at all, so I just hit everything straight down the middle. All I was hoping to do was stay in the match. Halfway through the second set I realized I was still in it. The score was three-all, and I began to think I had a pretty good chance. I was serving well, and I was able to put a little pressure on his forehand. If Kenny starts to go, that's where it'll happen."

What Stolle began to do was to exemplify the right strategy for playing in a strong wind: Take a little off your first serve to be sure of getting it in, and keep coming in to net behind it. The objective is to force your opponent to pass you or lob over you; either tactic requires particular accuracy to be effective, so either one is apt to be frustrated by wind.

Sticking resolutely to that plan, Stolle hung on and finally won a service game in which he had been carried to deuce no less than twelve times. In the next game Rosewall hit a beautiful crosscourt approach shot and came in behind it for the volley. It was *his* shot, and he had set it up almost perfectly. But he had to reach for it, and he was just a fraction of a second late in getting the racquet into the ball. And . . . he netted it. The error looked like the perfect illustration of Gardnar Mulloy's definition of the aging process.

Now, suddenly, Rosewall was down set point. A moment later, he hit another backhand into the net, and the match was tied, one set apiece.

Kenny was so disgusted that he simply blew his cool in a display worthy of a McEnroe. Taking two balls from a ballboy, he slammed one into the fence, then hit the other one clear over it. He flung his racquet down on the pavement and stared at it accusingly.

Stolle, after being completely out of the match, was now in command of it. He needed barely twenty minutes to polish it off, bearing in without letup behind his service and getting down to his volleys impeccably. As for his nemesis across the net, there was no sign now of the legendary Rosewall precision. He kept hitting wide or hitting long. The set went to Stolle, 6–1, and the match with it.

"That must be the worst Rosewall has played in a long time," the host pro, Robert Lansdorp, said afterwards in the clubhouse, where most of the scant crowd took shelter while awaiting the doubles. "Maybe the worst since Connors cleaned him out at Wimbledon and Forest Hills the same year. All those forehand errors! It's a shame to see a man get so upset with frustration, missing shots he used to get."

The ensuing doubles was mercifully restricted to one pro set, in which Laver and Rosewall mauled Scott and Krishnan, 10–4. The cheers were thin but grateful when the match ended —with a ball that blew so far out of court that nobody bothered to chase it. The ballboys just turned and ran, teeth chattering, to their parents' waiting automobiles.

Watching with Whitney

OVERNIGHT the gale mercifully died down to mere windsurfing velocity. The temperature still hung around mulled-wine levels, but for the West End finals I had the heartwarming company of one of the Grand Masters old boys—a former Number 1 American tennis player, the famous Whitney Reed.

The famous Whitney *who?* Former number *what?* Even among tennis scholars, the name is hard to place.

Over the years about seventy ex-champions of various nationalities have competed in the Grand Masters, and that roster includes a few whose names, while inscribed on significant trophies, are scarcely recognizable to the average tennis fan: Tom Brown, Hugh Stewart, Bob Howe . . . or try Giuseppe Merlo, better known as Beppe or "Little Bird." ("Merlo" is Italian for "blackbird.") He was an Italian clay-court specialist turned stockbroker. He was distinguished by a slight build, an ingratiating disposition, and an impenetrable accent that made his English grammar sound more skewed than it really was. "I prefer to spend my life in the tennis," he declared, upon renouncing the securities business. "I am more happy."

Merlo's style was as soft as his voice. You could barely hear the ball come off his loosely strung racquet. Yet he had given world-class players fits on the slow European surfaces, recording wins, for example, over Laver and Seixas. He hung on for six seasons in the Grand Masters.

Now what about Whitney Reed?

Whitney Reed is one of the most obscure champions of that

period in which American tennis was almost totally eclipsed by the brilliance of the Australians.

What was he champion of?

His titles include the 1960 U.S. Hardcourts (a crown also held by such distinguished players as Ted Schroeder, Alex Olmedo, Ramanathan Krishnan, Arthur Ashe and Stan Smith) and the 1961 Canadian Singles (succeeding a player whose name may be the ultimate tennis trivia answer: Ladislav Legenstein). Whitney was on America's 1961 Davis Cup team, which never got to play the Australians because it was defeated en route to the challenge round by Italy.

Whitney Reed's eminence, such as it was, lasted only briefly. In two years he climbed from Number 9 in the national rankings to Number 1. The year: 1961. Two years later, he was, in the phrase of tennis commentator Bud Collins, "returned to oblivion." That is, until his reemergence in the Grand Masters, in which he played for half a dozen seasons during the late 1970s and early 1980s, leaving behind him a trail of Whitney Reed stories almost as long as the literature about the deeds of Kenny Rosewall and the words of Torben Ulrich.

Whitney Reed stories are not usually about his tennis but about his distinctive personal style. In contrast to enthusiastic Jack Kramer and hustling Bobby Riggs, Whitney belongs to the modern, surfer-dragster breed of California kid. Even in his fifties, Whitney is so laid-back that he seems practically horizontal. His conversational manner has been compared with that of the comedian George Carlin's "hippy-dippy weatherman," the character who talks the cool jargon of the spaced-out 1960s. The stories Whitney tells about himself have the blurry quality of the morning after—of a man struggling, though not too hard, to recollect events of the night before.

Sometime after his abrupt decline from the top of the rankings, Whitney once recounted, he went to play a tournament in Las Vegas one weekend, but forgot to tell his wife.

"Couple of years later I was still in Vegas," Whitney said in his slurry style, "and she got in touch with me. I asked her 'When did you notice I was gone?'

" 'About a year ago,' " she said. Whitney went on without a

pause: "That's when I began to realize the marriage wasn't working."

About Reed's abrupt decline in the rankings, a theory has been seriously advanced that it was caused by his selection to the Davis Cup team. The training routine got him into condition, a state he wasn't accustomed to. Being in shape apparently threw him off his game.

One Whitney Reed story is part of the lore of "shamateurism." At a club tournament party a woman ingenuously asked Reed, then the top-ranking American amateur, how he managed to support himself while devoting so much of his time to tennis.

Whitney told her, "I have a paper route."

If you want to be serious about it (as Whitney never was), in the course of his tennis career he worked at a variety of sidelines, including driving a cab and tending bar. His playing style was almost as unfocused as his lifestyle. Or perhaps I should say *is* almost as unfocused, since he continues to play tournaments as a senior. He won the U.S. Hardcourts title for fifty-year-olds in 1983, some twenty-three years after his original championship on that surface, and he has also won the national doubles in that age group on grass and indoors.

When I watched Reed play during his Grand Masters seasons, I was struck by his long, somewhat flat-footed stride—a contrast to the slightly pigeon-toed short steps of most topflight tennis players. As Bud Collins observed in one of the few pieces of tennis literature devoted to Whitney Reed, he never had much regard for footwork or body position, and his preferred stroke seemed to be the half volley. That was because he was forever being caught a half step in too close for a ground stroke, a half step late for a volley.

"Get a little older," Whitney said from a relaxed position in an armchair on the clubhouse deck at West End, "you hit a lot of half volleys because you're not really getting down to the ball. Begin to feel your age around here"—he rubbed his midsection, which looked only a shade bulky in a sweater and warm-ups. "Get lazy about coming in behind your serve.

"Frank Sedgman once made me sign an oath," Reed went

on, recollecting his Grand Masters experience. "We were supposed to play doubles together—can't remember what happened to his regular partner. Sedg wrote out this oath on a paper napkin the night before. Made me sign it. Said I'd promise to come in on my serve. Didn't say how long. I came in the first couple of times. I was puffing so hard I decided that was it."

Reed was one of many players whose introduction to the Grand Masters, with its serious competition and its rigorous, eight-man format, came as a painful shock. After several early losses, he said, "I began to wonder when was I ever going to get an easy first-round draw. Then I realized—*I* was the easy first-round draw."

Whitney's recollections emerged fitfully, in brief, laconic bursts, with a little prodding from his companion, an attractive, athletic-looking blonde named Joanna Jones, with whom he sometimes teamed in mixed doubles.

"You needed an early-round win in the Grand Masters," Whitney added thoughtfully. "Otherwise you'd hardly make enough to cover your hotel, your food and beverage. Well," he added, "the hotel was paid for, and food didn't come to that much."

Joanna shook her head fondly.

On the exhibition court below us, Al Bunis introduced the two Grand Masters finalists: Laver and Stolle.

"That's a Wimbledon final," Whitney said, and turned his attention to the court.

Midbreak

LAVER AND STOLLE never actually met in a Wimbledon final, but the match at West End between these two forty-five year olds had just enough high points to suggest a Grand Slam level of play. Also just enough lows to remind you that time had passed.

The first set was full of surprises: Stolle attacking successfully behind his serve in the face of some blistering Laveresque passing shots; Stolle attacking Laver's service regularly, also with some success; Laver attacking too, producing situations in which they sometimes stood face-to-face at the net. But Laver was misplaying volleys in clustered errors.

Rolling up a lead of 5–2, Fred seemed to have the Rocket under his dominance. Then he eased up on a couple of volleys, letting Laver back into points that Fred had all but clinched. And now Rod became Hot Rod, with a sequence of terrific shots: an excellent rolled-over backhand service return that was simply unplayable; one of his old forehand topspin passing shots, slammed on the dead run as he covered the entire breadth of the baseline; then a lovely lob, setting up an overhead for a point that broke Stolle's service.

Laver followed the break with a quick flawless service game of his own. At the crisis point of 5–all, these two tough servers then broke each other's service. After all the ups and downs, the set remained to be decided by a tiebreaker.

It proved even more surprising than the pattern of events that produced it.

Laver ran off a series of four winning shots, collected two

cheap points on Stolle errors, then served an ace for an unusual 7–0 win of the tiebreaker—and of a set I never thought he'd pull out.

The second set was comparatively routine. Stolle had left the gate open, Laver had come driving through in high gear, and he never stopped. He put the match away, 7–6, 6–3.

We were now four tournaments into the 1984 Grand Masters circuit—about one-third of the way through the schedule—and it seemed easy to forecast the winner. Laver or Rosewall; it was bound to be one or the other. Rod would win all the hardcourt events, Kenny would take the slow-surface ones. In the renewal of their old rivalry they were playing about as close to dead even as ever. Each had beaten the other once; each had beaten Stolle in the remaining finals. And nobody else had won a tournament. There didn't seem to be any room in this race for a dark horse, especially not my long shot, Mal Anderson, with his sometimes deferential mindset and his gimpy, forty-nine-year-old legs.

Three weeks later, at a Grand Masters tournament in Hawaii, Anderson—his sciatica relieved by a chiropractor—became the tour's first non-Laver, non-Rosewall winner. He didn't have Laver to contend with. Rod skipped the Hawaii tournament because he and Mary were visiting his family in Australia. But still, to win the event in Hawaii, Mal had to beat both Stolle and Rosewall. That wasn't chopped liver. Or crushed pineapple.

I missed seeing my horse come in. I had returned to New York right after the Los Angeles finals, responding to a summons from my precircuit life—a television project that I didn't have the strength of character to resist.

Was there a chance that I'd get to see Anderson—or possibly some other contender, who could only be Stolle—repeat the unexpected stunt? Could it conceivably happen often enough to make a race of the 1984 Grand Masters?

I would have to wait a while to find out, because Hawaii was the last stop on the spring leg of the tour. The troupe was now scattering, most of them to wherever home happened to be—some back to their office desks, some to nonplaying tennis assignments. They would not reassemble until October, when they would begin the year's final series of seven more tournaments.

Between now and then, there would be the kind of hiatus that is known in the television business as the "midbreak"— the lengthy, suspenseful pause between the halves of the hour, in which your attention is maintained through a long sequence of commercials by occasional assurances that "we'll be right back!" The five-month midbreak in the Grand Masters would be usefully filled. I intended to pursue answers to some questions that had been provoked by a season of senior-tennis watching.

I realized by now that my original impression of the Grand Masters was impossibly romantic. This was not a troupe of Ponce de Leons in white shorts, discoverers of some athlete's fountain of eternal youth. I had seen enough late swings and flubbed volleys to know that age had indeed had its effect on the old champions' game. And I had heard enough invidious comparisons between today and yesterday by the players themselves to confirm this sad conclusion.

But I had also seen some glorious tennis, shots that would have done credit to almost any Grand Prix hot shot, feats of skill and daring on the court, moments of speed and strength that took the onlooker back a couple of decades.

I had been struck by one inescapable fact: how much more of an effect physical condition had on the outcome of a match between seniors than between younger players. The whole history of the Grand Masters could be viewed as a triumph of fitness over superior skills: of Torben Ulrich outlasting Pancho Gonzalez, Gene Scott defeating Roy Emerson, Mal Anderson holding his own against the best of his era.

So I couldn't help wondering: Exactly what is it that age does to a tennis player's body, and how much of the damage is really inescapable? How much of it can be deflected by conditioning, by competition—maybe even by attitude?

I decided I ought to spend part of the midbreak by seeing a doctor. Probably several different doctors, specialists in the fields of geriatrics and sports medicine.

Now *there* were a couple of subjects that were rarely linked in anybody's mind until overage athletes like the Grand Masters came along to make the connection.

PART VI

Improving with Age

39

The First Thing to Go

THE GERIATRIC FACTOR in tennis—how aging affects your game and vice versa—has become a matter of more than specialized interest. Of the twenty-five million active tennis players in the United States—those men and women who get out on the courts at least three times a month—four million of us are over the age of fifty, and well over a third of those are past sixty.

The annals of the game offer us a good deal of encouragement. The records are full of achievements at ages unheard of in most other sports. There were those remarkable Gonzalez performances in open tournaments after he'd reached his early forties, and Rosewall's two Grand Slam finals against Connors when Kenny was on the verge of forty. There was Mulloy achieving a Number 5 ranking at forty and winning that Wimbledon Doubles at forty-four. And there was Seixas competing in the U.S. Singles at Forest Hills just after his forty-sixth birthday.

Don Budge at forty—according to a qualified judge, Jack Kramer—was hitting the ball better than ever.

Gottfried von Cramm played on the German Davis Cup team when he was forty-four.

Jean Borotra, who won Wimbledon in 1924, played for France almost twenty-five years later, at the age of forty-nine.

The Grand Masters merely stretched the limits a little further.

But nobody in this distinguished company, it's safe to say, actually escaped the aging process. Everybody feels its effects, a little sooner, a little later, one way or another.

The old locker room cliché tells us that "the legs are the first thing to go." World-class seniors tell a different story—several different stories, in fact.

Vic Seixas was a player whose game pretty much depended on his wheels; speed and court coverage were his main assets. It was not until his midforties that he realized he had lost something. It was not his mobility, it was his first serve, which was coming back at him sooner and harder than it used to.

Frank Sedgman was another speedster—certainly one of the fastest in the history of the game—who should have been aware of any wobble in his underpinnings. But the first thing to go according to Sedg is the *return* of service.

Jack Kramer had that painful arthritis of the hip. But his first intimation of age, he says, was a tactical failure: He couldn't seem to finish off a point when he thought he had it clinched. The ball would come back, the rally would go on.

Gardnar Mulloy first began to measure the passage of years not by anything that happened on the court but by how he felt afterwards: by the loss of recuperative powers. At forty-five he noticed that after a tough match "my bones ached, my joints stiffened up, and next day my muscles would be sore . . . I began to feel it wasn't worthwhile any more." The aches persisted but the feeling didn't last. Twenty-five years later Mulloy was still playing.

His old doubles partner, Bill Talbert, thinks the first sign of age "isn't anything physical at all—it's the loss of the mental edge that often means the difference between winning and losing at the top levels of the game."

Most current members of the Grand Masters—all between their midforties and midfifties—seem to share one particular physical complaint. They all talk about being "late picking up the ball visually," as Rod Laver put it. They find indoor play and subpar lighting more bothersome now than they used to.

Not a word about the old legs.

Certainly it's not because aging tennis players are miracu-

lously free of problems with their wheels: Sedgman had those
Achilles tendon injuries, Anderson his sciatica, Seixas had bad
knees. Hardly any of the players were free of knee or hip pains,
and they were subject to pulled tendons and muscles: calves,
groin, hamstrings. But, perhaps because they lived with the
same problems all their playing lives, they tended to associate
the pains not so much with age as simply with tennis—with the
routine of a professional athlete.

Age, in the player's view, is something that happens to your
game—and only incidentally to your body.

Don't think for a moment that world-class players *ignore* the
aging process. In a way they pay more attention to age and its
consequences than most of us do. They factor it into their tennis
continuously, almost automatically. The very act of playing the
game competitively after forty-five is a matter of adapting to age
and compensating for its losses.

"You're compensating all the time without even thinking
about it," Gene Scott told me. "But it's also a conscious act. If
you're concerned about mobility as I am, with my bad hip and
my kind of game, then you're aware that you can increase mobility by losing some weight and by being sure to stretch your
muscles carefully before going on the court and after you come
off."

Scott's kind of game is not a bad model for seniors since it
depends less on power than on getting to the ball, meeting it
firmly and putting it in the right place. When it came to the
stretching routine, I noticed, he didn't just give it a lick and a
flex. He would go through a measured program of exercises,
one by one.

Most of the players will tell you they have also adapted their
strategy to age. They all claim to play more conservatively than
they used to. But in their book "conservative" doesn't necessarily mean "defensive." On the contrary, it sometimes requires playing more aggressively than you might have done in
the same circumstances when you were younger.

Fred Stolle came off the court one day after a match under
a hot Florida sun, and a very hip young woman reporter—she

had the look of a hitter herself—expressed surprise at how often Fred had serve-and-volleyed on the slow clay. Her tone of voice clearly indicated that she considered the tactic foolhardy.

"I'm an old man!" Fred protested, mopping his reddened face. "I couldn't stay out there and rally, could I? I was just trying to end the points as early as possible."

"Of course," says Sven Davidson, talking about the old boys' use of the attacking style, "you don't charge the net like a bull; you play within your physiological limits."

Sven, a man with a background in science and mathematics, is one of the few players who even refer to physiology when discussing age. And even he does so rather gingerly.

"The main difference between age fifty and age twenty-five," he once told me in his rather professorial style, "is a decline in the explosive power of your muscles. Whatever that means. It has to do with some kind of acceleration that occurs just before your racquet hits the ball."

I had never heard about that "explosive power" before. It sounded to me as if Sven was onto something. It was worth checking out with the sports scientists.

Sports scientists include researchers and practitioners trained in various special fields of medicine and biology, which they apply to exercise and physical competition. Some of them do indeed use the term "explosive power," meaning "the maximum use of all muscle fibers in arms or legs at a particular instant." In effect, it's what determines your strength and your speed.

That definition was supplied to me by Jack Engsberg, an associate professor in the Department of Sports Sciences at the University of Denver. His own special field is biomechanics, which is basically the study of muscular activity in movement and exercise. Some of his colleagues specialize in such areas as orthopedics (medical treatment of muscles, bones, tendons), nutrition and psychology.

I asked Engsberg how that critical muscular explosion was affected by age.

The answer was a one-paragraph course in basic biology. As you grow older, he explained, your metabolism slows down—the food you eat is less efficiently converted to energy and tissue, including that crucial form of tissue: muscle fiber. You actually start losing muscle fiber—losing strength.

"This aging process—it's inevitable," Engsberg continued. "A professional athlete, who has reached a high level of conditioning, is bound to decline, although there are exceptions. Some athletes have made their muscles more efficient by changes of technique."

I translated that into Gene Scott's late mastery of a topspin backhand—into the idea of learning at an advanced age to turn your shoulders for the backhand or taking the ball earlier on the rise. Engsberg didn't find fault with any of those examples. He went on to offer a further note of encouragement.

For the nonprofessional, or club-level athlete, who starts from a lower level of conditioning, it is possible not just to increase efficiency but even to increase the basic explosive force. You can do this, he said, by "strength training," which includes calisthenics, drills and playing the game, as well as the kinds of programs done on exercise machines.

"Muscles respond to training," he wound up cheerily. "It's possible to be stronger and faster at fifty than you were at twenty-five."

I tried that idea on Torben Ulrich, that remarkable specimen of fitness after fifty. He wasn't impressed. The importance of speed and strength, he said, is too easily exaggerated.

"Force is only one factor in putting the ball away, isn't it?" Torben said. "Control is another. Speed is only one factor in reaching the ball where it's been hit by your opponent. You don't need quite so much speed if you have anticipation—knowing where the ball is going to go from the memory of many previous times in the same situation. Some players have that to an extraordinary degree from the beginning. But with everybody it continues to improve with age. With experience.

"Krishnan, for example. He was always rather heavy, you know? Even when he was a semifinalist at Wimbledon, he was heavy. You didn't think he could ever reach the ball if you hit away from him. But he had such a marvelous sense of where the ball was going to land, from the instant it came off your racquet. He was always there waiting for it.

"Or myself. I don't know how often I've played Rosewall and found myself remembering, as soon as I saw his racquet meet the ball, 'Well, now, when he hits that shot in that way the ball goes crosscourt and it hits the sideline with just a little underspin.' All this in an instant, you know—it's thinking without thinking."

He gave a rueful little chuckle. "Unfortunately," he added, "I also remember that too many times there's no way to return the shot."

No question—strength and speed aren't the only important attributes in tennis. Or in most other sports. As another University of Denver expert, a former coach turned sports scientist named Dr. Marvin Clein, points out: Total performance in an athlete depends on two different sets of basic physical qualities. That "ability to exert an explosive force," says Clein, is only half the story. The other half he defines as "the ability to use oxygen . . . [which determines] the ability to sustain work over a period of time."

Unscientifically speaking: *stamina.*

That term "work" also requires translation. Science uses it to mean any kind of physical effort, including what the rest of us would call "play."

Oxygen of course is what the muscles require in order to produce energy.

This is the province of the heart, the organ that distributes oxygen to the muscles by way of the bloodstream. This is where the aging factor in tennis also becomes a risk factor. But not in the way—and not to the degree—that many people think.

Sven Davidson happens to know a lot about this part of the tennis/aging story. Not just as a matter of scientific theory but from personal experience.

31

Vital Signs

SVEN DAVIDSON is a tennis player to whom "sudden death" is more than a form of tiebreaker. It's a biographical episode.

At the age of fifty-two, en route to his eighth season in the Grand Masters, Davidson had the kind of experience that summons up the worst fears traditionally associated with playing strenuous sports in middle age. What sports medicine has been teaching us recently is that many of these fears are based on misunderstandings about the capabilities of the human constitution and how it is affected by exercise. The Davidson episode, dramatic as it was, can just as sensibly be read as a message of encouragement to aging jocks. As long as the reader doesn't overlook the caveats it also contains.

It happened on a tennis court, on a balmy January day in Los Angeles. Davidson, a Swedish expatriate living in the nearby town of Arcadia, was visibly in tip-top shape as always. A crew-cut model of disciplined athlete—six feet two and a half inches, a well-muscled 181 pounds—he had given up the computer software business at the age of forty-five to return to tennis as a professional competitor. The transition, extraordinarily difficult at best, might have been impossible if not for Davidson's lifelong habits of physical conditioning. His regime of running and calisthenics had helped make him Sweden's greatest tennis player before Bjorn Borg, Europe's best in the late 1950s and one of the top five players in the world at that time.

In the Tennis Grand Masters, Sven reached a second, late peak of success in 1979, beating Frank Sedgman in that year's championship final and finishing as overall runner-up in the tour.

The following year he had a scary experience during a trip to his native Sweden. At a railroad station he had collapsed under the weight of seventy-five pounds of luggage—normally no sweat for a man of his strength. He had keeled over backward, falling down a short flight of steps and smashing his head on a concrete pavement. In the emergency room of a local hospital, an electrocardiogram registered no heartbeat—he was cardiologically dead—until repeated jolts of electricity finally stirred the organ back into motion. He was diagnosed as suffering from an acute viral infection of the heart muscle, and stayed in Sweden for a month of recuperation. A month after that, he went back on the Grand Masters tour, winding up the season with moderate success.

Now, on his adopted home turf in Southern California, Sven was preparing himself for the 1981 tour by playing a local tournament in Los Angeles—a small open event he had won the previous year. His opponent was a teenager, and fifty-two-year-old Sven was winning without too much difficulty, 6–1, 5–4, 30–all, when something happened that he later described to his colleague Gene Scott, who told the shattering story in his *Tennis Week* column.

. . . The tall Swede came to the net behind serve and was passed cleanly down the line [Scott wrote]. "Nice shot," Davidson smiled. Quickly he realized he couldn't move his legs.

"In a flash I knew it must be my heart," Davidson recalled. [My first thought was] 'Please get an ambulance.' My next thought was 'Don't bang your head like last time.' Slowly I went down on my left side and over on my back. I felt very tired. As I rested my elbow on the court, I felt my head hit the pavement. And then total darkness."

A young man and woman kept Davidson going with CPR for the eight minutes it took the paramedics to arrive.

"I came to after ten minutes or so and heard a siren wail close by. It was an eerie feeling. The siren was for me. The ambulance drove me off. I drifted in and out. I could give my name and phone number. Jesus, I was sure I was going!"

[In] the Glendale Hospital's emergency room, Davidson's heart

started to fibrillate. This time the doctors understood the attack was
no viral infection.

Fibrillation is a kind of rapid, ineffectual twitching of the
heart muscle, in contrast to its usual rhythmic pumping action.
CPR, of course, is cardiopulmonary resuscitation—mouth-to-
mouth breathing alternating with chest-pumping movements
by hand. Davidson was in the throes of a myocardial infarction
—a heart attack causing damage to the organ. It had resulted
from blockages in the coronary arteries caused by a buildup of
plaque, or fatty deposits, on the interior walls of these major
blood vessels. As in most cases, the buildup had been going on
undetected for years. It is generally presumed to result from an
excess in the bloodstream of that notorious enemy of middle
age, the fatty substance called cholesterol.

When you exercise—when you exert your muscles to any
degree—your body consumes more than its normal, sedentary
quota of oxygen. But when the blood vessels are obstructed,
the heart may be unable to pump blood through the narrowed
passageway at a rate fast enough to meet the body's increased
demands. The heart, itself the most vital of muscles, is denied
the oxygen *it* requires. Sometimes, under this stress, the heart
is thrown into the kind of spasm that Davidson's suffered—a
fibrillation affecting the chamber of the heart called the ventri-
cle—which kills sixty percent of its victims outright.

Mainly by the administering of oxygen and massive medication, Davidson was pulled through that crisis. Two weeks
later he underwent bypass surgery, replacing no fewer than five
sections of the artery that had been found to be obstructed with
healthy transplants from a vein in his own leg. Again, from
Gene Scott's report:

"I wanted to get well and make a little money as quickly as possible—the various hospital bills added up to over $30,000," Davidson
said without a trace of pathos towards himself. "Two months later I
was out on the court again hitting for 20 minutes or so to strengthen
my arm muscles. I couldn't run, or didn't want to, at first. But slowly
I came back and—surprise—never got tennis elbow. I lost 25 pounds
in the process of the operation so I wasn't carrying around any extra

weight. I discussed the situation with my wife and with my cardiologists, and the consensus was 'Let him play to his heart's content.' "

[On other occasions Davidson has indicated that the doctors were dubious but that he talked them into it.]

Four months after the operation Davidson played his first Grand Masters event of 1981, losing to Alex Olmedo in the first round, 6–2, 6–3. Six months later he had picked up wins over Olmedo and Whitney Reed and earned enough points to finish sixth in the final point standings.

"I don't feel I gambled with my life," Davidson said. "I am an optimistic person by nature. I don't smoke, no hard liquor, but I don't really watch any special diet. I know for some years I have guaranteed clean pipes in my heart. On the other hand, maybe—though I hope not—some of my fellow Grand Masters may have problems they are unaware of. Next month I'm going to start running again—more rookies to battle next year, you know."

The next year, 1982, turned out to be Sven Davidson's last in the Grand Masters. His only win on the whole tour was over one of that season's rookies, Ramanathan Krishnan. Sven finished last in the standings. Last and out.

I wondered if his exit had been hastened by his damaged heart. Even more, I wondered if it was tennis that had caused the damage in the first place.

I was disabused of that idea by my own cardiologist. "You cannot 'strain' your heart," I was assured by Dr. Allan Schwartz, when I consulted him in his office at Columbia University–Presbyterian Medical Center in New York. "There's no exertion that's damaging to your heart at any age."

Allan Schwartz is not a tennis player. He is a runner. He enjoys the same sort of addiction to that sport as the one connecting me to tennis. At the age of thirty-seven and a height of six feet one, he was a stringy 160 pounds and going for 150 in preparation for his next New York Marathon. He customarily finishes that mass competition in the top quarter of the field— somewhere in the first 4,000 out of 14,000 entrants. Running, he volunteers, isn't as hard as tennis. It doesn't require specialized athletic skills, the agility and the hand-eye coordination of racquet sports. But he translates his experience easily from one sport to the other.

If there is any risk in middle-aged tennis, Dr. Schwartz said, it is neither in the sport itself nor in the age of the player but in the possibility that the player might have some undetected heart disease, as Sven Davidson did. That possibility, he conceded, is one that does increase with age.

"A fifty-five-year-old guy going to his doctor and saying, 'Is it okay for me to go out and play a tournament tomorrow? It's going to be ninety-five degrees, and I've never played before' —sure, that doesn't make sense from a cardiological point of view. But the main risk is simply this: that as you get older, the chances increase that you might have some heart disease even though it has not yet caused symptoms—you have never felt any angina."

The sharp chest pains identified as angina are of course the classic signal of heart disease and often the warning of an impending heart attack.

The doctor continued: "If you do have an underlying heart disease—and about one in twenty men over fifty-five have coronary artery disease, for example—and if you take up some vigorous sport in an unsupervised way, then you can develop a problem. You are susceptible to heart attack.

"But there are other things that can happen to you. The possibility is even stronger that you might go out there and get a slipped disc. But that's no reason not to play tennis, as long as you do it in a commonsense way.

"So," he summarized, "from the cardiological point of view, in the absence of heart disease, there is no problem in playing tennis when you get older. On the contrary, even with heart disease, if it's known, you can get into quite vigorous exercise, as long as it's in a structured way."

"Structure," in my own experience, means an organized conditioning program gradually building up the heart's defenses, plus a continuing regime of medication of the kinds that have been developed in recent years. Plus regular checkups.

Meanwhile, it has been argued, since regular exercise is known to lower the level of that damaging fatty substance, cho-

lesterol, in the blood, then sports like tennis may actually reduce the chances of developing certain forms of heart disease.
And thus they may reduce the chances of suffering a heart attack in *any* kind of circumstances, including just sitting at your
desk or entertaining your mother-in- law.

That seemed to be the implication of a report that was released in the summer of 1984, while I was in the midst of this
inquiry. It was issued by a combined group of Harvard and
Stanford experts after a study of some 17,000 men, middle-aged
and older. The ones who exercised regularly, even in as mild a
form as brisk walking four times a week, tended to have fewer
problems of high blood pressure and other cardiovascular
ailments. Regular exercise, the study concluded, appears to reduce the risk of coronary disease in general by almost twenty-
five percent. I have since seen other authoritative statements
suggesting that the odds may be improved by as much as one-
half.

Dr. Schwartz counts himself among the medical authorities
who are leery of any proposition suggesting that exercise actually *prevents* heart attacks. "That's controversial. But," he
quickly added, "it's less controversial that regular exercise will
make it more likely that you'll *survive* a heart attack if it happens to you. Arthur Ashe had severe coronary heart disease, but
he didn't drop dead. [Ashe, the former U.S. Open and Wimbledon champion, was forced to retire from competition in his
midthirties, after multiple bypass surgery.] Because he's conditioned, his heart works efficiently. It was able to do a large
amount of work—in his case, supplying the oxygen required
for a lot of strenuous running and hitting—without producing
the symptoms of angina."

In an individual less well-conditioned than Arthur Ashe was
by years of tennis, the heart might well have been thrown into
a fatal spasm by less of a burden than it took to stop Ashe. In
other words, Arthur Ashe's life (and Sven Davidson's) may have
been *saved* by tennis. Which is the kind of news I like to hear
—as if I need it to reinforce my affection for the sport.

When it comes to the risk factor in old folks' tennis, I like
Jean Borotra's attitude. In the autumn of 1985 Borotra played in

an international club match—French team against British team
—at Wimbledon, where he had first won the All-England championship all of sixty-one years earlier, in 1924. Borotra was now
eighty-seven years old, and a reporter asked if it didn't worry
him to get on the courts at that vulnerable age.

No, said Borotra, the only thing that worried him was "the
feeling that I may die without having played enough tennis."

I don't want to overstate the medical benefits of tennis. I
value it as a sport, not a therapy. As a heart conditioner, while
it beats golf and bowling by a lot, it rates somewhere below
swimming, running, bicycling, rowing and even brisk walks.
All these have the virtue of being aerobic forms of exercise, in
which the action of the heart is constant and regular. Tennis is
anaerobic exercise; its basic pattern is stop-and-go.

You can actually build up your ability to withstand the stress
of that stop-and-go action by practicing wind sprints and quick-
start agility drills, just as you can build up your aerobic capacity
(that is, your stamina for long rallies and long matches) by a
regular program of running, walking briskly, swimming, rowing
or riding a bike.

The bad news is that you can keep improving only up to a
point, because your heart's efficiency—that is, the rate at which
it can distribute oxygen—is something that keeps declining
with age—like your metabolism. You can reduce the rate of
decline by exercise—reduce it by as much as half—but you
can't stop the inevitable downward process altogether.

"There's no question that age does work against you," Dr.
Schwartz, the medic-marathoner summarized. "A fifty-year-old
can train all he wants, he's still not going to become like Alberto Salazar."

Alberto Salazar, one of Schwartz's heroes, is a champion
distance runner still in his twenties. I mentally translated the
name to John McEnroe.

"But lots of people just get started doing strenuous exercise
in their fifties," the doctor continued. "And as I said, there's no
basic reason not to do this. At least the cardiological factors are
not normally the significant ones. I think the orthopedic factors

are more important in running *and* in tennis. You become a lot less flexible with age—your tendons, your muscles. You have to be meticulous about stretching, and that helps. But even with stretching, you are much more likely to tear an Achilles tendon as you get older, if you're a tennis player. Runners tear everything. The frequency of orthopedic injuries increases with age.

"But if you want to know what I think about the things that limit improvement in sports, I don't think they're aging factors at all. I think they're economic factors.

"The major thing that limits me and most people I know who love doing sports is that we have to work for a living. Bill Rodgers says he never lost a race to anybody who held down a job. [Rodgers, the winner of both the New York and Boston marathons, is another of Schwartz's heroes.]

"And even if you had all the free time in the world, it's hard beyond a certain point to keep from losing the will to train the way you must—to make the sacrifices, to be as single-minded about training as the serious pursuit of a sport requires."

32

Rx for Tennis

WHEN IT COMES to the orthopedic problems of tennis players—
tendons, muscles, bones; pulls, tears, fractures—there is probably no man with more world-class experience than Dr. Irving
Glick, the orthopedist who serves as official physician of the
U.S. Open. Dr. Glick is a slight, mild man in his midsixties,
with a benign manner and a combination of steel-rimmed
glasses, gray mustache and combed-back hair that reminds you
of the 1930s. I looked in on him one day during the early rounds
of the Open, found him inundated by the normal tournament
caseload of groin pulls and muscle cramps, and made an ap-
pointment to consult with him about the training of aging tennis players sometime after the tournament, when the pressure
would be off.

The aging process in *professional* athletes, Dr. Glick began
by way of introduction when we regrouped some weeks later,
is partly a factor of injuries: "all that repetitive running and
jumping and banging around, all that wear and tear of the joints
and tendons."

But for most of us *part-time* jocks, he said, it's mainly a
combination of genetics with other, controllable factors, like
what we eat and how and where we live.

"We know that the cell membranes suffer a degeneration
over the years through the effects of many things like cigarettes,
alcohol, various pollutants in the air you breathe. Well, diet
also plays a very significant role in the aging process. Fats tend
to oxidize—a process that's injurious to the tissues over the
years. Deposits of fatty substances narrow the blood vessels in

time, and that slows down the circulatory system. I think much of the fatigue we associate with aging is a matter of nutrition as well as physical training or the lack of it."

Diet is a subject that both fascinates and repels people like me who have been fighting a lifelong battle against chronic overweight—and usually losing without even going to a tie-breaker. But win or lose, it's a subject that can't be avoided in the context of sports and aging.

Until only about the last decade or so, tennis players, like athletes in general, swore by red meat—lots of steaks, chops, hamburgers and other macho forms of protein—as the basic diet. Beef was regarded as the best source of strength with the least risk of gaining weight.

Perhaps the height of this misguided faith was achieved by Vic Seixas, in an incident he describes in his published reminiscences. When he went to England for the 1952 Wimbledon with, he figured, a reasonable shot at the title, he was concerned about getting enough protein to carry him through the tournament—meat being scarce in that country, which was still suffering severe postwar shortages. So Vic prudently took with him no fewer than thirty steaks, packed in dry ice. He turned them over to a restaurant to store and to serve as required—like medication or magic.

Seixas's careful planning turned out to be not only unscientific but overoptimistic. When he got bounced in the quarter-finals (by Herb Flam) he still had nineteen uncooked steaks left. He handed them out to other patrons of the restaurant before he left.

Seixas never blamed his defeat on protein, and it's probably just a coincidence that the following year, taking potluck with the British food supply, he won the tournament. Nevertheless, as nutritionists nowadays point out, and as everyone who has even been glancingly touched by the fitness boom has been made aware, protein is hardly a source of energy; it's the last form of nutrient the body draws on for fuel, the hardest kind of food to metabolize. Red meat, furthermore, tends to be high in fats, the stuff that sticks to you the most, building up unwanted weight.

Physical activity is no real antidote, and tennis even less so than a number of other sports, especially when it's played at a casual, hacker's level. Researchers have calculated that the average male, consuming the average American intake of three thousand calories a day and playing singles at an *above*-average pace using five hundred calories an hour, would have to get in an hour of singles every day just to lose a single pound in a week. Granted, that's more than you'd take off sitting around a pizza parlor or fishing or playing cards—still, it's less than you can shed in an hour of jogging, squash or cross-country skiing.

At the world-class level the consequences of being overweight are obvious and they are severe. You can't help notice that it's the players who have gained the most around their waistline who have lost the most in their games.

In spite of that fact, when it comes to diet, the Grand Masters seem to cheat like the rest of us ordinary mortals. Beer remains the Aussies' staff of life. And though all the players pay some attention to the current emphasis on the lighter forms of protein—fish and chicken—the standard tournament lunch, and often the postmatch supper, is a hamburger or a hot dog. Hamburgers, of course, are one of the fattiest forms of protein, and hot dogs have been rated X—flat out unacceptable—by a panel of nutritionists dealing with diet for active individuals over fifty.

The one rule the players seem to take seriously is the rule of moderation. They do not overeat. But otherwise they remain captive to the old training-table eating habits.

"We were victims of ignorance about training techniques," Gene Scott says about his years as a young player on the circuit and in the Davis Cup. "It's annoying to think how much things have changed. Not just diet but the whole subject of conditioning."

When Scott first started to work out with weights, some years ago, it was contrary to the traditional training methods in tennis. The official wisdom held that weightlifting and other muscle-building exercises would inhibit the flow of your tennis strokes. Scott took up weights originally to combat a case of tennis elbow that resisted other forms of treatment. He became aware that any time he began to feel a twinge, he could get over it in a couple of weeks by exercising with light weights. "Conversely," he recalls, "after a few months without weights, I'd begin to get elbow again." Now weight workouts are part of Scott's routine.

Not all of the seniors are converts to muscle building, but they all have been affected to some degree by the fitness revolution.

"We do some things now for fitness that were practically unheard of in our own Davis Cup days," Neale Fraser, the Davis Cup captain, told me. "Stretching, for one thing. Our idea of loosening up in the old days was to go out on a court and hit for five minutes before a match. We used to do all our gymnasium work prior to the season or prior to a tournament. Now you exercise along with your match play. I still don't do as much of it as I should."

"Years ago," chimed in his old teammate, Mal Anderson, "when you pulled a muscle, first thing you did was put heat on it. Now you treat it with ice—keeps the swelling down. We didn't even know that! About weights, though, I wouldn't recommend that for a tennis player. I think Neale will agree."

Fraser nodded. "The playing that you do is much more important, as far as building up your strength."

Dr. Glick, the U.S. Open tournament medic, agrees with that proposition, especially as it applies to older club players.

"At that level of the game," he told me, "weights are not terribly useful. It's not that weight lifting will make you 'muscle-bound' as some people think. But you don't need that much buildup in strength to swing a twelve-ounce tennis racquet, and the risk of injury from using the weights is more than the potential benefits.

"Same thing with running," he volunteered. "We see a lot of muscle tears and stress fractures, mainly involving the bones of the feet."

For aerobic exercise, to build up stamina on the tennis court, Dr. Glick recommends jumping rope or using a small trampoline, either of which jars bones and joints less than running, especially when the running would be done on city pavements. He is also an advocate of fast walking—"an excellent form of exercise, good for the heart, easy on joints and tendons." He doesn't push, but doesn't discourage, the agility drills favored by some sports-medicine experts, a standard one being to sprint the width of the court, bend the knees and touch the sidelines or pick up and lay down a racquet.

Half of Dr. Glick's private practice consists of tennis players and their musculoskeletal problems, and the greatest numbers of injuries he is called on to treat among club players consist, not surprisingly, of knee and shoulder traumas and that old favorite, tennis elbow. A lot of these injuries, Glick says, result from faulty technique. This is especially true of elbow, which in the professional player is usually caused by overuse. In the club player it most often develops when shots are hit with a flexed wrist instead of a firm one, especially on the backhand. The tendency to wrist the backhand, in turn, most often reflects a stance that is too open—a failure to make that crucial turn of the leading shoulder toward the net before stepping into the ball.

There seems to be no sure and simple remedy for tennis elbow. Some victims respond to rest, others to a program of graduated exercises, with or without light weights, with or without cortisone shots to deaden the pain while the remedial exercises are undertaken. The one common factor seems to be that the problem is likely to recur unless the faulty stroke is corrected.

I asked Dr. Glick if he had any general advice to offer the club player of advanced age who wants to make the best possible use of his declining physical resources. The answers fell neatly into a list of Do's and Don't's:

· *Do drink a substantial amount of water both before and during a match.*

"Hydration has been one of our major problems in taking care of players here at the Open, to avoid muscle cramps and fatigue. What we've learned is that water is as good as any fluid, better than most. Half an hour before you play, you should have two or three cups of water—don't wait until you've started to perspire heavily during the match, which may be too late. But you should continue to take maybe half a cup of water during changeovers.

"Also, it's important to drink *cold* water, which is absorbed into the bloodstream more readily than warm water."

· *Don't take salt pills.*

"You need a certain amount of salt in your diet, but you probably get it with all the fast foods and prepared frozen foods that most people eat. We've learned that salt tablets really have a negative effect. The increased salt puts a burden on the kidneys. It tends to thicken the blood, and it makes you sluggish. It draws the potassium out of the cells—potassium is crucial to energy—and causes fatigue and possible muscle cramping."

· *Don't depend on sugar—a soft drink or a candy bar—for a quick energy pickup.*

"Sweets cause a temporary lift in the blood sugar, but then there is a sudden dropoff: a loss of energy, often hunger pains. Also, if you have a heavy sugar concentration it tends to lodge in the stomach instead of passing into the intestine, where it can be usefully absorbed."

Fruit and fruit juice are better sources of energy than any food containing processed sugar because the natural fructose is broken down more gradually—less of a sudden lift, less of a sudden drop. But even so, if you drink fruit juice before or during a match, Dr. Glick recommends diluting it with three or four parts water.

· *Do include plenty of fresh fruits and vegetables in your daily diet.*

The foods Dr. Glick emphasizes are dark green vegetables like spinach, along with fruits like bananas, melons, oranges.

These are all good sources of potassium, the energizing, anti-cramping mineral.

And as an "antiaging factor" the doctor recommends carrots and yams—vegetables rich in the substance called beta carotene, which deters oxidation of the cells and thus, he says, "keeps the tissues young." That is, it keeps the muscle fibers pliant.

· *Don't overload on beef and other forms of protein.*

Australian Davis Cup teams, the doctor concedes, reached their zenith on a diet based on steak, even for breakfast. "But I sometimes think they succeeded at tennis in spite of it rather than because of it. Red meat once a week—that's enough. Take it easy on other forms of fats, too, like butter and cheese. Use skim milk.

"The best source of energy, we've learned, isn't protein and it isn't sugar, it's a complex carbohydrate—something in the starch family like pasta or potatoes, as long as you don't load them down with butter or sour cream or something like that. Carbohydrates metabolize into a substance that can be stored in the liver, so that as it's needed it can be brought out by the body's mechanism and put into use to fuel the muscles."

Dr. Glick's idea of a healthy diet for a tennis-playing adult is a far cry from the average American's daily fare. Our ravenous appetite for junk foods has raised the consumption of fats to the point that they now represent no less than forty percent of the average diet, and protein represents thirty-five percent; carbohydrates the remaining twenty-five. A Senate committee study concluded that the carbohydrates figure ought to be raised to fifty percent. Dr. Glick would go even further, revolutionizing the diet to achieve a level of about seventy percent for carbohydrates, with only twenty percent fats and ten percent protein. That's a good balance, he thinks, for adult tennis players.

Irving Glick himself looks trim and fit enough to make you think he just may have hit on the right formula. He regards tennis as one of the consolations of age, and he is happily convinced that the quality of senior tennis keeps improving, both at the world-class level and among club players. He is equally convinced that individual club players can continue to lift their games even after they've passed fifty or, for that matter, sixty. He cites himself as an example. He must have been on some kind of roll at the time of our meeting because he talked about his game in the euphoric tone by which you can always recognize a club player who has been hitting the ball well lately.

The remarkable thing about Glick's improvement is that it came after a disabling injury. In his midfifties he was hit in the eye by a tennis ball and lost his depth perception. "It took me a year, year and a half," he said, "to pick up new visual clues. But I must say I am now playing at a level I didn't think possible for me. I'm hitting the ball harder and better than I have for a long, long time."

Glick thinks examples like his are partly explainable by the improvement in equipment as well as in conditioning methods. "The larger-sized racquet and the new racquet materials— that's been a renaissance for me. We senior players are also in much better shape than we used to be. We stretch properly, we're conscious of fitness, we're not carrying around all the obesity we used to."

He sounded to me like a man who was getting ready to join those elbow-braced, baseball-capped codgers on the senior tournament circuit, but he demurred.

"I don't play tournaments," he said. "If it got to be that serious for me, then I might as well spend the time working instead of playing tennis. Tennis to me is *play*. It's physical therapy, it's emotional therapy, it's recreation. I've been playing for fifty-some-odd years now, off and on. It helps me work better. I go back to my practice with less pressure, feeling relaxed. I'm able to get more professional reading done. I can keep up with research better.

"They talk about a runner's high. Well, I get a tennis high. So many of us do. That's enough to keep us seniors playing. We don't need the tournament trophies."

33

Survivor

THE 1984 RUNNING of the U.S. Open may have been a lively couple of weeks for Dr. Glick—all those dehydration cases and groin pulls—but for most tennis fans it was a dull affair, rescued from total forgettableness at almost the last possible moment by one day of total, exhausting, gratifying drama. That, as television viewers will remember, was semifinals day, an eleven-hour TV spectacle during which John McEnroe finally wore Jimmy Connors down in five sets after Ivan Lendl had done the same to the young Australian, Pat Cash. The final—McEnroe's wipeout of Lendl—was more of a footnote than a climax.

Until that one day of glorious battle, I would have said that the highlight of the 1984 Open for me was a second-round women's doubles match played on an obscure field court the Saturday before. What made it memorable wasn't so much the quality of play (although that wasn't bad at all) but the company I had for the match. I watched it with that fifty-six-year-old tennis didact and sports-medicine phenomenon, Sven Davidson, survivor of nine years in the Grand Masters and a massive heart attack, and, incidentally, the only player who ever volunteered for the Saturday morning clinic because he likes instructing people. *Drilling* them, some of his colleagues said, comparing his style to that of an Army sergeant at boot camp.

When I met Sven in the scoreboard plaza outside the stadium, I found him looking fitter than ever in his brightly colored warm-ups, with his graying blond crew cut. He had purposely kept off some of the weight he'd lost a few years before during his coronary episode, so the impression you got now was not just one of well-maintained muscle but of lean, tough rawhide.

He was carrying a tall paper cup full of some unappetizing orange fluid, which he kept stirring carefully like a chemist's formula. It was something he had to take, he explained, as part of an experiment involving heart patients for a medical research project. He sipped at it with an expression of cheerful tolerance belying a state of inner rage. It wasn't the drink he was sore at, or the researchers, he told me, it was the United States Tennis Association, which ran the U.S. Open.

"There is corruption and prostitution at the highest level of the USTA and at the second foremost championship in the world," he declared, fixing his eye on me like the scourge of God. "For TV advertising reasons, the ninety seconds' limit on change of court have become forty-five or sixty seconds longer. Which means that the weaker of the two players benefits more than the other from the changeover. Therefore," he went on, "the possibility exists that a player might have won a match that was televised who shouldn't have won it if they enforced the rule.

"Now that very thought is shameful! Despicable! And I am very sad that it has happened in this country because my wife is American and my children are American. [Davidson, a Swedish expatriate, lives in Southern California, and his son happens to be a career Marine officer.] But the fact is that the rules of tennis, which are universal, are not being enforced here. They are enforced in *non*televised matches—players are penalized there if they take thirty-two seconds between points or ninety-five on a changeover. But when it comes to televised matches —two minutes or more for a change of court! And for what? For money!"

I could have pointed out to him that a more basic corruption has been visited upon the game in the interests of TV bucks without bringing the sky down upon us. I'm referring to the tiebreaker, which was widely adopted in order to make the length of the tournament matches more predictable and thus better suited to the relatively inflexible programming schedules of the networks.

The tiebreaker introduced the alien idea of a limit into a game that had the beauty of being infinite—theoretically capable of going on forever if neither player could get the two-game edge required to end the final set. The twelve-point "lingering death"—the form of tiebreaker that has become prevalent—*is* theoretically endless in that the winner can't close it out until he's achieved a two-point margin. But it fixes a limit to the length of a set; in standard matches, the score can't go beyond 7–6. Therefore, as hardshell critics point out, the tiebreaker diminishes a factor that was once considered almost as important as strokes and tactics. That is the factor of stamina, both physical and mental. The tiebreaker, these critics argue, has made a tennis match less of a test and more of a crapshoot.

I might have raised this point with Sven Davidson. I miss those old 10–8 or 18–16 fifth sets that Pancho Gonzalez and Vic Seixas seemed to thrive on. But I have become reconciled to the tiebreaker, not so much because it has facilitated tennis on television but because it originated as a tennis idea not a media idea. Also because it fits in with the realities of the game as most people play it. Most tennis matches—that is, recreational tennis matches—do have limits. They must be played within an hour or two of available court time. The tiebreaker originated as a way of reaching a decision not just in a televised match but also in friendly competition, or within the restricted schedule of a weekend club tournament.

But as for the stretch-out of changeover time to accommodate TV commercials—now, that's a different matter. There's an issue on which I just might be willing to join Sven Davidson on the barricades.

For there is no *tennis* reason whatever for that change, only a media one. Also, it is not done openly and aboveboard—the USTA to my knowledge has never announced any such variance in the rules.

But finally there is no real necessity for it. The extra advertising is only an example of Parkinson's Law of commercial television: commercials expand to fill any amount of time that can be pried loose from program content (in this case, an athletic contest) without actually driving customers away.

Davidson's outrage at the corruption of his beloved sport wouldn't keep him from his daily seat at the U.S. Open. He was there not just as another spectator but as part of a new job. After leaving the Grand Masters in 1983, he had been engaged by the Swedish Tennis Federation to coach a group of that country's most promising young women. He was making a success of it. The Swedish women had burst onto the international scene that season on the heels of the young Swedish men who had invaded the top ranks of the Grand Prix tour. They were then en route to their stunning 1984 victory over the formidable American team of McEnroe, Connors and Peter Fleming in the 1984 Davis Cup.

Like the Australians in the 1950s, the Swedes in the 1980s kept coming on in a continuous wave: Mats Wilander, followed by Anders Jarryd, followed by Henrik Sundstrom and Joakim Nystrom and Stefan Edberg, with more promising kids visible in the wings. And now Sven's girls—in particular, Catarina Lindqvist and Carina Karlsson—were starting to attract attention, too, and not just for their blonde good looks. Like their male compatriots, their instincts favored the baseline (Edberg, an exception, is a relentless serve-and-volleyer), but I had no doubt that Sven would soon have them playing an all-court game.

Tall and imposing, Sven moved through the Saturday morning crowd at the Open with an energetic stride. I followed him to the bleachers flanking a field court where a pair of American women, Andrea Leand and Mary Lou Piatek, were hitting warm-up shots against Catherine Tanvier of France and a Scandinavian named Tina Scheuer-Larsen.

The Americans were seeded, the Europeans were a pickup team. But Sven had more than an ethnic rooting interest in the underdogs. For Scheuer-Larsen, though actually a Dane, was traveling as a member of Sven's Swedish contingent.

Sven's girl-by-adoption got off to a good start. A rather small, sweet-faced brunette, she did a nice job of setting up plays for her partner. Tanvier, a striking blonde with a macho style, did her part by putting away the winners. The European women earned themselves an early service break, and then hung on against a surge of pressure from the Americans.

It was Tanvier who put a crimp in their attack. Running a hot streak, she scored on two successive volleys hit solidly down the middle. Then she changed pace, stroking a perfect offensive topspin lob off her two-fisted backhand. It looped over her opponents, catching them both flatfooted as they charged the net.

An offensive lob hit with topspin off the backhand is not a routine shot. I remembered Gene Scott's pride at having pulled that shot off in his first match of the Grand Masters tour against Roy Emerson in Nashville. When I expressed my admiration for the way Tanvier had executed the shot, Sven Davidson nodded. But during the next change of court he launched into a Sven-like diatribe against the excessive use of topspin in general, especially the muscular form of stroking practiced by many current players.

"All this grunting that goes on with every stroke!" he exclaimed in a kind of angry whisper. We had taken seats in a high corner of the bleachers, and he was keeping his voice down so as not to disturb the other spectators or the players. "When I say, 'This is awful, this grunting,' I get the answer nowadays, 'Well, this is the power game.' And when I hear that, I retire from the conversation because I realize that they don't want to listen to anything.

"But I think they have missed the point entirely. Tennis is a game of harmony, of movement. It is ballet. Figure skating. It is not—pardon my English—fucking weight lifting!

"Look at this little Swedish girl, Carina Karlsson, who played such a good match here the other day. [Karlsson had drawn plaudits for her performance in a first-round loss to one of the best young American hopefuls, Patty Fendick.] She's very small and very light, still she hits very powerful shots. Why? Because she has exquisite timing. You don't have to have big bulging muscles to play tennis.

"To hit the ball in front of you, at the head of your swing—
that is what will carry the ball on its farthest trajectory, not to
hit it with the force of a blacksmith! Gottfried von Cramm explained it to us already forty-five years ago. 'The mark of aris-
tocracy in the tennis stroke, the mark of quality,' he said, 'is
neither force *nor* rotation' "—here Sven's voice, even at low
volume, took on its old professorial, Saturday-morning-clinic
tone—" '*neither force nor rotation. It is depth!*' "

Well, yes and no. Bill Tilden, who preceded von Cramm,
once devoted a whole book to "The Spin of the Ball," and his
key statement was that "the mastery and complete knowledge
of spin and curve of the ball is of paramount importance to a
tennis player." I would leave that argument to the ghosts of
Big Bill and the Baron, but I would not presume to argue
strokes with the tall Swede whose flat, fluid forehand I could
picture as it landed time after time in the deepest corners
of the court in Grand Masters matches against Ulrich and
Sedgman.

By invoking the name of Baron von Cramm, Sven had summoned up an era—the 1930s—whose style now seems almost
as foreign to tennis as long white pants. The German Davis
Cupper was not only a model of elegant stroking; he was not
only an outstanding competitor, a potential world champion
thwarted only by the presence of Perry and Budge, but he was
also a sportsman of exquisite sensibilities. He always introduced himself to other players simply as "Cramm" because the
aristocratic "von" and the noble title might give him a psychological edge. And in an era when a player would sometimes
throw a point deliberately to make up for a bad call in his favor,
Cramm raised sportsmanship still one notch higher—he *declined* to throw a point because that would insult the judgment
of the official.

Sven Davidson wasn't part of the 1930s scene—he missed it
by two decades—but he feels more closely attuned to the earlier era than the current one.

"I don't think I'm *too* conservative," he said, "but I definitely believe that the intellectual level of the game today is appallingly low but for a few guys—McEnroe and a few others.

"And as far as athletic skills are concerned, they say there are much better athletes playing the game today. Well, I don't know how they measure it, and I don't think they should underrate the athletes of previous years because they have been pret-ty solid guys!"

Down on the court Tanvier and Scheuer-Larsen had run out the first set with surprising ease, 6–2, but I don't think the coach had even noticed. "You know," he said, pursuing his argument, "they sometimes tell you, these advocates of the so-called modern game, that in all other sports the world records have been improved, so today's tennis players must be better than the players of previous generations. Well, I have been told by fellows that know a lot about golf that the clubs and balls are better, the courses are better. Then professional golfers should play a round of eighteen in about sixty strokes today. So isn't it funny that they still struggle around in sixty-six, sixty-eight, seventy, just like the champions did fifty years ago. So where does that leave you, young man?"

In defense of the older generation, he could also have cited boxers like Dempsy, Tunney and Joe Louis, for example, whom no one would hesitate to match against recent champions like Ken Norton and Larry Holmes. There are no current baseball players a manager would rather have than Ruth or DiMaggio. And a sports scientist, Gideon Ariel, has concluded from studies that Jesse Owens, wearing current shoes on a modern track with modern starting blocks, could beat Carl Lewis, the 1984 Olympian.

Sven Davidson preferred to pick his examples from other fields. "If everything progresses," he said, "then why are there not one hundred or more Mozarts or Bachs or Handels or Beethovens? And writers and painters and what have you? I do not choose these names foolishly, because there is something in tennis that is artistic that you don't have in some of the more measurable sports.

"I compare it with the capability to read. Now in Sweden

we have a literacy rate of close to one hundred percent. Does this mean that kids today read so much better than I did? In fact, there is a lot of evidence pointing out that maybe they don't even read as well as our generation. You have kids in your American school systems who come out after twelve years and they can't even write their own names.

"I think we all start from scratch. We don't build on the previous generation, not as individuals. Maybe the literacy rate is higher around the world today. And certainly I agree—there are *more* good tennis players now than there used to be. But the *peak*—is the peak higher or is it lower?"

The umpire announced: "Tanvier and Scheuer-Larsen win the first game of the second set."

Sven Davidson nodded but went on and answered his own question. "I would like to see Lew Hoad, Ken Rosewall, Frank Sedgman, Rod Laver against today's competition. I don't mean the way they are today, but the way they played at their peak, twenty or thirty years ago. I think they'd do very well. McEnroe, Connors, Borg—I don't know how the older group would fare with them"—he was being deliberately cautious now—"but most of the others? They'd be cut up in small pieces!"

Tanvier and Scheuer-Larsen now went on another roll, but Sven was scarcely paying attention—he was wrapped up in remembrance of games past.

"Ken Rosewall was the player I enjoyed playing against the most," he said, "because he made it such a *beautiful* game. But I mention Hoad, as I did a moment ago, because of his special quality of aggressiveness. He had a blacksmith's arms! He just put out his racquet and—Jesus! Two hundred miles an hour! Pancho Gonzalez told me once, when we were in the Grand Masters together, the toughest player he ever played against for a series of matches was Jack Kramer, for day in, day out consistency. But for one match, he said: Lew Hoad. He had tremendous respect for Hoad. I'd like to see Hoad—the *old* Hoad, the way he was in 1957—slug it out with any one of these big hitters today. I think he might hit right through them!"

It was the same story I'd heard from Gardnar Mulloy, back

in Boca Raton, and from a number of the other old players: The current generation has the depth, but the old-timers had the quality. Open tennis has produced professional players in great numbers, but the best of them—the McEnroes and Connorses —are no better, and probably not as good, as the best of the past: the Tildens and Budges, the Kramers, Gonzalezes, the Hoads and Lavers.

I asked Sven Davidson the question I had asked the other Grand Masters, and got the same kind of answer. How would he rate Sven Davidson, the fifty-year-old Grand Masters star, against Sven Davidson, the Wimbledon standout at age twenty-five?

"Oh," he said, "I don't think the latter-day Sven Davidson would have gotten a game. It's like the question Gerulaitis raised about women's tennis—could Martina beat the hundredth-best man? I am positive there are at least ten *thousand* men players that would beat her. That would *toy* with her. I mean, you *know* that. Men are simply better than women in tennis. Young players can beat old players in tennis. So what? That doesn't mean women's tennis can't be terribly interesting. Or senior tennis. I think even *mixed* can be a beautiful game. Any tennis match can be terribly exciting, even when the tennis is played at a low technical level, as long as the opponents are bloody evenly matched—when every ball is painfully important to the players."

Something caught his attention—something I missed—and he interrupted himself and leaned over to reprove a man sitting in front of us who had apparently been giving signals to the American women.

"Look here," said Sven, gently but firmly, "Tina Scheuer-Larsen is on my team, but I don't think we should do any coaching, either of us. You know there are penalties for that."

The man nodded, blushing. It's only in the Davis Cup that coaching is permitted during a match.

Within the next ten minutes or so, Sven interrupted himself several more times—once to exchange a few words in French with a Tanvier rooter, then to answer a question in Danish from a reporter for one of the Copenhagen papers, finally to express his disapproval of the practice of appearance money—expressing himself in fluent German to a tournament promoter from Cologne, who said he couldn't agree more.

I remembered something Neale Fraser had said once about the way that 1950s generation of Australian tennis stars had been developed: "Tennis was all we knew!" I hoped the Swedes, in developing their new breed of superstars, were paying attention to one of their own earlier models—to Sven Davidson, a tennis player who had also become an expert mathematician, selected his own models of excellence from the field of great music, regarded literacy as a matter of paramount social significance, and was articulate in five languages including his native Swedish.

It was interesting that, with all this—and after a career in one of the most dynamic fields of business, the computer field —in the end it was tennis that won him back. First and last, Davidson, no less than Fraser and Laver, Kramer and Riggs, was a tennis player.

For Sven, at fifty-six, taking on the coaching job was almost as venturesome a career move as the one he had made ten years earlier, when he quit the computer business to go back to tennis as a profession. The new job took him away from home— away from his wife and his two grown daughters in California —even more than the Grand Masters tour did. He had been traveling most of the spring and summer, first in Sweden, then on the women's tournament circuit.

I asked him how he liked his new role—whether it didn't bother him to be back on the sidelines after almost a decade of competitive play in the Grand Masters. He gave me a rather complicated answer.

"I enjoy getting out on the court with young players when they practice," he said, "to share with them whatever knowledge I have. I am still terribly concerned with the sport of tennis. But I am not *playing* tennis any more. It would *bore* me." He gave the four-letter word an emphasis worthy of a West End actor in a drawing room comedy. "I am not interested in tennis for exercise. Once I was out of the Grand Masters, I didn't have something to look forward to and practice for, so it became boring for me to play. I think that has to do with the competitive spirit.

"Perhaps you didn't see it in my behavior on the court, but that's because I learned something very early from my father. My father was very clever. He was an athlete, and when I had won something and I tended to be a little bit too enthusiastic, he told me, 'Sven, take it easy, you might lose tomorrow's match.' On the other hand, when I was depressed because of a loss, he told me, 'Sven, just practice hard and beat this guy the next time you get a shot at him.' So the end result of that is, I never looked jubilantly happy about winning, nor did you ever see any tears on my face when I lost.

"As far as my health was concerned, I could have kept playing in the Grand Masters after my heart attack. But I was Number eight on the tour—I was the weakest player. And as you know, I was used to being at least in the semifinals in singles and the finals in doubles."

The problem, in other words, wasn't playing with a damaged, aging heart. The problem was *winning*.

"I don't think we would have reached the point we did as tennis players," he said, "if we had not had the competitive instinct. I think that's something you have with you all the way through. And that's the way we played in my nine years in the Grand Masters. We fought like hell on the court, but we were good fellows after the match. We laughed with each other in the locker room, and then we went out and had beer and a poker game. And we didn't hate each other on the court, even when we slugged it out.

"And that," he concluded, "is why I am not playing tennis at all any more."

The final score of the doubles match was posted near the umpire's stand: 6–2, 6–2.

"Look!" said Sven. "Tina and Tanvier have brought it off! Straight sets!"

He stood up and applauded with the crowd, but he stood out from the rest of us—a tall, handsome, fifty-six-year-old man, his damaged heart concealed by the look of an athlete, the uncompromising style of a champion.

PART VII

Going for It

34

Fall Campaign

THE FRONT PAGE was full of embarrassing questions about the family finances of the Democrats' Vice Presidential candidate, Geraldine Ferraro—full of political trivia and hints of the impending Reagan landslide.

The sports pages rang with the season-ending feats of the Detroit Tigers and the Chicago Cubs, who seemed likely to meet in the World Series.

But the item that leaped out at me from the papers was an ad nestled among the box scores of the baseball playoffs. "They're back!" it said, as if announcing the reappearance of your favorite movie stars. Then: "Mutual Benefit Grand Masters. Braidburn Country Club. Florham Park, New Jersey."

It was the announcement signaling the start of the fall tour —the second and last leg of the 1984 tournament schedule. I sniffed at it happily, like a boozer waking to the smell of whiskey being poured.

Five months had passed since the troupe scattered following the last spring tournament. But during the hiatus I had caught an occasional glimpse of the old campaigners in the background of the tennis news.

For instance, when Pat Cash, the young Australian star, reached the semifinals of the U.S. Open (as he had at Wimbledon), his Davis Cup coach, Neale Fraser, was watching closely from the sidelines. Neale had been traveling the Grand Slam circuit, sizing up talent for the next round of Cup competition.

Fraser made a little news in his own right that summer. He was inducted into the Tennis Hall of Fame at Newport, joining the august company of Kramer and Gonzalez and Sedgman, Talbert and Riggs and Mulloy, not to mention historic figures like Bill Tilden and the turn-of-the-century Doherty brothers.

I knew that Krishnan had been in the stands at Wimbledon when his son Ramesh made a brave but disappointing third-round exit after eliminating the previous year's finalist—the climax of Krish Senior's annual month in London.

A couple of purely personal items caught up with me via the grapevine:

The Lavers had sold their ranch and bought a house farther down the California coast in Newport Beach. That made them neighbors of Roy and Joy Emerson.

And Whitney Reed, the old hippy-dippy tennis player, had married his good-looking mixed-doubles partner, Joanna Jones, in a ceremony performed on a tennis court. They sent me a wedding picture showing them emerging through an archway of crossed racquets held aloft by their attendants. With it came an announcement that the bride and groom were setting up shop as a team of teaching pros in a town south of Los Angeles.

The way Gene Scott had spent his summer vacation was doing what he called "the gritty business of finding sponsors" for his New Jersey Grand Prix tournament. Being a tournament promoter was obviously no piece of cake. I'd gone to that tournament, and I'd seen Scott, emerging from his office looking as played-out as if he'd just finished a fifth-set tiebreaker.

That same day I ran into several of the old alumni—Talbert, Riggs, Seixas. They were paying their dues to the game, playing in some sort of pro celebrity event at Scott's tournament, all doing their best to look interested in the desultory proceedings. Seixas was also working the tournament as a paid official of the Grand Prix organization—a kind of inspector, policing the event to make sure the international code was enforced.

I thought it was interesting that Vic, like Sven Davidson, had chosen to stay in tennis instead of returning to civilian life after his Grand Masters playing days were over. But Seixas made it plain that in his case, too, tennis had permanently won out over business.

"I didn't think I really missed tennis during the time I was away from it," he told me during a break in his official chores. "I had been a tennis player, period, until my midthirties—it was amateur tennis in those days, of course—and then I just had to start thinking about a career. I didn't want to turn pro, not against Kramer, and not against younger guys like Gonzalez, Sedgman and Trabert. I wouldn't have been able to make a living in that competition.

"I had majored in business at the University of North Carolina, so I surveyed the possibilities in that field. I rejected the insurance business because I tended to duck insurance salesmen myself. So I became a stockbroker. At the age of thirty-four. That was 1957.

"It took me a year to get used to an office routine, keeping a set schedule and wearing suits and ties. But for fifteen of the seventeen years I was a stockbroker I enjoyed it. I reconciled myself to being a weekend tennis player. I played an occasional big tournament—Wimbledon, Forest Hills. And then I got too old for that.

"But when the market went sour and I stopped enjoying being a stockbroker and the Grand Masters came along, I went back to tennis. It was really too late for me—I was fifty. I was giving away five years to guys like Sedgman and Gonzalez. My knees were shot. I had some other physical problems.

"But," he concluded, "I enjoyed it while it lasted. It made me realize I had missed the game, and I didn't want to leave it again."

He looked like an extraordinarily fit and youthful sixty-one-year-old in his tennis whites—not a hint of flab around the middle. And when I saw him a little later, conferring with the tournament's director-promoter, Gene Scott, near the trailer that was the front office, he looked like a very contented sixty-one-year-old in his tennis official's blazer and flannels.

Since I had spent part of my own summer break in the company of the sports medicos, living close to the subject of physical conditioning, I returned to my place on the sidelines of the senior tennis wars with a sharpened eye to the fitness factor.

After my first autumnal glimpse of the Grand Masters in action at the Braidburn club, I doped the field in terms of what shape they seemed to be in:

Laver—best record but looks a little soft.
Anderson—coming on and match-tough.
Stolle—always keen and fit.
Emerson—looking slightly trimmer.
Scott—lean if not mean, but needs practice.
Krishnan—still carrying too much weight.
Fraser—game but lame.

If Rosewall had been present, I'm sure I would have been able to place him right up there with Laver, with an entry something like this: "as always, hard as nails and just as tough."

But Kenny was still back home in Australia, detained by some personal business that would keep him from playing the first couple of events on the fall schedule. His absence probably disappointed a lot of New Jersey fans, but it had one happy effect. It made room in the draw for one of my sentimental favorites. A hurry-up call had been sent out to Frank Sedgman in Melbourne, and he had flown in, looking about as fit as a fifty-six-year-old grandfather can without being downright freakish.

"I keep myself in fairly good shape," he told me with more than a touch of pride. "It's all a matter of habit. I do some of the Nautilus thing, and I run four or five miles, about five times a week. I suppose I could do it better than what I do—run wind sprints and all that stuff. But the main thing is to keep your weight down.

"I generally do my running before breakfast—six-thirty or seven in the morning, before I go to my office, get behind my desk and get involved in all the daily phone calls and letter writing and all that sort of stuff. I might play a bit of squash two or three times a week. I don't play much tennis because there's not many people around for me to play.

"But I don't have any problem getting back into the game for a Grand Masters tournament. I hit backhands and forehands the same as I've been doing for twenty years." He caught himself and grinned, a curiously boyish expression coming over his weathered roundish face. *"Forty* years," he said.

In his first-round match Sedg gave an excellent imitation of a much younger man. The opponent he drew was Emerson. Sedgman went on the attack immediately, not just behind his own service but also against Emmo's—the old pro tour style in action. He was standing well inside the baseline when receiving—moving forward with the return, straining toward the net.

But in the end it was *only* an imitation. His legs just couldn't seem to carry him far enough forward to execute his game plan. Not fast enough or often enough. Serving at 3–5 and deuce in the first set, he became tentative, hung back for an instant, and got passed by Emmo's return. On the next point—set point— he got caught at the T by a return at his feet.

The Sedgman of even twenty years ago would have taken that return and converted it into a winner. That was Sedgman's signature—the winning volley from a deep position. In Jack Kramer's catalogue of the best shots in tennis (Vines's first serve, Segura's forehand, Budge's backhand, Gonzalez's half volley), Sedgman led the field in the first volley. According to Kramer, he seldom had to hit a second, because the first was always a putaway, especially off the backhand.

Frank Sedgman, age fifty-six, watched Emmo's return tick off the wooden frame of his Oliver racquet, shook his head and walked to the sidelines for the change of court. Set to Emerson, 6–3.

In the second set Frank began crowding Emmo's service even closer, so that he was often half-volleying the returns— and was actually making something out of the shots. But Roy, with a nine-year advantage in age, was in control and playing solid tennis.

At 2–5, Sedg pulled himself up for one last valiant effort, and salvaged the game with a booming service ace down the middle. That was as far as he could go. In the next game Emmo served out the match 6–3, 6–3. Sedgman picked up his racquets quickly and headed for the locker room, looking just a bit grim.

By the time I joined him for a beer in the players' lounge, he was viewing the result philosophically.

"I don't feel that much different today at fifty-six," he said, "to what I felt at forty-five. And at forty-five I still thought I could play with the younger kids. In fact, I played a few tournaments when open tennis started. I was forty-three then, but I beat a few of the good young players.

"But what happens is, your sighting of the ball sort of slows down, and you don't react as quickly as you used to. I used to stand in close for my returns all the time, the way I did tonight. I'd take the ball early and hit it hard. But I could do it better than I do now."

Again, the youthful, slightly bashful grin. Like a kid who's afraid he just said something immodest. The first time I met Sedgman, at a Grand Masters tournament party a half-dozen years or so earlier, he blushed when I asked him if he ever felt the impulse to test himself against some of the current young players.

"You mean *Connors?*" he said. "Or *Borg?* But they hit so *hard!*"

I was reminded then, and I was reminded again now, of an old photograph I had once seen in a tennis book—young Frank Sedgman, the likeable blue-eyed, auburn-haired Wimbledon singles champion, looking very debonair in white dinner jacket and black tie as he poured champagne for the women's champion, Maureen Connolly. Little Mo looked terribly young in a strapless evening gown, like a girl playing grown-up in her mother's clothes.

The year was 1952.

"That year I was superconfident," Sedgman recalled. "I was riding a high. You know, you get that feeling you're going to win, no matter what. I must have played ten months of the year, and I was in the final of every tournament I entered, singles, doubles and mixed. That was my great quality: consistency of performance. I think I lost four singles matches all year, and I lost two doubles. My partner was Kenny McGregor, and that's all we lost all year. Sometimes I try to figure out how much money I would have made nowadays, with that kind of record."

There was no reticence in Sedgman now, no fear of being

immodest. He wasn't bragging about himself, after all. He was talking about somebody else—a tennis player of three decades ago, who also happened to be named Frank Sedgman.

It was in 1952 that Sedgman and McGregor came within an eyelash of duplicating an extraordinary achievement they'd recorded the year before—a Grand Slam in doubles, the only one in the history of the game. They missed the second when they were beaten in the 1952 finals at Forest Hills by an Aussie-Yank duo, Mervyn Rose and Vic Seixas.

A year later, Frank Sedgman was a professional tennis player, making his living by challenging Jack Kramer two or three times a week, head to head, on a barnstorming tour. Sedgman had caught his first glimpse of Kramer in 1946, when Big Jake was starting to make a run at the amateur laurels, and young Sedgman was just a promising Australian junior, Harry Hopman's discovery. Kramer, leading America's first postwar Davis Cup team, had made a lasting impression on the young Aussie.

"He was head and shoulders above the best Australian players of that time," Sedg recalled. His statement encompassed some outstanding talent—Jack Bromwich, Adrian Quist, Dinny Pails, all members of the Aussies' squad. "Everybody thought Kramer was frightened of our players, because he didn't play any of our tournaments, he just practiced. And then he came out in the Davis Cup and killed them all. He was just too good for them."

Sedgman's respect for Kramer was confirmed by his experience on the pro tour. Kramer had the shots—that devastating forehand approach down the line and a service that Sedgman ranks close to Gonzalez's fearsome weapon. Kramer had the smarts—his command of the court, based on that poker-table knowledge of the odds on various strokes and situations, was like Hannibal the Great's command of ancient battlefields.

But what made Kramer too good for the pro challengers, as he'd been for the amateurs of his day, was a quality above and beyond tactics and mechanics. That was his ability to keep up the pressure, keep up the attack without suffering wild streaks:

strings of errors or lapses of concentration. Kramer was able to maintain a high level of performance, game after game throughout a match, match after match throughout the tour.

That's the way Sedgman describes the special quality of Kramer's game, but he firmly declines to name Big Jake—or any one else—as the best he ever played. When it comes to that favorite game of picking the "All-Time Best," Sedgman doesn't participate.

"You get asked that a lot," he said, "but it's really hard to compare, isn't it? You'd see Kramer play very well, but I also saw Budge play very well indeed. And Lew Hoad—I saw Hoad play a great Wimbledon final, when he just blasted Ashley Cooper off the court. [It was the same awesome performance that Krishnan once described to me in detail.] But on some days Hoad would play just terrible—his concentration wasn't good."

That was a comment frequently heard about Hoad—one Lew subscribed to himself. Once, he told an interviewer, after winning two sets in an important match, he found himself trying to think of the name of a boxer—one of those Thailand bantamweights with multisyllabic names that sound like the repeated striking of a gong. He never came up with the name and never got the third set either, losing the match in the fifth.

Jack Kramer, who called Hoad "potentially the greatest tennis attraction of all time," said that what Hoad lacked was "intensity" and a sense of the odds. Like Jimmy Connors and Evonne Goolagong, the graceful Australian women's champion of the 1970s, Lew Hoad was, in Kramer's phrase, "always drawing for an inside straight."

Sedgman thought of another candidate for his pantheon of outstanding players. "Rocket—I played against him when he played real well. For a period of two years there, he was like McEnroe today; nobody could get near him. He'd hit those passing shots on the run—whoosh! This high over the net"—he held his hands close together, palm above palm—"and this far from the line"—the hands held vertically, not much farther apart—"and he'd hit 'em either way, crosscourt or down the line."

The beer supply in the clubhouse bar hadn't been exhausted, even though the place was full of Australian tennis players, so we ordered another while I directed Sedgman back to his own experiences on the pro tour. He is another one of those players for whom that subject evokes no nostalgia.

"The tour was not entirely fair to the players," he said, "because you played maybe five or six times a week, you traveled maybe two or three hundred miles between stops, you'd be playing under different conditions. I hurt my shoulder halfway through the 1953 tour, and for six or eight matches I couldn't serve. And then Jack got the flu, and I ran off a string of wins. You just hadda keep playing.

"It was a tough life because you had all the dates booked, so you couldn't *not* play. You just sort of went out there even though you were hurting. You couldn't play at your best. That was the bad part of it. The other part was that you were guaranteed a lot of money. I was making my future secure. I'm quite comfortable now, and it was because that first year or two on the tour gave me a good start."

Sedgman's contract for the 1953 tour guaranteed him $75,000. He wound up making almost twice that much. But—although he came closer than any other challenger to knocking the old champ off, winning forty-one matches against fifty-four losses —he wound up just another also-ran. That was Kramer's last year as a full-time player, after which the title was tossed into the ring for a scramble among Sedgman, Segura, Gonzalez and Budge. Finishing second to Gonzalez, Sedgman figured that was it—two seasons on the tour, end of the line as a pro.

"After that," he told me, "I just sort of filled in a bit every now and then when somebody got hurt. I sort of played until 1962.

"But the thing was that after that first couple of years I had something to fall back on. I'd gone into business; I'd bought a gymnasium with squash courts in Melbourne, and I started to invest in various real estate deals. Hotels and so on. And now it's paying off. I've sold the gymnasium, and we've just sold off the hotel interests. I've educated all my kids pretty well, and we've lived pretty well. I've got four daughters and one grandchild—one more on the way."

Roy Emerson, who had just eliminated Sedgman in Frank's first tournament of the year, came by with his gear bag slung over his shoulder, and asked if Sedg wanted a ride back to the players' hotel. I squeezed in one final question as Frank tipped up his glass and pushed his chair back from the table. I asked him how much longer he expected to keep playing in the Grand Masters.

He stopped. His answer, when it finally came, was carefully evasive. "Not too long," he said.

Well, maybe he was just that cool about it. Maybe the grandchildren, the investments, the daily mail and phone calls would be enough for him. That and the occasional game of squash. For all I knew, the prospect of a Grand Masters tour without Frank Sedgman—it would be the first—bothered him a lot less than it bothered me.

Maybe. But I had my doubts.

35

Scramble

"I GO into every match looking for a win," said Mal Anderson. "I've beaten them all often enough so I know I can do it. I don't mean this to sound cocky, but that's the fact."

For a man who was runner-up to Krishnan in the modesty sweepstakes, who had psyched himself out of a couple of big wins earlier in the tour, Mal was showing surprising self-confidence. Maybe it was a carryover from his winning tournament in Hawaii, the last stop on the spring schedule. He was sizing up his prospects not just for the New Jersey Grand Masters but also for the rest of the tour.

The outcome of these final two months of competition among the senior players appeared to hang on two questions. One was whether Laver or Rosewall, either of them, could establish any clear-cut advantage over the other in the remaining half-dozen tournaments. The second question was whether Anderson, the only outsider so far to break into the winner's circle, could maintain any pressure on the two front runners.

This was semifinals day in New Jersey, and Anderson's optimism was about to be tested against the toughest of opposition: Laver.

The crowd was just filtering into the Braidburn club, a large, newish but somehow seedy-looking building in whose bowels the tournament court was buried. In the cramped lobby an improvised bar was just setting up operation. The players were circulating among the civilians. Neale Fraser, in street clothes, gave me a medical report as full of hope as his partner's mindset. Kept off the courts by his Davis Cup duties in recent months, he had given his ailing elbow a complete rest. Before heading back to the Grand Masters, he'd had a cortisone shot. "Right into the nerve! That's where I wanted it, where it would do the most good. Hurt like bloody hell, it did! But it's done the job! Feels okay for the first time in months."

Near the entrance to the stands, Krishnan stood chatting amiably with a couple of well-dressed gentlemen who looked as if they might have originated in Bombay or Delhi or some other Gandhian metropolis. No doubt they were making arrangements for one of those get-togethers in honor of India's old tennis hero. Never mind that he had begun the fall season with another straight-set loss.

Rod Laver came bustling through the crowd with one arm full of racquets and the other draped companionably around the shoulder of his son, Rick, a slender teenager with a profile like a happy compromise between his father's and his mother's. Rick had come east to enroll at the Hun School, a prep school in nearby Princeton, and his father had driven down to get him so they could spend the tournament weekend together.

Anderson seemed bent on spoiling the family reunion.

Both players were hitting big serves, which skidded off the fast indoor surface. They played even through the first set. But when, at 6–all, they moved into a tiebreaker, Mal ran up a quick lead.

At 1 point to 4, Rocket served an ace, but followed it with the first double fault of the match. He tried to make it up in one stroke with one of those patented "crashing" returns of his. It missed. And now Anderson hit a big serve down the middle of the court for a winner. Set to Anderson, 7–6.

Laver began having trouble with his service in the second set, and Mal attacked his second serve, breaking him with a lucky crosscourt that dropped unexpectedly on the sideline. Laver's strokes began to look a little rough, as if they needed work, as if his sharpness in the first set had been a mistake.

Anderson moved into a 4–3 lead. Both players held service. Finally, on match point, Laver hit a perfect lob, which Anderson managed to retrieve with his back to the court. Laver, in perfect position to put the ball away, netted the overhead and lost the match, 7–6, 6–4.

There was one obvious explanation for the upset. Mal looked fit and ready to play; Rod didn't. He'd been preoccupied with the sale of the ranch and other personal business during the off-season, while Mal had stayed reasonably sharp, playing exhibitions.

Another reason—something purely psychological. All due credit to Mal, his opponent's concentration was faulty. Rocket never seemed to get *into* this tournament. It was as if he were waiting for something to happen before he could take it seriously—and it never did happen.

A hunch on my part: What Laver missed was the presence of Rosewall. A tournament just didn't count quite as much unless the guy waiting for him in the finals was his old archrival, Muscles.

The other semifinal was nothing short of a revelation. Roy Emerson, whom I would have rated a no-chance underdog against Fred Stolle, played straight out of his own scrapbook. None of that "waffling" on service that Gene Scott called to my attention at the beginning of the tour. He served crisply, attacked decisively—never mind that Stolle was hitting some excellent service returns.

Once, in the middle of the first set, Emmo aced Fred on a second serve. On the next point, with Emerson at the net, Stolle hit one of the hardest, flattest shots I have ever seen anybody hit on a tennis court: a backhand that went right through Emmo. If it had hit him, it would have left scorch marks. The shot was pure retaliation, no question about it. Not mean, but awfully firm.

Emmo didn't flinch, he just grinned. Serving at 5–4, he hit three service winners in a row for the set.

He even seemed to have rediscovered some of his lost schoolboy speed. Early in the second set he reversed course to catch up with a sharply angled drop shot that had wrongfooted him, and returned it at an equally sharp angle, winning the point. Soon he was in command as I had never seen him in any match on the tour, anticipating Stolle's shots repeatedly and cutting them off with expert volleys. Racing to a 5–2 lead, he saved himself from a service break with a spectacular shot: a backhand overhead return of a fine topspin lob, which he caught and smashed away just as it appeared to be getting beyond him. He followed that with a slashing crosscourt volley, then blasted in a service winner. Emerson: 6–4, 6–2.

"Vintage Emerson," pronounced Al Bunis—a perfect caption for the flashback we had just witnessed. It was a reminder of the player who, after all, had won more Grand Slam tournaments in his time—singles and doubles—than anybody in the history of the game.

It seemed an opportune time to ask Roy a couple of questions that I'd been hesitating to ask, because they were about the past, and he usually seemed to be giving such a pale imitation of the Roy Emerson who appeared in the record books. I was afraid I might embarrass him by any implied comparisons.

In a winner's mood, Emmo didn't mind reminiscing. There were a couple of matches in particular, he said, that he still enjoyed thinking about. "The second Wimbledon was pretty gratifying," he said, referring to his second straight All-England Singles title, in 1965. "Both were against Fred, you know. If you won it once, you could have been lucky. But two—well, then it's not a fluke.

"But my *favorite* tennis match was in the 1964 Davis Cup final against America. We were down two matches to one going into the last day. We had to win the two singles. Well, Fred goes out and plays Dennis Ralston. He's down two sets to love—we're that close to losing the Cup—and he pulls the match out. It's now between me and Chuck McKinley.

"We used to grind it out against each other, Chuck and I. This time I lost the first set, 6–3. One service break. I'm in trouble."

The book on Roy Emerson, even in his heyday as World's Number 1, was that if you could jump out in front then you had a good shot at him. Because what Emerson's game lacked was flexibility, the capacity to change with circumstances. He was strong and speedy as hell—always had been since he came off his father's dairy farm in Queensland as a schoolboy track star. But his shots lacked variety and strategic purpose. He was described even by respectful observers as a fine player with one game and no particular game plan.

But not that day against the Yanks.

Having started by trying to outslug McKinley from the baseline, and having failed, Emmo now uncharacteristically changed course. He went on the attack. In each of the next three sets he broke McKinley in the first game, taking control of the net.

"I turned the match around," Emmo recalled. "I beat him in the next three sets, and we won the Cup back. Kept it three more years."

For all his remarkable twenty-seven Grand Slam titles, you rarely hear Emerson's name mentioned among the all-time greats of tennis. His game lacked that special brilliance of a Kramer, a Gonzalez, a Sedgman or a Laver. But he does qualify for one particular superlative. He has been described as one of the best right-court doubles players, possibly *the best* ever—so described by two experts who ought to know a good deuce-court man when they see one. The experts are Jack Kramer, four-time winner of the U.S. Doubles, and George Lott, whose name appeared on the doubles trophy no less than five times, in the 1920s and 1930s.

Their encomium puts Emmo in or above the company of Billy Talbert, Australia's nonpareil Jack Bromwich, Don Budge's partner Gene Mako, Kramer's partner Ted Schroeder, not to mention George Lott himself.

Now, everybody knows what it takes to be an *ad-court* player. The guy on the left is the scorer, the player with the crushing volley who crosses over to put the points away. But what, I wondered, did it take to make your mark in history as a *deuce*-court player? At the club level, what did it take to keep from embarrassing yourself when paired with the club champion as your partner—with the champ normally playing the left-hand court?

"The main thing for the right-court player," Emmo said, "is

always make the service return, no matter what serve comes in. The first point of the game is important, and it starts with you. So is the thirty-all point. If you make a good return, you can have them at break point. If you don't, then they're serving for the game.

"The principles you have to keep in mind are: First serve—don't try to do too much against it. Second serve—attack it. Lots of people stand back too far on return of serve. You want to be ready to move right in behind it. Get to the net where you win the points."

I asked Emmo's brother-in-law and frequent doubles opponent, Mal Anderson, what made Roy an outstanding right-court player, and got a completely different answer. It was what Roy did when his *partner* was receiving, Mal said. "Roy's so quick on the backhand volley," said Mal. "He cuts off the ball you play off his partner's return [that is, the ball after the return of service]. He keeps you from knocking off that point, so you never can really take advantage of a good service and an ordinary return."

In the battle of the brothers-in-law, the Sunday afternoon singles final, age would not be a factor—there was only a two-year gap between Emmo, at forty-seven, and Mal, forty-nine—but fitness could well decide it. And there Mal had an all-too-visible advantage.

But this was a new Emmo (or a new-old Emmo) and he was still on a roll, his unique corkscrew service zipping in with extraordinary accuracy. For most of the first set he was getting his first serve in about seventy-five percent of the time.

At 4–all, Anderson suddenly broke him, then held on to win the set.

Emerson simply dusted himself off and started over again. He was playing like a kid—stretching and lunging for volleys, making half volleys and scrambling retrieves. He was taking Mal's sharply angled services, rifling them back at equally tough angles, turning them into winning returns. A pair of those returns—one forehand, one backhand—decided the set in Emmo's favor, 6–3.

But after an early exchange of service breaks in the third set, there was a change of tactics. Unlike the fondly remembered 1964 Davis Cup final, this time it was Emmo's opponent who switched course. Anderson, burned by the angled returns, began serving straight into the receiver instead of away from him. And it worked.

The change of tactics enabled Mal to take control of the net, and his success seemed to give him momentum. He forged ahead 4–2, hit a couple of aces in the next game. Now, with Emmo serving at 2–5, Anderson attacked, took Emerson's volley *on* the volley. Mal's point.

Next service, Anderson catches his brother-in-law at the T with a crisp return right at his feet. Emerson is unfazed, keeps attacking, brings himself up to 30–40. It's match point against him.

Now Emmo winds up that distinctive service. Fault. On the second service I'm looking for him to come up with a good, deep ball. He does—*too* deep, not good. It's a double fault, and Emerson, after reaching his first final on the tour, has lost it 6–4, 3–6, 6–2.

The crowd thinned out some, but I stuck around to watch the doubles final, in which Roy, partnered by Stolle, got another shot at his brother-in-law. Mal was playing with Laver in this tournament as a substitute for the absent Ken Rosewall.

I didn't have to wait long to see right-court doubles principles put into action.

Midway through the first set, against Laver's formidable lefty service, Emmo cracked two excellent returns right at the server's feet. In between, Stolle hit another of the same from the ad side of the court. And then Roy, as if making a nod to Mal's analysis of the doubles game, crossed over to cut off a volley by the server—cut it off with a pretty backhand volley of his own. That completed a service break. Emerson-Stolle hung onto that margin and won the set.

There were a lot of pyrotechnics in the second set. Rod and Mal ran up a 4–1 lead, mostly on vicious, spinning lobs off Laver's racquet and a string of Laver's crashing returns. Stolle-Emerson caught up to them and sent the set into a tiebreaker.

It was a typical Grand Masters doubles windup: all four players at the net in point after point, plopping surprising little dinks at each other's feet or slicing shots away from each other, instead of slamming the ball 1980s-style. Everything fell Stolle-Emerson's way, and they came off the winners, giving Roy some measure of revenge for his singles loss.

As I was leaving the Braidburn club a few minutes later, I ran into Laver and his son Rick, the visiting preppy, heading toward the locker room. I had seen them together a lot in the players' lounge during the tournament—munching postmatch hamburgers or shooting a little inexpert pool or watching the baseball playoffs on TV. They were trying to root their home state team, the underdog San Diego Padres, into the National League pennant. (The California entry made it, too. It was the Padres, not the favored Chicago Cubs, who met the Detroit Tigers in the World Series the following week.)

As I passed the Lavers, *père et fils,* Rod was scurrying up the stairs at his usual man-in-perpetual-motion pace. Young Rick, while panting to keep up, was trying to console his famous father, so untypically a two-time loser in this tournament —singles and doubles.

"Well, you *played* good, anyway," Rick was saying, as they headed into the locker room together.

The Last Chance Open

WELL, I had my horse race, after all.

The Laver-Rosewall competition had turned into a three-way affair. Anderson's win, Laver's loss—however you wanted to look at the outcome of the New Jersey Grand Masters, it had widened the opening in the field, and Mal had come storming through.

What's more, in the next month of play, he kept right on coming.

As the fall tour followed its eccentric orbit—from New Jersey to Toronto, Kansas City, Salt Lake City, Tucson—form generally prevailed. Krishnan and Fraser continued to take their lumps. So did the elderly fill-ins, Sedgman and Ulrich—though Torben once took Laver to three sets, and he and Frank managed to reach one doubles final. It seemed like the last, brief flare of light that astronomers ascribe to dying stars.

Anderson's performance was the one exception to the rule of the odds. He won the Tucson tournament by beating Rosewall (now back on the tour) and Laver on successive days. In two of the other tournaments, he came *that close*—once against Kenny, once against Rod—in each case holding four games in the third set before losing out to the favorite.

"What happened in those third sets, anyway?" I asked Mal. "What went wrong?" I was wondering how seriously to take his chances as the competition headed down toward the wire.

"Nothing went wrong," he said simply. "Except up here." He tapped his skull. "It's all up here."

We were standing at the bar at a cocktail party for the play-

ers and their fans in Naples, Florida, on the eve of the tournament that would decide the winner of the 1984 tour. The
festivities were being held in a large, handsomely furnished
condo on the grounds of the Naples Bath and Tennis Club, the
tournament site. The stars drifted through the premises, making polite chat. They were a natty bunch in their dress uniform
—all wearing blazers, a few in the abhorred red-piped "band
costumes." Some of the wives had joined the tour as it neared
a ceremonial ending: Daphne Anderson, Joy Emerson and,
again, Wilma Rosewall.

The singles were in swinging form. Neale Fraser, coming
in from the balmy air of a November evening in Florida, waved
with his one free arm. The other was firmly engaged by a pretty
auburn-haired woman in a cocktail sheath slit seductively up
the sides. She was every bit the equal of the women I had seen
attached to Fraser in Florham Park, New Jersey; in Boca Raton,
Florida; in Nashville, Tennessee. I was beginning to understand what Neale meant when he told me that his five years in
the Grand Masters were the best five years of his life. When
you're a twenty-one-year-old jock on the circuit, that sort of
female attention is fun; when you're fifty-one, it's an ego trip.

At the cocktail party some of the players were talking about
a couple of intramural subjects that had been coming to the
surface during the late stages of the tour: standings and bonus
points. The tournament starting tomorrow would be the last
one in which players could earn the points that would determine their order of finish on the tour and their shares of the
bonus pool.

At the end of this week the points awarded throughout the
tour would be toted up: a basic two points for playing a tournament, so much more for reaching a semifinal, for a final, for
winning the event. The money accumulated in the bonus pool,
tournament by tournament, would be divvied up according to
each player's point total. The top finishers then would go on to
the Grand Masters Championship Finals, a ceremonial playoff
with extra prize money.

Traditionally, only the leading five or six players qualified for the playoff, and the remaining places in the eight-man draw were filled by new talent: the rookies, just turned or just about to turn forty-five, who would be joining the tour the following season. But this year there would be no new blood in the Championship Final; the draw would be limited to the top eight finishers on the tour.

But there was something at stake besides the bonus money and the playoff draw. For the player with the most points for the year would go into the records as the winner of the tour— Number 1 in the Grand Masters and by that distinction the best over-forty-five tennis player in the world.

For players at the bottom of the list, points could be equivalent to survival. The Naples tournament, for Krishnan or Fraser, would be the last chance to pick up a win that could keep one or the other out of the Number 8 position. Below that rank you could fall into the category of substitute, like Sedgman and Ulrich, or even out of the competition altogether: out of world-class tennis.

And if you were shooting for the middle of the pack like Gene Scott, then Naples would be your last chance to rack up enough points to beat out Roy Emerson.

Neale Fraser had arrived in bad shape to make a stand at Last Chance Gulch. Momentarily detached from the auburn-haired beauty, he set his glass down on the bar, slipped his left arm (his working wing) out of the official red-piped blazer he was wearing, and displayed an ugly inflammation that ran along the inside of his well-muscled forearm. The effects of the cortisone shot he'd taken for his tendinitis had worn off somewhere beyond Toronto, and so had the euphoria it briefly induced. Now he was about to play the Last Chance Open with the worst case of tennis elbow—to call the affliction by its everyday name—that I had ever seen.

"It's a good thing I'm going home in a week or so," Neale said. "I think I'm going to need surgery for this." With some difficulty he worked his arm back into the sleeve of the jacket.

I asked why he kept playing—why he hadn't simply dropped off the tour and gone home before this. He looked at me as if I'd just asked him what a Wimbledon was.

"Because I need the points," he said. "I want to play next year."

I knew that Neale was way down on the totem pole, but I hadn't been keeping precise track of the point totals.

"Check with Mal," Fraser advised me. "That's what we all do. Mal always knows the standings."

Anderson gave me a rundown on the situation as it stood now, on the eve of the last tournament before the playoff. It was somewhat less complicated than the NFL postseason football matchups leading up to the Super Bowl.

One thing was clear: Ulrich and Sedgman were out of the picture—they hadn't played enough tournaments to earn the necessary points. So all eight regulars on the tour—everybody *except* Torben and Frank—would be moving on to the Championship Finals in Miami a week later.

But when it came to the tour standings, the Grand Masters rankings for the year, there was a pileup both at the top and bottom of the group.

Fraser and Krishnan were tied with the minimum twenty points for the ten tournaments they'd played. Neither of them had managed to win a match all year—not even a set.

Farther up the ladder, Emerson had an edge on Scott for the Number 5 slot, but Gene was still within striking distance. Fred Stolle was solidly entrenched in fourth place.

And at the top, by Anderson's calculations, it was a complete scramble—practically a three-way tie. Of the ten tournaments played so far, Laver had won four, Rosewall and Anderson three each.

"So it comes down pretty much to Kenny and I," Anderson summarized cheerily. He carefully looked over a depleted trayful of canapes before selecting a skewered shrimp. "Whichever one of us wins this tournament wins the tour. I don't mean to say somebody else couldn't win the tournament, but . . ." Clearly he had pretty much ruled out that possibility.

It struck me that he was leaving out a very significant factor. "What about Laver?" I asked him.

"Rod's taken himself out of the running. Some sort of personal problem. Torben's coming down to fill in for him in the draw tomorrow. Right now Rod's ahead on points, of course, but without playing this week there's nothing he can do to keep Kenny or I from passing him."

Laver's "problem" was hardly more than a small domestic situation—something that belonged more to a TV sitcom than to big-time tennis. The weekend of this decisive Grand Masters tournament in Florida was also Parents' Weekend at the Hun School, Rick Laver's new school in New Jersey, and Rod and Mary had opted to spend it by showing the family flag on campus. With the Number 1 ranking at stake, the leading contender was bowing out by default.

It was not the kind of choice you would have expected of a Grand Slam champion—not unless you happened to remember how full of regrets he sounded when he reminisced about how tennis had kept him separated from his own family when he was a teenager playing the tournament circuit. Call it one more sign of age—that period in a tennis player's life when, in Rod's words, "family definitely assumes the Number one position."

Naples is to the west coast of Florida in the 1980s what Palm Beach was to the east coast in the 1920s: the place where the big money goes to build its vacation hideaways. The differences reflect our economic history. Palm Beach was a monument to the Gilded Age, built by the last generation of robber barons with their accumulated family fortunes. Naples is a product of the Age of Merger and Acquisition, built by corporate executives preparing to retire on their golden handshakes or their golden parachutes.

Naples Bath and Tennis Club, the site of the Grand Masters tournament, lies outside that special orbit. It's a rather modest condo-style tennis resort erected on landfill in the marshy outskirts of town. Its residents are doctors, dentists, businessmen from places like Cleveland, Pittsburgh and Worcester, Massachusetts—people with a few bucks to invest in a Florida pied-à-terre that throws off a few bucks in tax benefits.

But for the week of the Grand Masters tournament, the Bath and Tennis Club borrows from the community's upper-class tone. It is a special event, staged by Naples honchos as a benefit for one of their favorite charities, the Naples YMCA. As often happens with undertakings of this kind, charity becomes the occasion for a lot of competitive zeal.

You can see it in the parties thrown by rival hostesses, with players and sponsors heading the guest lists; in the jockeying for choice table locations on the clubhouse terrace—the choice vantage point for watching the matches; and most of all in the unique Naples version of the pro-am tournament.

The competition is limited to a select field of eight local club players, each of whom pays $1,000 into the Y kitty for the privilege of teaming up with one of the pros in a daylong elimination tournament preceding the Grand Masters itself. That narrows the field down to two teams, which meet at the end of the week, on the day of the Grand Masters finals.

The local players' pictures appear in the tournament program, along with Kenny and Emmo and the rest. The matches are umpired, and they are conducted with none of the usual pro-am horseplay. The principles of social tennis go by the boards as the pros smash overheads not at each other but at the opposing amateurs. Because the idea in this event is not to keep the ball in play but to score. To win.

"That's the way they want us to play it," Neale Fraser explained to me with a shrug. "Hell, they insist on it!"

One year an amateur hired the pro he'd drawn as his partner to come down to Naples a week in advance to work out with him for the pro-am tournament.

For all the seriousness of the event, the quality of play didn't strike me as particularly high. Not bad, just average club doubles on the amateurs' half of the court. But they all showed good doubles sense and a willingness to attack in the face of fire from across the net. There was no flinching from the pros' overheads. All the matches were long and tough.

At the end of the first day's competition there were two court-weary teams looking forward to a matchup in the final three days later. Emerson had come through in partnership with a short, rather solemn fellow in his forties, with an impressive mane of blow-dried hair—a New Englander who, somebody told me, had made enough of a bundle in real estate so that "he can afford to spend a lot of time working on his tennis game." Their opponents would be Krishnan in tandem with a local resident—a lanky stockbroker with rather ungainly strokes but remarkable qualities of persistence.

I hadn't seen any actual fights on the court (I was told there was one, a few years back) but there weren't a lot of laughs, either.

Maybe it was this unusual atmosphere of competitiveness, sometimes bordering on acrimony, that spilled over into the ranks of the Grand Masters themselves. Maybe it was fatigue catching up with the troupe as they neared the end of the campaign trail. Or maybe it was just my imagination. But I sensed bad vibes at Naples. Or bad temper. Or bad *something*. It seemed to affect not just the spirit of the matches but even the quality of play.

I could feel it in the oppressive Florida air when Scott and Emerson met in a first-round match. Here were two players, once separated by at least ten notches in rank, whom the years had leveled out to an even-money bet: Emmo, the former world's Number 1 amateur, now at forty-eight carrying excess weight on a bum knee; and Gene, once eleventh-ranked in the world, and now a forty-six-year-old gamer with improved strokes but a degenerating hip. All they were playing for was the bragging rights to fifth place in the Grand Masters—that and the accompanying bonus money. Roy was a few points ahead but even if he won would have no chance of overtaking Fred Stolle in fourth place.

Scott and Emerson not only seemed determined to beat each other out in the standings, but they also seemed bent on making each other look bad in the process. Under the hot sun on the slow clay court, they exploited each other's bad side relentlessly.

"I knew what he was going to do," Scott said afterwards. "He was going to make me play off my forehand. Well, okay," he added grimly, "I'm going to play *his* forehand!"

It was a match filled with long forehand exchanges from the backcourt, interspersed with punishing drop shots, also delivered pointedly to the forehand side. Sometimes there were drop shots played off the drop shots.

Finally, Emmo simply wore out. Winning in straight sets, Scott was now just one point out of fifth place, and he could clinch it by winning his semifinal while Roy sat powerlessly on the sidelines.

In another first-round match, Torben Ulrich, filling Laver's space in the draw, found himself repeatedly pinned into the corners by Rosewall, who then kept hitting winning placements into the open court. Nothing remarkable about those tactics. But there was a sequence in the second set that struck me as mean-spirited.

It began with Rosewall, comfortably ahead by 6–1, 2–0, hitting a beautiful, feathery drop shot that just cleared the net. Torben was way out of position, but with a tremendous burst of effort he managed to reach the ball and returned it for the point. It was such a terrific get that Kenny tucked his racquet under his arm and joined the crowd in applauding it.

But it was as if he begrudged Torben the applause, because on the very next point he repeated the ploy. This time Torben didn't move for the ball. He simply turned his back on the net and walked away from the point in a gesture of disdain.

After losing the second set almost as quickly as the first, Ulrich was in a downbeat mood. The role of substitute was weighing on him. His Zen approach to tennis told him that winning and losing were irrelevant; the experience of playing well was everything. But playing as little as he did made playing well an impossibility.

"Should I have agreed to play for Laver?" he wondered aloud as he pulled on his tatty sweat suit after the match. "I think the question is either to play more often or not at all."

On his flight from the West Coast to Florida, Torben had brought with him a sample of some paintings he'd done recently at his studio in Seattle. He invited me to walk over to the condo he was sharing with Krishnan to take a look at them. Ulrich's art turned out to be a kind of action painting which he achieved by hitting tennis balls dipped in acrylic paint against Japanese rice paper pinned to a wall—hitting the balls repeatedly so they formed random patterns of exploding little circles, which he then ornamented with calligraphy. The lettering consisted of Zen-like captions: "These balls are not grounded in fact" . . . "Can you dance to this? [Check one:] Yes? No? Don't be silly." . . . "Spectators will please not resume watching until the airplane overhead has come to a complete stop."

After I used up my scant resources as an art critic, we got back onto the subject of the Grand Masters and Torben's disillusionment with his benchwarmer's status.

"The trouble is," I ventured, "you don't really have any choice, do you? Either you play once in a while, whenever they call you, or else you don't play in the Grand Masters at all."

"Well," Torben said, as if he'd been giving the matter some serious thought, "that's not out of the question, is it?"

Even the unflappable impresario, Al Bunis, seemed out of sorts and not his usual benevolent self. It was an unfamiliar, brooding Bunis who said one day, apropos of nothing in particular, "Anybody who thinks I started the Grand Masters out of some missionary impulse has got the wrong idea. I love to play tennis, and I love to watch tennis, but I couldn't care less if I ever convert a single person to the game. And people who watch these guys and look at their age and assume that it's some kind of health crusade. . . ." He shook his head. "Healthwise, you could achieve the same results on a rowing machine. You'd probably do yourself more good, in fact." He picked up his racquets and sauntered out toward the courts to meet Krishnan for the daily workout, leaving the rest of us tennis nuts to find our own rationale for the hours we spend on the game.

Krish was the only one who seemed to rise above the Naples miasma. In his first-round match with Mal Anderson he mounted an attack that had Mal backed against the wall for a while—a streak of aggressive shotmaking in which points flowed off his racquet as if he were inspired by his favorite example of Lew Hoad at Wimbledon. I could hardly believe the scoreboard when I realized that the match was tied at one set apiece. It was Krish's best performance all year—the first set Krish had won on the whole tour!

Or was it Mal who had lost it, a victim of Naples and its malign vibes?

Whichever, that was as far as Krishnan's streak would carry him. Anderson suddenly roused himself and wrested control of the match, running out the third set quite easily. Now he was just one round away from the match that could make him Number 1 in the Grand Masters. All he had to do was get by Stolle in the semis. Then he and Rosewall would be fighting it out head-to-head for the top spot in the annual rankings. Conceivably, he could even back into the title if—granted, a big *if*— Gene Scott could finally figure out the formula for winning games as well as points against Rosewall and knock him off in their semifinal match.

Sitting at the Naples clubhouse bar on the eve of the semifinals, I watched a tableful of tennis players and other VIPs break up in an explosion of hilarity and then head out to somebody's party in town. I went back to the calculations I had been making in the margins of my tournament program—various possible effects of the next two days' matches on the point standings.

When I did so I realized that something had happened to me and my point of view in the course of the tour. I was no longer the pure scientist, the objective student of the game, probing it for data about technique and tactics and the pitfalls of age. I was a fan with a rooting interest.

I raised my glass in a silent toast before draining it. "Go for it, Mal!" I found myself thinking.

37

Prizes

THE UNCERTAIN MENTAL FACTOR in Mal Anderson's admirable game had been noted by other observers long before I got into the act.

When the twenty-two-year-old Queensland cowboy unexpectedly won the 1957 U.S. Singles Championship over top-seeded Ashley Cooper, *The New York Times* expert, Allison Danzig, wrote that Mal's performance "ranks with the finest displays of offensive tennis in recent years." But he went on to wonder at Mal's curious compulsion to "make every shot look too good."

"Mal's trouble," as Kenny Rosewall once analyzed it, "is that he's a perfectionist. He has to make the perfect shot each time with perfect style and put it perfectly on the line instead of giving himself a margin of error."

The consequences, when he missed, were often drastic. In the 1958 Davis Cup classic he lost to Alex Olmedo, 8–6, 2–6, 9–7, 8–6, Anderson held set point on the Chief's service in each of the three sets he dropped. And a reporter at that scene was moved to comment on "the strange complexity in Anderson's makeup that makes him so despondent at losing an opportunity . . . that he presents himself as a sitting target in the next couple of games."

The problem didn't go away. In 1974, almost forty years old, Anderson had two match points against the world's Number 1 player, twenty-two-year-old Jimmy Connors, and blew them both by trying for the perfect volley. Instead of landing at the baseline, both balls went out.

It was hard to identify that sometimes jittery performer with the off-court Mal Anderson—a forty-nine-year-old gentleman of such composure, such an unflappably even disposition that you would have said he didn't have a nerve in his body. He radiated confidence.

On the morning of the Anderson-Stolle semifinal, I ran into Mal at the Naples club pro shop, where I had gone in search of help for a severe personal problem. Unlike Mal, I was suffering an acute attack of the heebie-jeebies. Gremlins had taken over my service during the week at Naples, leaving me feeling like a Jonah in the doubles games that were part of the daily routine among the rabble at the Bath and Tennis Club's acreage of well-kept Har-Tru courts. I guessed I might have caught some hacker's form of the Naples malaise, and was looking for a club pro to give me an hour of therapy. Mal was picking up some balls for a morning hit with one of his colleagues.

He was in his usual benign mood, chatting almost nostalgi-cally about the tour, as if it were already over. It had been a damn good tour, he said. Rosewall always forced you to play your best. And Laver's presence this year had certainly added something to the competition. Too bad Rocket couldn't be here for the last shot at the bonus points, but. . . .

I ventured to ask Mal just how good a tour it had been for him from a purely financial standpoint. The total prize money for the year was a matter of record. It was $400,000, spread over the entire schedule of twelve tournaments. But individual earn-ings had not been publicized at all during the tour. That was certainly a contrast with mainstream tennis—just by reading the Grand Prix stats in the sports pages, you can practically track John McEnroe's bank balance. But about the Grand Masters winnings, IMG remained resolutely closemouthed. Maybe it was out of some vestigial amateurism, maybe it was a conviction that gentlemen (as distinguished from young tennis millionaires) simply do not discuss money. What-ever the reason, a chronicler of the tour was left wondering how to translate tournament wins and bonus points into pay-checks.

Mal had an answer at his fingertips, and he didn't seem to feel any of the official inhibitions about sharing it.

When it was all added up, he told me, he figured he'd average around $4,000 per tournament—somewhere between $40,000 and $50,000 in prize money for the tour.

"McEnroe's probably making that much this afternoon—if he loses," Mal said, almost apologetically. "But it's not bad for twelve weeks' work. Better than you can make in a lot of other ways, and most of them wouldn't be as much fun." He added over his shoulder as he headed down toward the practice court, "Anyway, it beats coaching, doesn't it?"

The trouble with Anderson's candid arithmetic is that it didn't make sense.

Even at $50,000, his earnings would be no more than average for the troupe—eight players per tournament splitting a total of $400,000 in prize money averaged out to exactly $50,000 a share—and Mal's record was distinctly *above* average. It appeared to entitle him to something more like the lion's share of the loot. I wondered if Rosewall and Laver could be playing the tour for such relatively modest rewards. Rod, the first tennis millionaire? And Kenny, the canny investor? Surely they didn't have to worry about the dreaded alternative of becoming a teaching pro!

Putting mere lucre out of my mind, I settled down with the crowd a few hours later, prepared to watch Anderson stroke his way toward a title shot against Rosewall. Our "grandstand" was a grassy slope extending from the clubhouse terrace, where the chosen sat at their high-priced umbrella-shaded tables, down to the edge of the exhibition court. By custom, if you were sitting on the slope, you brought your own beach chair, a supply of sunscreen lotion, and a plastic glass full of something comforting in case the sun's vicious rays penetrated your defenses.

I was prepared, as I said, to watch Anderson stroke his way into the finals. I also had to be prepared to see Stolle come out gunning and take the play away from my personal favorite, since Fred was capable of doing that against anybody in the world outside the Grand Prix category—and a lot still in it.

What I could not anticipate was the bizarre sequence of events that actually took place that sunny November afternoon.

To begin with, in the first five games, neither of these two extraordinarily effective servers could manage to hold serve. Anderson was the first to climb out of that rut, finally capturing a service game with an ace. Then, with Stolle serving at 3–5, Mal broke him for the fourth time. A double fault handed Anderson the game and set.

The second set began with a change of tactics on the part of both players, almost as if they'd made some kind of pact during the change of courts. Now, instead of trying to hit their way in to the net, they started to throw high lobs into the glaring sun. They seemed to be just trying to survive their own errors.

I took some comfort from the low standard of play. The fact that Mal was beating Stolle even while playing below par was promising, and it made his chances against Rosewall tomorrow look good, because a player as mechanically sound as Anderson wasn't apt to have two bad days in a row. And the problem of temperament seemed to be under control. When Mal broke a string and had to go to a backup racquet, it barely threw him off stride. He made the adjustment and got back into the game.

But at 2–3, on Anderson's service, something happened— something that didn't seem overwhelmingly important at the time. It settled the outcome of the match.

What happened was that Mal broke a second racquet. His third was a Yonex boron-graphite, like the other two, but it was obviously strung looser. And from the moment he picked up the third one, his game changed almost beyond recognition. His usually impeccable sliced backhands flopped repeatedly into the net. Flat forehands sailed deep or wide. His service died, he rarely got in to make a volley. Even the high defensive lobs were landing short—easy prey for his opponent's overhead.

I had never seen Mal so befuddled on a tennis court—not by Rosewall's angled ground strokes, nor by Laver's cannon-shot serves and whizzing placements. From the time he broke his second racquet, Mal never won another game—not a single

one! Stolle hung back only briefly, as if he couldn't quite believe his luck. Then he began charging the net and finished off
points almost brutally. Fred simply ran off with the match. The
scores were 3–6, 6–2, 6–0.

The winner stood toweling off at courtside, with a slight air
of disbelief still showing on his face. "It wasn't up to me to tell
him this," Stolle told me, as he gathered up his gear, "but if it
was me, I'd have sent the first racquet up to the pro shop to be
patched as soon as it broke. I tried some things in the last set
that worked, but the main thing was, he couldn't hit with that
last racquet at all."

Mal, slowly collecting himself on the other side of the umpire's platform, looked nothing less than dumbstruck. He was
staring at the offending racquet. "It was the only one I had
left," he said, "and I'd never tried it before. It had no life in it
at all."

I murmured something meant to be consoling. I tore up my
imaginary pari-mutuel ticket with a shrug.

No question, I had just witnessed an example of the Naples
hoodoo at its most potent. Yet I couldn't help wondering if the
racquet might have had such a drastic effect on anybody but
Mal—anybody other than this amazingly even-tempered man,
this veteran of the tennis wars at their toughest, with his air of
confidence and his command of every technical aspect of the
game, who was still so much at the mercy of things that went
on inside his skull.

The mental part of the game, as Mal had once referred to it
—it's what gave tennis its beautifully unpredictable quality.

And drove players and rooters nuts.

Even an immortal like Rosewall was not immune.

Kenny beat Gene Scott flawlessly, almost surgically, in the
other semifinal. But the next day, in the final against Stolle,
Kenny committed errors on every possible kind of shot, just as
if he were an ordinary fallible human being. Stolle moved out
to an early lead.

It was at Naples the year before that Fred Stolle had staged
his remarkable comeback from the verge of defeat and beaten

Rosewall in the first of two successive tournaments—two rare triumphs over his old nemesis.

As his normally meticulous shots flew over the baseline or into the alleys, Rosewall began hanging his head between points, like a small boy sulking. "I had him looking for dimes," in Stolle's description.

But Rosewall had Stolle looking up at the heavens, muttering terrible things under his breath, as Fred—committing tactical errors as bad as Kenny's mechanical ones—let himself get maneuvered into hopeless positions on the court. A Rosewall backhand return of service down the line went for a winner, followed by a forehand passing shot off a chancy approach shot. And then Rosewall took a service on the rise and drove it at Stolle's feet in midcourt for a crucial break. Another Rosewall break—in spite of more Rosewall errors—and Kenny had the first set 6–4.

There was one nice episode in the second set—a terrific exchange of forehands that went on for something like a dozen shots until Rosewall abruptly altered pace and direction, and caught his opponent moving the wrong way. Otherwise, neither man was able to lift his game above a pedestrian level of erratic play. Stolle double-faulted on crucial points. Both players repeatedly missed the lines with attempted placements. Both were bouncing their racquets on the court in frustration and disgust.

The shambles ended unremarkably with Rosewall on top— or Stolle on the bottom—6–4, 7–5. Fred, commenting on the errors and faulty serving in a postmatch speech to the crowd, assured them, "You don't usually see that in the Grand Masters."

Kenny also made a little speech as he accepted the winner's check—amount unannounced. Five thousand dollars? Seventy-five hundred? The speech was nothing more nor less than a public apology both for his sulky behavior and his erratic play. "Win or lose," he said, "you like to feel you played reasonably well. Even at our ripe old age, we still get disappointed when we don't play the caliber of tennis we think we can play."

Old age! I suddenly remembered that just a few weeks earlier Rosewall had passed his fiftieth birthday—the watershed, in Al Bunis's fateful calculations.

Was it possible that the laws of nature had finally caught up to Rosewall and that what we had just witnessed was the first step on the downslope?

I wouldn't bet on it. Anyway, it would probably take years to find out. And, meanwhile, at fifty, Kenny was still King of the Grand Masters.

The most interesting tennis of the day in many ways was—would you believe?—the pro-am finals. Not very stylish but gritty and dramatic. Everybody was making great saves. Point after point sprang back to life after apparent putaways. The club players showed a commendable willingness to cover their full share of the court instead of leaving all the tough ones to the pros. In the end, Emerson and his partner, the short, well-coifed New England real estate promoter, outlasted Krishnan and the gangly local stockbroker. The scores told you just how tough it was: 7–6, 4–6, 7–6.

I saw the winners afterwards toasting each other with a congratulatory brew in the clubhouse bar. Emmo's partner looked tired, but he had the satisfied expression of a Yankee who feels he got his thousand bucks' worth. I found out that was the fourth time he got his name on the Naples Bath and Tennis Club pro-am trophy.

Myself, I had nothing to show for the day—nothing but another losing encounter with the local jinx. That morning, in my final appearance on the bewitched Naples courts, I had blown what should have been an easy singles against a scrawny, baselining condo owner from New Hampshire.

When the points were toted up by Mike Savit after the Naples finals, the ten best tennis players in the world for their age had their 1984 rankings.

Like a delayed replay of the 1964 pro tour standings, it was Rosewall Number 1 and Laver right behind him.

Mal Anderson, by reason of his quirky loss in the Naples semis, not only blew his chance to be on top, but also lost the Number 2 spot to Laver—by the margin of a single point. Mal had to settle for Number 3 behind the two superstars. And that, I suspected, is where in his mind he really belonged.

Fred Stolle was unexpectedly far behind Anderson in the Number 4 position.

Gene Scott, who had aspired to a modest Number 5 ranking, had to settle in the end for sixth behind his rival, Emerson. Gene also missed out by a single point.

Winless Krishnan and Fraser occupied the 7 and 8 slots in a tie.

And Sedgman and Ulrich, also with no wins but fewer appearances, were stuck where they started: ranked 9 and 10, or nowhere.

When I commiserated with Gene Scott on his narrow setback, he shrugged. I made some sympathetic remark about the loss of bonus money. There was a moment's hesitation. Then Gene said, in a tone of mild embarrassment, "Well, you know, there's only a difference of—what?—I think it's a thousand dollars a man. A thousand between positions in the standings. The whole bonus pool is only $25,000."

I expressed some surprise that there had been so much concern about the point standings when there was so little money at stake.

"That's not what the Grand Masters is about," said Scott.

What was it about then?

"Competition," said Scott.

When I referred the subject to Al Bunis, he assured me that no player had ever refused a check for his share of the bonus pool. But, he said, even the overall prize money, involving much larger amounts, is not the primary incentive. "It may not even be the main *financial* incentive," he added, explaining that the ancillary benefits of the tour for most of the players are probably as great as the prize money itself. Some of the players need to maintain an active connection with tennis in order to keep endorsement deals, to maintain their value as coaches or tennis directors for clubs or resorts. Furthermore, Bunis said, there are all those opportunities to earn extra money from company outings and other personal appearances in the course of the tour.

As for amounts, Bunis wouldn't talk. The code of *omertà* remained inviolate.

I tried Kenny Rosewall on the idea that the ancillary benefits are the Big Payoff for a Grand Masters player. Not necessarily, he told me. The tour, he said, is really useful only to players who live in the United States.

Useful in what way?

"Making business contacts," said the newly recrowned Grand Masters Number 1. "You meet people in the business world, like you did on the old amateur circuit. It leads to investment opportunities and playing opportunities if you live in the States. That's why so many Australian players live over here. There's not so many of those opportunities in Australia."

I asked how come the Rosewalls had never joined the expatriates.

He glanced fondly toward Wilma, who was chatting with a cluster of women wearing Florida-colored dresses and holding plastic cocktail glasses. "Oh," said Kenny smiling, "we decided to stay in Australia because we had kids in school. And then it got too late to move. It was too late for us to take advantage of the opportunities. But I'm not sorry how it turned out."

I knew Rosewall couldn't be playing *just* for the sheer love of competition. Surely, that's not what Gene Scott meant. For all Kenny's teenage enthusiasm for the game, it took some incalculable combination of that *plus* money to define an old pro's status, feed his ego, and gratify the competitive athlete that survives in everybody who has ever played sports seriously.

The monetary factor in that formula remained elusive. If it wasn't the ancillary benefits, then, I reasoned, Rosewall must be getting some sort of appearance money—a guarantee that would make a tournament worthwhile for an old pro of his means and stature. And if he was getting guarantees, then so was Rod Laver. Appearance money was outlawed in the Grand Prix, but there was nothing to prohibit it in the Grand Masters, which was independent and made its own rules.

I tried out my theory on Mike Savit. He shot it down, sort of. "Everyone on the tour plays for prize money," he said.

That could have been a technicality. It didn't preclude the possibility that Laver and Rosewall were playing for more prize money than the rest of the troupe under some sort of bonus arrangement, for example. That might be the explanation for Mal Anderson's surprisingly small share of the $400,000 kitty. Maybe a sizable chunk of that purse came off the top earmarked for the two superstars. A winning tournament for Anderson might be worth only $5,000 or $7,500, but for Rod or Kenny the same tournament might be worth twice as much.

One way or another, I assumed, Laver and Rosewall were probably assured of making perhaps $10,000 apiece at every stop on the tour—let's say $100,000 for the year, allowing for the couple of tournaments each of them missed.

I found that some of the other players in the troupe shared my assumptions, not necessarily about the amount of money involved but about the existence of some sort of bonus or guarantee, however it might be structured. Nobody professed to be offended by the idea.

"It's dead-on appropriate," Gene Scott said firmly. "Laver and Rosewall are the reason we're playing. That fact has a certain market value."

If Scott was right, and if the people were going to get what they paid for, then it would surely be Laver versus Rosewall again in the one last act of the 1984 tour, the Grand Masters Championship Finals in Miami.

38

Winning

THE ANNUAL GRAND MASTERS CHAMPIONSHIP TOURNAMENT has an extralarge winner's prize of $10,000. There is no secrecy about the amount—it is announced. I guess anything in five figures is respectable enough for gentlemen to talk about in public.

Rosewall and Laver were the names that sold the tickets. Rosewall and Laver were ranked 1–2, and they were seeded 1–2. But at the end of a dozen tournaments spread over eight months of the year, it could have been two other guys mixing it up for the tour's biggest prize and the title of champion. Anderson, Stolle, even Emerson could have hit a hot streak in Miami that week and ridden it into the finals.

Only history wouldn't have permitted it.

For twenty years history had been looking for a winner in the Laver-Rosewall rivalry—from their first meeting on the 1964 pro tour on through the early open tournaments, the dramatic WTC Finals, and beyond.

And as the 1984 Grand Masters tour wound down to the very end, history was still looking. Kenny had locked up first place in the overall point standings, but the two were precisely tied in tournament victories with four apiece. They were also deadlocked in their personal competition. They had met four times in tournament finals, and each had won twice. The 1984 season would have ended in an anticlimax if the matchup had turned out to be anything but Laver versus Rosewall for the last and biggest prize of the year, at Fisher Island Tennis Club in Miami.

Laver versus Rosewall was what we got.

In a decade of competition, the Grand Masters had played tournaments in twenty different countries—three times at Wimbledon, once at the U.S. Open, many times in exotic spots like Hong Kong, Manila and Johannesburg, South Africa. Occasionally, they played at sites so bizarre as to stir up painful memories of the old professional barnstorming tours.

Once they traveled to an island resort called Itapica off the coast of Brazil to perform before hordes of Club Med revelers in matches that had to be played before breakfast because soon afterwards the temperature reached 130 degrees on the asphalt court. It was the last event before a break in the tour, and it left the players stranded in a place so remote that after thirty-six hours of travel by a combination of boat, car and unscheduled airline, the Australians were still three days from home.

Fisher Island, a resort to the windward side of downtown Miami, was not so remote as Itapica, but it had a certain unreal air about it.

You could get out there in no more than a twenty-minute boat ride; and in case your boat was laid up for refitting or was off cruising somewhere in the Virgin Islands, there was a flotilla of launches waiting at one of the downtown hotel landings —waiting to take the daily tennis crowds out to the matches.

Once you got to the island, though, you were confronted by an underdeveloped-looking vista of architectural framework, scaffolding, raw concrete. It reminded you of the setting for some early Antonioni movie. Fisher Island was not actually a resort—not yet, anyway—but a multimillion-dollar promotional work-in-progress. Literature distributed with the tournament program described the place in terms suggesting a kind of high-tax-bracket Shangri-la, with a central lodge and outlying villas, all surrounded by landscaped parks. There would be docking space for the private boats and there would be a helicopter pad and a seaplane ramp for people accustomed to getting places in a hurry, never mind the cost.

The centerpiece of all this drawing-board luxury had nothing unfinished or merely promissory about it. Fisher Island Tennis Club was a going, glowing center of activity in the

shadow of all that framework. The clubhouse was a former Van-
derbilt mansion, a beautifully refurbished spread in the Spanish style, with stucco walls and tiled roofs, around which some
lovely clay courts had been laid out and a stadium seating a
couple of thousand had been built.

The place was throbbing with the sound of television
trucks, the camera crews were checking their shots, and early
spectators were picking their way in over the TV cables when
I came up the dusty walk from the launch landing. It was the
last day of the Grand Masters tour, the Sunday of the championship finals.

I had been obliged to miss the preliminary rounds of this
tournament. It was another Naples situation. Semifinal day was
also my son's wedding day, and the ceremony was held in Connecticut. I had toyed with the idea of asking the bride and
groom to change the date or move the proceedings south, but
that seemed presumptuous, even for something as serious as
tennis. So, following Rod Laver's example at Naples, I gave
family matters the Number 1 priority, and spent Saturday in
Connecticut as a member of the wedding. On Sunday morning,
with the taste of champagne still in my mouth, I caught an early
flight to Miami, arriving in time to survey the scene of battle
before the hostilities got started.

Some of the early casualties had already been cleared from
the field. Gene Scott, bumped by Anderson in the first round,
was already back in New York, ready to get to his desk first
thing Monday morning. Neale Fraser had suffered a severe
muscle pull in his leg, adding to his elbow miseries. He had
had to quit in the middle of his doubles match. In sheer disgust,
and once more in defeat, he immediately caught a plane and
was on his way home to Australia.

Krishnan, likewise a loser, was staying on to watch the finals
from the clubhouse terrace, where the tournament patrons and
other VIPs were seated at umbrella-shaded tables. Krish looked
relaxed in his blazer, and every jet-black hair was slicked back
as usual. He reviewed his season's dismal record with an air of
Eastern patience.

"This is a very hard competition," he said. "They are a

tough group at any age—Laver, Rosewall, Stolle, Anderson. If my game had only stayed as it was and they had aged, I would have been all right. But as things are, it's very hard to win.

"But I'm satisfied. Financially it doesn't bother me so much that I haven't had a win on the tour. I don't play the Grand Masters for a living. I didn't play for money then, and I don't do it now. This is not even the main part of my tennis life. The main part now is my son's career. Whatever I make from the Grand Masters I spend on tennis somewhere else. Traveling to Wimbledon. Taking a house in London for the month. I watch my son play. That's enough. And I would do all that anyway, with or without the Grand Masters earnings.

"So . . . no," he concluded, "I didn't do as well as I would hope. But I'll continue to play the Grand Masters as long as I'm invited."

He gave Laver and Rosewall each a little comradely tap as they made their way across the terrace to take their bows and their warm-ups on the court. They had gotten to the finals without much trouble. Laver had beaten Anderson in the semis. Rosewall had disposed of Stolle.

They were both wearing baseball caps to ward off the blaze of the Florida sun, and as I watched them begin hitting slow, deliberate, warm-up strokes, I had a kind of premonition or preview of things to come. I was conscious of time, of their ages, of the deep creases in Rosewall's lean face and the slight thickening of Laver's waistline. I saw the two heroes as they might be in the next stage of the aging process: two old coots in their baseball caps swatting balls in some supersenior event because that was the only tennis game around.

In his introduction of the two featured players, Al Bunis invoked the hallowed memory of the 1972 WCT final in Dallas, the whole long history of the Laver-Rosewall rivalry, and Rod's double Grand Slam—"a feat achieved only once in the history of the game, and I doubt it will be again." He cited Rosewall's extraordinary longevity—his two U.S. Singles championships, sixteen years apart; his two French championships, fifteen years apart; his first and last Australian titles, separated by nineteen years.

Laver walked over to the courtside and went through a little ritual of preparation, roughening his racquet handle against the net cable, then wiping the handle elaborately with a towel. Now he was ready to start serving against the player he had faced too many times to count, with results too close to measure. Laver, now turned forty-six, against his fifty-year-old mate, antagonist and sparring partner, Rosewall . . .

Writers have described the special drama of great sports encounters—Joe Louis versus Schmeling, Ali versus Joe Frazier, Koufax versus Bob Gibson—in terms of atmosphere and occasion. There is a humiliation to avenge, a heavyweight title at stake, a pennant race pumping adrenaline into the contestants' nervous systems. It takes another athlete to explain just what goes on inside the ring, on the diamond, on the tennis court, when two great champions square off against each other.

Gene Scott once explained Laver versus Rosewall to me in player's terms. "Laver is a power hitter," he began, "and Rosewall, of course, is not. But Kenny is not just a retriever in the classic sense. He doesn't just get Laver's ball back. He tries to do something with it that'll put a little pressure on Rod.

"Now Laver sees the ball coming back at him. It's not just a return, it's got depth or it's coming at an unexpected angle. And he thinks, 'I'll have to give the little bugger something better the next time!' And he does.

"So every time these two guys meet on a tennis court there's a mutual pressure that raises the level of the game."

Mal Anderson once said pretty much the same thing in trying to explain the special quality of a Laver-Rosewall match. He said it in a single line: "It's not just the shots, it's the shots played *off* the shots!"

I looked for that quality on the Fisher Island court, but if it was there, it was in a form too subtle for an ordinary hacker to recognize.

The players themselves were hard to recognize. In place of Laver the brisk, experimental power hitter—the often impetuous "crasher" of his own description—what I saw was a patient clay-courter. The famous whiplash topspin? That was hung somewhere in his trophy cabinet, along with the youthful memories. The onetime Rocket came out hitting middle-aged backhands, deliberately, carefully sliced. From the forehand side he hit *looping* topspin shots that looked to be just this side of the moonballs that are a standard feature of women's tennis.

The clay court was new and soft—extremely slow—so it seemed inevitable that Rosewall would take control with his accuracy and his moderate pace. Kenny was returning Laver's shots, but without the vaunted Rosewall depth and angles. He kept lobbing into the sun, drawing errors or overly cautious returns. Troubled by the glare, Laver couldn't get his service going. Kenny broke him twice in a row, running up a 3–1 lead.

Now I expected to see Laver start gunning his engine, revving up the game. He did no such thing. The backhands were sliced all the more deliberately, the looping backhands only went a little deeper and bounced a little higher.

The way most players hit topspin, it slows the ball down. Not the way Laver does it. The special sting in Rod's shots, as an old circuit player, Julius Heldman, once pointed out, comes from the fact that his form of topspin actually speeds up the pace of the ball. That, says Heldman, is because Laver hits so hard and hits on the run. *I* think it's because of the exaggerated wrist action in Rocket's shots.

At Miami, Rod wasn't hitting those looping forehands with a great deal of force, but he was giving them his characteristic wrist action. The bounce was giving Rosewall trouble, reaching him at eye-level, where he couldn't put anything into his return. Time and again Kenny returned that shot into the net.

It was all part of Laver's resolute plan. "Kenny likes the ball low," he told me later. "I wasn't going to give it to him. I was patient. I wasn't thrashing around as I sometimes do. I was trying things.

"Sometimes you give your game away by experimentation. You try something, fail, try it again—and now he's ready for it. But this time I didn't have the failures. Whatever I tried worked."

Rosewall was having the same trouble as Laver in serving against the sun. Rod began to attack the service. The un-

Laveresque ground strokes kept paying off. And with the increasing effectiveness of his game plan, Rod's confidence grew. At 3–all, he camped under a high Rosewall lob and instead of playing it the way every other player in the world would have —with a standard overhead—he turned away from the sun, waited for the ball to bounce, and smashed it away with his backhand. In all my years of tennis watching, I don't think I ever saw a shot hit quite like that before.

That game seesawed between deuce and ad. One exchange ran the whole gamut of offensive and defensive tactics—lobs, drives, approaches, volleys—as the two antagonists sparred for position on the court. But Rosewall, trying to get back to the net, hit an approach shot over the baseline. Next he got handcuffed by another one of those deep looping shots that he had to reach up for.

Laver got the service break . . . played a crucial point by intercepting a Rosewall passing shot and returning it with a reflex stop-volley . . . brought a nice crosscourt exchange to a sudden end with a delicate crosscourt drop shot. A few minutes later, on a big serve down the middle and then a couple of Rosewall errors, Laver pulled out the first set, 6–4.

The second set went fast. Rosewall was struggling; Laver was in command. Rod maintained his pattern of slices and loops, but now he risked an occasional cannon shot and threw in the odd embellishment, as if to maintain his franchise for power and innovation. A shot that began as one of his patented crash returns—a lashing topspin off the backhand—changed in midstroke to a perfectly disguised drop shot, winning the point.

With a 4–1 lead, Laver tried a boomer down the line off his backhand, netted it, tried it again—made it. Rosewall tried a drop shot from deep in his own court. It failed, and Rod had another break and a 5–1 lead on his own service.

At 15–all, Laver tried another flamboyant shot—a topspin lob hit on the run. It dropped long. But he proceeded to stroke a couple of careful, winning placements. And then Rosewall netted a routine backhand, and the Grand Masters Championship went to Laver, 6–4, 6–1.

The insiders' comments on the match had a certain defensive tone, I thought, as if they were covering up for a performance that, while perfectly effective and workmanlike, had not really lived up to the high expectations of a Laver-Rosewall match.

"I've seen Kenny hit better backhands," said Mal Anderson. "But Rod was hitting with good pace—maybe more than it looked like."

"I felt like I had a lot more penetration on the ball than Kenny realized I had on it," Laver said when I caught him at courtside a few minutes afterwards. He looked around for someplace to put the winner's envelope he was still holding in his hand. Finally he stuck it in the pocket of his jacket.

"I was hitting fairly heavy topspin, but my idea," he confided, "was to try and get the ball to lift with some speed on it, rather than just flipping it and having it bounce high. That's what made it work."

The almost ladylike moonballs, he was telling me, were not so innocuous as I may have thought. They had something on them that made them land deceptively deep in the court, and with a little bite on them—some special Rod Laver quality.

I didn't doubt it. But that wasn't what I saw from the clubhouse terrace. For me, the story of that match was the story of the Grand Masters. It was about growing old without being defeated by age. How? By keeping alive the idea of winning.

There was a time, apparently not so far back, when Laver would have played that match differently, when—as Gene Scott once put it—Rocket would have insisted on winning his own way. Now he only insisted on winning. And that's what would keep him in the game.

A lot of people might be distressed by that idea. *Winning!* What a crass objective! What kid stuff!

But wasn't it the essence of competition—the measure of excellence in sports? And wasn't that simple fact the special glory of sports, the secret of their enduring appeal? It was the experience so uniquely satisfying that it kept these exceptional athletes in the game or brought them back to it long after their prime.

It was the lesson the amateur hot shots learned on the pro tour: Not how to look good or make the great shot, but how to win.

It was what Fraser had missed sitting behind the desk in his insurance office; what Seixas discovered he still needed after a taste of being a loser in the stock market; and what Laver said he'd still be trying to do at eighty or as long as he could still play at all.

And Sven Davidson: It was the end of winning that finally sent him into retirement.

Even Ulrich: In his expressed disdain for winning, Torben was only beguiling himself with some classic Zen word play. For, in the end, wasn't winning simply the measure of playing well?

None of the players would argue, in the cynical language of football, that winning was *everything*. Laver didn't even rate it Number 1 in his list of adult priorities. *Losing* a match against Laver or Rosewall was hardly considered a disgrace. Tennis is a sport in which players speak of "a good loss."

But clearly it was the *effort* of winning that gave these admirable athletes their lead over the rest of us in the common search for the Fountain of Youth. The closest thing we would find to the ephemeral Fountain was the search itself—the training and practicing, the continual perfecting of near-perfect techniques, the manipulation of tactics and strategies, all to be measured by the finite arithmetic of game, set and match.

Along with most of the Fisher Island crowd, I waited for Laver and Rosewall to shower and then come back on to the court to play Stolle and Emerson in the doubles final. It proved to be a strange match, with seven service breaks in the first eight games. Stolle said afterwards that the extraordinary pattern could be explained in two words: "Shitty serving."

Laver and Rosewall, simply by being broken one time less than their opponents, won the first set 6–4. In the second set the four Aussies gave a reasonable demonstration of traditional doubles as against the modern crash-and-bash style. They pulled out the whole catalogue of chip-and-charge, angled dinks, and beautifully placed, exquisitely timed lobs. Laver-Rosewall put the second set away also, 6–2. In singles and doubles both, they had asserted themselves as the class of their tennis generation, just as they'd done two decades before.

I had a couple of farewell beers and caught one of the last launches back to civilization. The next morning I was on a flight for New York.

On the plane, I was trying to figure out the real winner of the Grand Masters phase of the Laver-Rosewall rivalry. I decided that the nod had to go to Laver because the Championship at Fisher Island gave him an edge of three to two in the five finals they played against each other during the 1984 tour. But then I remembered that they had also met in one *non*final —the exhibition in Seattle, where Anderson defaulted and Rod filled in. That match was won by Kenny. So, after another year of touring, after a dozen tournaments, after crossing the continent a couple of times, they had wound up even again.

Laver and Rosewall were probably going to go to their graves in a dead heat.

39

The Golden Age

By a freak of scheduling, the 1985 tour of the Tennis Grand Masters actually began in 1984. There were two year-end tournaments before the troupe disbanded for the winter, to resume the competition the following April. I caught the final event, which was held at Saw Mill Racquet Club, a lavish, well-run indoor facility in suburban Westchester County, only about an hour's drive from my home in New York City. It was a chance to check out the new crowd of rookies who were joining the 1985 competition.

I checked in at the Saw Mill club one day well in advance of match time, hoping to catch the new talent in practice. The first face I saw was a familiar one. Mal Anderson was just on his way in with a case full of Yonex racquets slung over his shoulder.

"How're you hitting 'em?" Mal asked by way of greeting.

"I'm still getting over Naples," I told him. On impulse, I added, "Maybe you can help me work it out."

"Any time," he said genially with his hand on the locker room door.

I stopped him. "Mal," I said, "I keep trying to describe the shots you guys hit in the Grand Masters, but I've never had to return any of them. How about hitting a few tennis balls with me so I'll know what I'm talking about?"

Outsider or not, if I was ever going to have that experience, then time was running out. It was this weekend or never.

"Any time," Mal repeated.

"How about tomorrow? Eleven a.m.?"

"I'll book the court," he said.

We didn't play any games—I wasn't looking for a scalp to display in the bar of my own club. Mostly, we traded ground strokes in long leisurely rallies from the back court. I kept the ball on Mal's backhand. I wanted to see that perfect, fluid underspin stroke coming at me. Mal obliged with shots that skimmed the net but invariably traveled to within a foot or two of the baseline. Even off the slow Har-Tru surface, they came at me with a low, skidding kick.

"You've got to hit that ball well out in front of you," Mal said, giving a perfect demonstration of the stroke. "And you've got to take it early—take it on the rise. That's the key to the whole thing."

The ball came whizzing down the line, and I got just enough of it with my racquet to send back an ineffectual forehand into midcourt. In a match, Mal would have pounced on it for an easy volley.

In trying to emulate Anderson's perfectionist strokes, I soon became aware of a tic in my own shots. It was the old familiar club-hacker's malady: Lack of preparation. On the forehand, I only *thought* I was getting my racquet back. On the backhand, I wasn't really turning my forward shoulder far enough into the shot; and I wasn't taking the ball far enough out in front of me. I made some adjustments. My shots began traveling deeper, the rallies lengthened.

After we had been hitting for twenty or thirty minutes, Rod Laver came over from an adjoining court carrying an unsheathed racquet—a player looking for action. "Ready when you are!" he called to Mal, indicating a couple of other players obviously getting ready for some four-man drill.

"Just a few more minutes!" Mal called back, and slashed another lovely backhand approach shot.

Well, I had my story for the clubhouse bar. *I was having a hit with Mal Anderson the other day. You know, the old Davis Cup player. Beautiful strokes! . . . Did I take any games off him? Well, we didn't keep score. I was just warming him up for Rod Laver.*

There were two rookies in the draw at Saw Mill, both Spaniards. One was Andres Gimeno, a tall, balding man with a kind of jaunty, slightly flat-footed stride and a solid attacking game. He was a veteran of the professional wars of the mid-Sixties. The other was Manuel Santana—Manolo to his friends and fans —a holder of the U.S., British and French singles. They would be joined in the spring by two more youngsters. One was Cliff Drysdale, the tall, personable South African, whose two-handed backhand was rare in its time. The other was Ron Holmberg, a Sixties-vintage American with a history of long matches, including a six-hour-and-twenty-minute doubles match in the U.S. Indoors with the rousing score of 26–24, 17–19, 30–28.

The verve with which Gimeno took a practice set off Laver the first day I watched him made me think that Andres just might turn out to be the revelation of the 1985 tour. But when they met in an official match, Rocket turned up the heat and played perhaps the best tennis I'd seen in the Grand Masters all year.

Santana, meanwhile, gave a series of crowd-pleasing displays of his highly individual flamenco style. He is rather slight, cocky, and inventive. Some observer once wrote of Manolo that he had more varieties of forehands than Heinz had pickles. That would make it at least fifty-eight, which may be only a slight exaggeration.

When Santana and Laver met in the final, there was the kind of tension in the air that you used to feel when a new challenger climbed into the ring for a heavyweight title fight. He proceeded to taunt the Grand Masters champion with some of the most flamboyantly played drop shots I have ever seen—hit with elaborate, misleading preparation from the weirdest positions on the court. Laver covered them, turned them into winners, then began to top them with even better drop shots of his own.

Santana, changing course, started to hit curious, deep chopped forehands down the line to Rod's left-handed forehand corner. Laver whipped them back with ferocious topspin. Santana was trying to attack the net, but Laver drove him back with beautiful passing shots off both wings.

Sometimes Laver would fill the empty space with more of those little drop shots. Almost casually, Rod took control of the net and scored time after time with beautiful volleys. It was even better than the match against Gimeno. It was the kind of performance that reminded me of an encomium written just about the time Laver was passing from the big-time tennis scene by an Australian tennis expert named R. L. Whitington.

In what may have been the ultimate example of generational favoritism—the mindset that makes people overload their All-Time lists with players of their own era—Whitington wrote:

Tennis has gone as far as it can go in skill, physical fitness and strength. Nobody will ever serve faster than Pancho Gonzales, nobody will rush a net more swiftly than Sedgman, Newcombe, or Connors; nobody will drive, volley, half-volley or smash better than Laver. *There is nowhere to go.* [Italics his.]

Whether any of that was true or not, Laver at Saw Mill was the Laver I had been looking for all year—the player I had seen flashes of almost everywhere on the tour, more in some places, little in others.

It was the Rod Laver that, I knew, would always continue to exist in his own mind—the creative, risk-taking crasher of returns. Sometimes that player would also appear on the court.

His son, Rick, was with him in the locker room when I poked my head in. The day before I had seen them hitting together on the practice court. Rick's style was pretty much standard teenager: hard and wild. I could be wrong, but it looked to me as if he didn't regard tennis as his game. That didn't affect Rod's patience.

"I had to be pleased with my level of play in this tournament," Rod responded when I complimented him. It was player's jargon, a postmatch press conference cliché, and he suddenly stopped himself in midsentence, flushed slightly, and laughed. Obviously he agreed that he'd put on a hell of a good show.

Gratified as I was by Laver's display, it delighted me no more than one of the first-round matches. That one had ended with Ramanathan Krishnan—he of the magic anticipation, the once-supple wrists and the once-supreme overhead—trotting up to meet Roy Emerson at the net with a huge smile on his dark-skinned face, as the umpire announced Krish the winner in straight sets.

Emerson was having a beer in the players' lounge afterwards when I went up to him with my hand out in a congratulatory gesture.

He looked puzzled. "I lost," he said.

"I know," I told him. "But you must have made an Indian very happy."

Emmo broke up. "You know what he said to me when we finished the match? He came up and threw his arms around me and said, 'Emmo! That's the first match I won all year!' "

No news to me. Hadn't I been keeping track as closely as Krish?

Before the tournament ended and the troupe broke up for the winter, I checked in with Al Bunis, asking him about the players' roster for the 1985 tour proper.

"It'll be pretty much the group you're seeing here," he said. "Plus Rosewall and Stolle, of course. Andres and Manolo will be regulars. Weren't they interesting? They'll give us some good matches."

The Rosewalls had gone straight home to Sydney from Miami. Stolle had commitments that had forced him, too, to pass up Westchester.

"What about Ulrich?" I asked.

"Oh, I think we'll find some way to work Torben into a tournament every now and then. As you can see, there's always somebody missing for one reason or another."

"But there's no way he can play regularly?"

Al shook his head.

"And how about Sedgman?" I asked.

"Basically, Frank is retired."

Sedgman? Retired? The old hero of Wimbledon and Forest Hills? The speediest man on a tennis court, the tennis player's tennis player? The point man of the Australian wave of the Fifties? Sedgman retired—without a fanfare? A ceremony? A gold watch inscribed with the good wishes of every tennis fan of our mutual generation?

Sedgman—the first king of the Grand Masters.

I went to say goodbye to Mike Savit. "I hear Sedgman won't be on the tour at all next year," I said.

"Well," said Mike, "basically, Frank is retired."

"Whose decision was it, yours or his?"

He looked slightly uneasy. "It was mutual," he said. "It was just time."

A few weeks before the start of the 1985 spring circuit, I heard that Sedgman had asked to play one tournament on this year's tour. He did. Bombed out in the first round of singles, but won the doubles with Rosewall.

About the same time I heard about Sedg's one-shot unretirement, I got a phone call from Torben Ulrich. He was calling from Philadelphia, having just returned to this country from a visit to his native Denmark. It had been a very productive trip, he reported with enthusiasm. Very promising, anyway.

I could picture Torben at the other end of the line, fingering his beard or his beads as he talked.

He had taken some of his Zen/tennis action paintings with him to Copenhagen, he said, to show to some gallery people, and they had expressed an interest in his work. Even as we spoke, some of the paintings were being exhibited at a tennis tournament in Philadelphia. There was a likelihood that he would be going back to Copenhagen in the spring or summer to conduct some seminars, something like the ones on sport and gender that he'd been running in Seattle.

"So you see," he concluded, "it might be the best possible solution to my dilemma. Maybe I won't have to worry how can I play well when I don't play often enough. Maybe I'll be too busy to play the Grand Masters at all!"

But when a place opened up in the draw of a Grand Masters tournament a couple of months later, Torben packed his Prince Graphites into his racquet bag and went out on the court. He lost. He and Sedgman both wound up playing a few times on the 1985 tour, which was won by Kenny Rosewall, now fifty-one. Laver was the runner-up again. Drysdale and Gimeno gave the front-runners some trouble. Holmberg, young but out of shape, was no match for the fit old-timers. Krishnan and Fraser struggled through the tour. Ulrich and Sedgman wound up at the bottom of the point standings again and were not expected to play on the 1986 tour.

Ulrich and Sedgman—the last survivors of the Golden Age of tennis, that halcyon era that keeps advancing with every new generation. For me, it ended with the 1950s, only to be miraculously revived, two decades later, with the birth of the Tennis Grand Masters.

Now my second Golden Age was over.

INDEX